DECISIONS OF DESTINY

DECISIONS

CLEVELAND AND NEW YORK

OF DESTINY

by Richard L. Tobin

The World Publishing Company

PUBLISHED BY *The World Publishing Company*
2231 West 110th Street, Cleveland 2, Ohio

PUBLISHED SIMULTANEOUSLY IN CANADA
by Nelson, Foster & Scott Ltd.

Library of Congress Catalog Card Number: 61-6649
FIRST EDITION

ACKNOWLEDGMENT IS HEREBY MADE FOR PERMISSION TO QUOTE FROM:

White House Profile by Bess Furman. Copyright © 1951, used by special permission of the publishers, The Bobbs-Merrill Company, Inc.

Seven Ages of Washington by Owen Wister. Copyright 1907 by The Macmillan Company, by permission of The Macmillan Company.

Woodrow Wilson by Arthur Walworth. Copyright © 1958 by Longmans, Green and Co., Inc.

Makers of a New Nation, Vol. 9, The Pageant of America. Copyright 1928 Yale University Press.

You're the Boss by Edward J. Flynn. Copyright 1947 by The Viking Press, Inc. and reprinted by their permission.

Harry S. Truman *Memoirs*, Vol. II. Copyright 1956 Time Inc.

The Autobiography of Theodore Roosevelt. Copyright 1913 by Charles Scribner's Sons, Centennial Edition. Copyright © 1958 by Charles Scribner's Sons.

Grover Cleveland, a Study in Courage by Allan Nevins. Copyright 1932 by Dodd, Mead and Co.

TO HELEN ROGERS REID,

the best newspaperman I know.

CONTENTS

ACKNOWLEDGMENTS

I SHOULD LIKE to express my special thanks to Lewis G. Vander Velde, director of the Michigan Historical Collections, for his guidance and many helpful suggestions in my preparation of this manuscript. Professor Vander Velde is, moreover, responsible for my initial interest in American history, which he taught superbly at the University of Michigan. I never knew a finer teacher; and the seed he planted in my youthful brain became in later life a nightly reading habit which has given me more pleasure than anything else I know.

Secondly, I should like to thank Peter Levin, my Wilton neighbor and friend, whose excellent book *Seven By Chance* is one of the undiscovered gems of American historical writing. Mr. Levin's careful scholarship has saved me I cannot calculate how many hours of drudgery, particularly in research on Arthur, Cleveland, and T.R.

I also acknowledge with gratitude the following permissions: Bobbs-Merrill, Indianapolis, for Bess Furman's *White House Profile;* Columbia University Press, New York, for a host of reference favors from *The Columbia Encyclopedia;* Dodd, Mead, New York, for Allan Nevins' *Grover Cleveland;* Doubleday, New York, for Harry Truman's *Memoirs;* Farrar, Straus and Cudahy, New York, for Peter Levin's *Seven By Chance,* and for other help from the author; Harcourt, Brace, New York, for Henry Pringle's *Theodore Roosevelt;* Harper and Brothers, New York, for Margaret Leech's *Reveille in Washington;* Houghton Mifflin, Boston, for Henry Cabot Lodge's

ACKNOWLEDGMENTS

George Washington, Arthur Schlesinger Jr.'s *The Coming of the New Deal,* and William Allen White's *Woodrow Wilson;* Alfred A. Knopf, New York, for Adrienne Koch's *Jefferson and Madison;* Little, Brown, Boston, for John Morton Blum's *Woodrow Wilson and the Politics of Morality,* Frank Freidel's *Franklin Roosevelt,* and Arthur Schlesinger Jr.'s *The Age of Jackson;* Longmans, Green, New York, for Arthur Walworth's *Woodrow Wilson;* McGraw-Hill, New York, for Herbert Hoover's *The Ordeal of Woodrow Wilson;* Macmillan, New York, for Owen Wister's *Seven Ages of Washington;* Oxford University Press, New York, for John W. Ward's *Andrew Jackson: Symbol for an Age;* Viking Press, New York, for Edward J. Flynn's *You're the Boss;* Yale University Press, New Haven, for material from Vol. IX in the "Pageant of America" series. Also Brandt & Brandt, the New York agency, for Raymond Moley's *After Seven Years; Life* magazine for Harry Truman's *Memoirs;* and *Look* Magazine for further articles and material by President Truman; to the *Congressional Digest,* Washington, D.C., for material on the Korean War debate in Congress; and the *New York Herald Tribune* for permission to reprint material from its files.

In addition, I should like to acknowledge the great help rendered by the New York Public Library, the Westport, Connecticut, Library, and the Pequot Library of Southport, Connecticut, for research material, much of it from contemporary sources. Further, I should like to thank Grace Horvath for aid in preparation of the manuscript and Theodore Carlson for unique material on Chester A. Arthur, given to me along with much encouragement and aid.

R. L. T.

Wilton, Connecticut

Who knows only his own generation
remains always a child.

CICERO

DECISIONS OF DESTINY

George Washington

IN FESTERING camps near the Atlantic seaboard, particularly at General Washington's headquarters at Newburgh, just sixty-five miles up the Hudson from New-York, the miserable Continental Army lay impatient and mutinous that frigid early spring of 1782. It was morose, hungry, forgotten—and unpaid. Lord Cornwallis had surrendered the autumn before at Yorktown in southeast Virginia, and the War of the Revolution was supposed to have come to an end. Yet, somehow it was not over.

Valley Forge, five timeless years ago, had been a ghastly nightmare of bloody frost and starvation, but also of incredible fortitude and vibrant hope. There had been many difficulties, almost impossible ones, and men had deserted hourly across the rolling winter hills of Pennsylvania. But there had also been sufficient challenge and heroism to keep a ragged corps of 11,000 patriots together. The Cause was the glue that had done it, a catalytic agent which gave adhesive power to what appeared a crazy human mixture. But now that Cause seemed a thing of the past: the glue was becoming unstuck in idleness and despairing gossip. Surrender of the British at Yorktown in October of 1781 had insidiously dissolved the catalyst.

A new and subtle poison had begun to eat into the heart of the Continental Army. The men wanted desperately to go home. There seemed no reason to stay any longer—particularly without food or pay, even if at the absurd rate of only four pennies a day. If the war were over, the men asked, why

14

1

Rejects a Monarchy

shouldn't they go home? Some hadn't seen their families for half a decade of wandering, starving, bleeding, hurting, and fighting. Homes of many a ragged Continental were now desolate, families in dire want. As never before or after in the history of our nation, the gaunt and hideous specter of starvation was haunting America that winter.

Were there any more campaigns to bewitch and excite? Was there any reason to stay in camp? The men in faded buff and blue had ample time to ask such questions, to share their complaints, to worry about their deserted and hungry families, to bemoan the incredible futility of the Continental Congress. How absurdly disorganized and poverty-stricken appeared the tiny nation to which they had given birth in an extended agony of frustrating forced marches, fighting, and bloodshed.

Despite the increasing flood of dissatisfaction and complaint, Washington ordered his soldiers to remain with him. The incandescent star of Valley Forge, whose name was pronounced in tones reserved for some Messiah, was still a hero to his men; yet now he began to seem more and more incompetent to them. He was unable, on the one hand, to let them go home because Britain's King George obstinately refused to acknowledge the loss of his best colony and Washington feared new encounters.[1] On the other hand, however, the six-foot

1. Most historians believe that Yorktown need not have ended the war. That it did is largely because the British ministry following Lord North's fall was friendly to America.

three-inch hero could not persuade that absurdity, the Continental Congress, to send sufficient money to take care of his men. So the once great champion stubbornly required that his men stand ready to fight battles they could not imagine, even at the cost of the personal luster he had gained the autumn before with the surrender at Yorktown.

The arrival in New-York, just down river from Washington's headquarters at Newburgh, of Sir Guy Carleton confirmed the General's disquiet and forebodings. Washington knew about Carleton's diplomatic skill and acumen in the handling of the Canadians. Sir Guy had upset Montgomery and Arnold in their early expedition against Quebec. And it was Carleton's beguiling peace talk that Washington had had in mind when he wrote Robert R. Livingston, then Secretary for Foreign Affairs:[2]

> We want no fresh opiate to increase that stupor into which we have fallen, but I much fear that the idle, and delusive offers of Peace with which the Country resounds, will, if it is not powerfully counteracted, be exceedingly injurious to us; not (I apprehend) from any disposition of the people to listen to improper terms, but from a misconception of what is really meant, and the arts which are used to make them believe that Independence and what not, are preferred to them.

Washington could painfully remember Sir Guy's adroit measures placating the Roman Catholic Church—activities which gave both English-speaking and French-speaking Canadian settlers sufficient autonomy to save their country for the crown. If Carleton had succeeded in the north he might (Washington thought) succeed in Tory New-York, the lone British garrison of any consequence still holding out against total union with the revolutionaries. Washington shuddered at what might have been had Wit and not Stupidity been King, Prime Minister, and General throughout the Colonial War. Almost any palpable conciliation to the Colonies, like Carleton's to Canada, might have shattered the revolutionary effort, never whole-

2. John Dos Passos, *The Men Who Made the Nation* (Garden City, Doubleday and Company, Inc., 1957), p. 36.

hearted nor unanimous and always subject to periods of black doubt.

Sir Guy was in New-York, less than three days' march from Newburgh, backed by Admiral George Rodney's magnificent post-Yorktown conquests in the West Indies, where Rodney had lately captured St. Eustatius and thoroughly whipped the French fleet under De Grasse. It didn't matter for the moment that De Grasse's disaster in the Caribbean would inevitably take pressure off French claims for American aid during the Revolution and make the peace treaties easier to negotiate. New-Yorkers would surely read of Admiral Rodney's great West Indian conquest and toast King George anew. Rumor had it that settlers in the Green Mountains, eager to rid themselves of the border fight between New-Hampshire and New-York, were negotiating secretly with the British. Peace, peace, but there was no peace!

In the circumstances, no general, least of all a tenacious redhead from Virginia, could disband his army, theoretically victorious though it was. He could not disband it; also he could neither feed nor pay it.

A nineteenth-century British book gives us a brisk and disarming account of how difficult things must have been for Washington prior to the preliminary peace talks the following November. It also suggests the startling conclusion colonists and soldiers drew from the apparent anarchy of their time:[3]

> The years 1782–83 saw discontent become quite prevalent throughout the (Colonial) Army. The whole Army suffered from arrearages of pay, and in various ways had long been exposed to disappointment and irritation from the vacillating and fluctuating course of policy of the various colonial governments upon which they depended, and also from the impotency of Congress under the Articles of Confederation. These discontents naturally produced dissatisfaction with the civil authorities as then constituted. In meditating upon their wrongs, some of the officers and soldiers were led to the conclusion that justice could only be done to them, or the

3. C. W. Upham, *Life of George Washington*, Vol. II (London, The National Illustrated Library, 1881), pp. 91-92.

affairs of the public managed with efficiency and success by introducing a strong government.

The idea of a Monarchy became a favorite one with persons who entertained these views, especially in the unpaid Army. They believed that it would be vain to attempt to preserve the prosperity or establish the power of a nation without a King, and, as a matter of course, they fixed upon Washington as the man on whom alone the honor and the burden of Royalty could be placed.

The Continental Army was not alone in feeling the need to plant the seed of American monarchy to replace the unworkable muddle of an impotent Continental Congress and a useless constitution. Beyond the garrison bugles of New-York, King George's royal forces, it is true, exercised little or no formal authority in the Colonies. During 1782 the Southern ports would be abandoned and the Continental Army become theoretically supreme—so long as it remained intact. But politically considered, the Colonies were losing their unity and their peace and out of this chemistry the reversion to monarchy soon gained headway.[4]

In March, 1781, certain Articles of Confederation had been adopted, but they were merely a "league of friendship" lacking police power of enforcement. No true national executive existed, therefore; nor were there national courts in which a man from Connecticut, for example, could find redress for a Federal[5] wrong done him by a man from Pennsylvania. Why should a Pennsylvania jury decide in favor of a stranger from New England whom they would never see again? Without Federal law enforced throughout the whole country in Federal courts under a powerful Federal executive, each colony had to take care of its own people and ignore the Articles and Continental Congress. There was no other regional choice.

Common people, whom the Revolution was to have benefited most, were the first to be disillusioned by the replacement of the British monarchy with self-government. The Continental

4. Allan Nevins and Henry Steele Commager, *A Short History of the United States* (New York, The Modern Library, 1945), pp. 108-34.

5. The word "Federal" is here used in the post-1787 sense. In the pre-1787 sense it denoted Confederation relationship.

Congress consisted of only one house in which each state had a single vote, regardless of size. Huge Virginia or Massachusetts had to swallow legislative equality with tiny Rhode Island or Delaware. Twenty Bostonians were the equivalent of one New Hampshire farmer. This wasn't equality, as everyone knew, but worse still it wasn't even common sense.

The Continental Congress could levy no taxes, punish no men who broke laws it passed, compel no state to observe its foreign treaties if it didn't like them, or enlist a single troop. Worst of all, it couldn't raise sufficient money to pay interest on a large and insolvent national debt, which daily increased, nor carry on the simple functions of what toothless government there was. The American Revolution had given a new people independence in the family of nations—a radically altered social order in which privilege, wealth, and heredity counted for less and human equality for more. But the American people had yet to show they possessed a genuine capacity for self-government. Their loose league of friendship amounted to no more than an ocean of frustrations, dissensions, and imperfections.

Though no group suffered more intensely from this chaotic babel than the army, disgust with The System was universal. In every colony at one time or another from 1782–1787 were introduced resolutions pleading for a change of Federal procedure and aegis. These resolutions, it is important to note, did not seek more democratic systems of government. The most frequent toast of 1782 was, in fact, "Here's to a hoop for the barrel," and when Washington's officers at Newburgh said it they meant a Strong Man—one who would give less emphasis to equality and more insistence on order in government. They wanted Washington—the hoop without whom, many felt, the barrel of thirteen separate staves would quickly collapse— to be a king and they wanted him to begin the reign of a royal family.

As the country's situation rapidly deteriorated in early spring, 1782, there was a concerted drive to make Washington King George of America. On May 13, 1782, news of the birth of a Dauphin in France ignited an absolute paroxysm of rejoicing in freedom-loving America, celebrations exploding without restraint wherever the happy news was told. It seems likely this was the spark which set off the timing device of as strange a letter as any American has ever sent a national hero, strange yet somehow natural in setting, date, and circumstances. To plumb Washington's thinking about the subject of a monarchy, a letter was addressed to him May 22 by a distinguished Philadelphian, an Army officer of renown and standing, Colonel Lewis Nicola.[6] The Colonel was a highly respected officer, no young hothead, an elderly Philadelphian of Huguenot extraction who had risen to Major in the British army before emigrating to America. Before the war he had published and edited the first regular magazine in Philadelphia, become one of the founders of the American Philosophical Society, and had written a drill and conduct manual for the use of Colonial troops. During the war he had become well known as Town Major of Philadelphia.

In his carefully written proposal Colonel Nicola first summed up the grievances and discontents of the Army:

> The injuries the troops have received in their pecuniary rights have been and will continue to be too obvious to require a particular detail, or to have escaped your Excellencies [sic] notice, tho' your exalted station must have deprived you of opportunity of information relative to the severe distress occasioned thereby.

Washington read this well-aimed salvo[7] at "the eternal ignorance of top command to problems that beset the lower ranks," and he must have gone cold in the stomach since he himself knew the truth only too well. The General's correspondent (the ingenuous memorial was written in Colonel Nicola's hand with covering letter enclosed) next pointed out that the Continental Congress had taken no effective action to find money for the arrears owed the Army. Not only was the Army's paper "not worth a Continental," but it was for the most part nonexistent.

6. Dos Passos, *op. cit.*, pp. 37–39.
7. Joseph Dillaway Sawyer, *Washington*, Vol. II (New York, The Macmillan Company, 1927), pp. 84-94.

This gives us a dismal prospect for the time to come
[Washington read on] and much reason to fear the future
provision promised to officers, and the settling and
satisfying their and their men's just demands will be little
attended to, when our services are no longer wanted, and
that the recompense of all our toils, hardships, expense
of private fortune will be, to those who cannot earn a
livelihood by manual labor, beggary; and that we who
have borne the heat and labor of the day will be forgotten
by such as reap the benefits without suffering any of the
hardships.

Washington's petitioner then stated that officers as well as
men were selling their pay certificates and paper money to
speculators at enormous discounts. To keep body and soul together, the worn heroes of American liberty were having to
settle for a small part of the value of the paper, "never more
than one-tenth, but often less." The Army's patience was
running out, wrote Colonel Nicola, and an explosion seemed
imminent. He went on:

I believe it is generally intended not to separate after the
peace until all grievances are redressed, engagements and
promises fulfilled . . . God forbid that we should ever
think of involving that country which we have, under your
conduct and auspices, rescued from oppression, into a new
scene of blood and confusion, but it cannot be expected
we should forego claims on which our future subsistence
and that of our families depend.

Nicola then began a carefully reasoned argument against
democracy as a workable form of government (the word for
democracy was more popularly "republick" in those days).
Said he: "I own that I am not that violent admirer of a republican form of government that numbers in this country are."
He cited the disasters to the aristocratic municipalities of
Genoa and Venice, and the weakness of the Dutch Republic
as proof that republicanism was flaccid and unworkable, as
that parody on good government, the Continental Congress,
was amply proving.

"Does not the great similarity there [the Dutch Republic's

failure] between her form of government and ours give us room to fear our fate will be like hers?" he asked. The truth of this sally must have made anguished reading for the patriot of Valley Forge. He knew better than most how impotent were the Articles of Confederation and the Continental Congress, and he must have been able at this point to guess what Nicola was about to suggest: a return to monarchy in limited form similar to the English style. Nicola rammed home his point:

> This war must have shown us all, but to military men in particular, the weakness of republicks. . . .
> The same abilities which have led us, through difficulties apparently insurmountable by human power, to victory and glory, these qualities that have merited and obtained the universal esteem and veneration of an army would be most likely to conduct and direct us in the smoother paths of peace. Some people have so connected the ideas of tyranny and monarchy as to find it very difficult to separate them; it may therefore be requisite to give the head of such a constitution as I propose some title apparently more moderate, but if all things are once adjusted I believe strong arguments might be produced for admitting the title of King.[8]

Nicola even had a suggestion for solving the Army's terrible pay problem under the new American monarchy. Congress would, on the day of the coronation, pay arrears owed to men and officers, one third in cash, the remainder in public lands to the West where the Army's families would pioneer a new state as a military buffer against British and Indians—a sort of frontier police force at the rim of the colonial stockade.

Though Washington had been raised an aristocrat and had sworn fidelity to the crown as a young colonial officer, his Virginia upbringing had taught him the necessity for the military to be subordinate to the civil power. From Douglas Southall Freeman's biography of Washington, it is clear that the essential equality of man and man had somehow, somewhere penetrated the very core of George Washington's thinking at an early age. He was an instinctive gentleman in the finest sense

8. Revolutionary Archives, Pequot Library, Southport, Connecticut.

of that noble word, but he was also an instinctive democrat. He had too often seen colonial interest sacrificed to British Toryism to hold any great love for the third George and if he had ever supported the House of Hanover it was certain that a man of his character superseded this fealty the hour he took command of the Continental Army by his oath of allegiance to the revolution.

A military man, Washington doubtless had the same black doubts about representative government that the army mind always harbors. Nevertheless, as the years wore on, he saw more clearly that The Cause had become indissolubly intertwined with the equality of man and he had given his solemn word to champion in every way "the support of the Glorious Cause." When the war was finally at an end and the peace treaty signed, he planned to ride back to his beloved Mount Vernon and to remain there forever. And as a final gesture of love and affection for the cause of independence and liberty he had served so magnificently, Washington had decided, it is now known, to lay down his command without any payment or reward. For such a just man, Colonel Nicola's proposal of kingship must have been chastening and shocking.

Early Americans were well acquainted with the various proposals to make George Washington a monarch and the subject was common table talk throughout the trying period between revolution and constitution. One of the most popular books of its time was Parson Weems's famous, if imaginative, schoolboy account of the life of George Washington. In it was born the wholly untrue but delightful story of George Washington and the cherry tree ("Father, I cannot tell a lie. I did it with my little hatchet"). Yet, besides complete fabrication, Weems's precious volume contains much that reflects the age of Washington, and from its pages, which went through forty editions after 1800, the thread of the seriousness of the agitation to create an American monarchy with Washington as King George the First is markedly evident.[9]

9. M. L. Weems, *Life of George Washington* (Philadelphia, Joseph Allen, 1800), pp. 131–32. The Rev. Weems was formerly rector of Mount Vernon Parish, and the book was sold by J. Grigg, No. 9 North Fourth Street.

Weems writes that, around the time of Nicola's formal offer to support or launch a monarchial system with Washington its king, the man who was "first in war, first in peace and first in the hearts of his countrymen" became "suddenly alarmed by the appearance of an evil which threatened to put an end to all his well-meant labours for ever—this was the incipient dissolution of the federal government!!!" Weems's report quotes Washington as saying: "We cannot long exist as a nation, without lodging somewhere a power that may command the full energies of the nation for defense from all its enemies, and the supply of all its wants. The people will soon be tired of such a government. They will sign for a change: and many of them already begin to talk of Monarchy, without horror!!"

Owen Wister's more authentic *Seven Ages of Washington*[10] underlines the father's concern for his country as an incipient dictatorship. Between Yorktown and the signing of the peace, Wister writes, "to men's angry minds it occurred that there were not many steps to march between themselves and the control of government and they talked of their beloved leader as Dictator. Washington's words (to Nicola) quickly burst the bubble."

In response to what Dr. Freeman calls "the preposterous and plundering suggestion"[11] of Colonel Nicola amid the public clamor for a monarchy, Washington took immediate action. He wrote so that no one, then or ever, could misunderstand. In addition, he took the precaution, for purposes of record, of asking both Humphrys and Trumbull, his military amanuenses, to sign an attestation that the copy of his letter they sent off in reply to Nicola was a true one. If the matter ever came out (as it was bound to amid much sentiment along these lines) he wanted to be in the position of being able to counter the "animadversions" he dreaded.[12]

This is his letter to Nicola in full. It begins "Newburg [sic],

10. Owen Wister, *The Seven Ages of Washington* (New York, The Macmillan Company, 1907), p. 194.
11. Douglas Southall Freeman, *George Washington*, Vol. V (New York, Charles Scribner's Sons, 1952), p. 416.
12. Dos Passos, *op. cit.*, pp. 38–39.

22 May, 1782," two months after the new British cabinet had recognized American independence, yet more than six months prior to the signing of the preliminary agreement in Paris on November 30:

> *Sir,* — With a mixture of great surprise and astonishment, I have read with attention the sentiments you have submitted to my perusal. Be assured, sir, no occurrence in the course of the war has given me more painful sensations, than your information of there being such ideas existing in the Army, as you have expressed, and I must view with abhorrence and reprehend with severity. For the present the communication of them will rest in my bosom, unless some further agitation of the matter shall make a disclosure necessary.
>
> I am much at a loss to conceive what part of my conduct could have given encouragement to an address, which to me seems big with the greatest mischiefs, that can befall my country. If I am not deceived in the knowledge of myself, you could not have found a person to whom your schemes are more disagreeable. At the same time, in justice to my own feelings, I must add, that no man possesses a more sincere wish to see ample justice done to the Army than I do; and, as far as my powers and influence, in a constitutional way, extend, they shall be employed to the utmost of my abilities to effect it, should there be any occasion. Let me conjure you, then, if you have any regard for your country, concern for yourself or posterity, or respect for me, to banish these thoughts from your mind, and never communicate, as from yourself or anyone else, a sentiment of the like nature.
>
> I am, sir, your most obedient servant
>
> *G. Washington*

If the General had been aghast and chastened at Colonel Nicola's[13] memorial to him, his reaction was as nothing compared with Nicola's when he received Washington's stern reply. So shocked was the Colonel at the tone of his commander and the flagrant lashing his proposal had received that he wrote

13. Washington spelled Colonel Nicola's name "Nichola" in the salutation of his response.

three separate letters of apology in the next few days. All had different dates and it is even likely, historians say, that he wrote others which he subsequently destroyed. All expressed profuse sorrow for misdoings, all were forthright and gentlemanly, and all of them backtracked rapidly. Yet somehow none ever really came to grips with the General's fundamental point. Without precisely retracting anything about the glories of monarchy, they bowed to General Washington's superior judgment—and rank: "Since I find your sentiments so different from mine I shall consider myself as having been under a strong delusion and beg leave to assure you it shall be my future study to combat, as far as my abilities reach, every gleam of discontent."

From that hour onward, the man his people would unhesitatingly call the Father of his Country knew that, just as he had spent his life's vigor in raising a makeshift army and keeping it alive over seven intrepid years, his energies must now be focused wholly on getting that army home again without a calamity. Nicola's letters had dramatized it as nothing else could.

There are those who like to believe that Washington was actually not averse to such a royal scheme. Many modern patriotic societies based on blood descent from revolutionary heroes have mirrored such sentiments. Such groups speak of how Washington was first President of the Society of the Cincinnati, where a well-grounded effort, one which gained considerable headway after the revolution, sought to create a permanent nobility. Nor, they also point out, was Colonel Nicola's proposal the only one. So monarchial was the atmosphere of this country in 1782 that Gouverneur Morris, the superpatriot whose family name was signed to the Declaration of Independence and had long been a votary of the common man, wrote to General Nathanael Greene in the Carolinas: "I have no hope that our union can subsist except in the form of an absolute monarchy."

Even so sterling an American as John Adams was dubious about democracy, and he spoke of its questionable stability and leaned for a time to a stronger executive. John Jay supported for a while the idea of an American monarchy. The King bee buzzed in many a patriotic brain and colonists had no sooner thrown one monarch into discard than they began to yearn for another in the muddled morass of do-nothing self-rule. Would-be courtiers, possessed of more ardor than common sense, made several abortive attempts to establish royalty in a new nation that had just rejected and repudiated it.

A popular song of the time, "No King But God," composed by Nathaniel Billings, is said to have aided materially in killing the monarchy idea and restoring the democratic logic of Paine and Jefferson. But that Washington might have become King George was apparently possible at almost any hour between Yorktown and the Constitutional Convention.

Henry Cabot Lodge the elder wrote in his biography of Washington:[14]

> This incident has been passed over altogether too carelessly by historians and biographers. It has generally been used merely to show the general nobility of Washington's sentiments, and no proper stress has been laid upon the facts of the time which gave birth to such an idea and such a proposition. It would have been a perfectly feasible thing at that particular moment to have altered the frame of government and placed the successful soldier in possession of supreme power. The notion of kingly government was, of course, entirely familiar to everybody . . .

Thomas Carlyle wrote disparagingly of George Washington because he let events take their natural course and did not "seize the tottering government with a strong hand." But Lodge feels this is woeful misunderstanding of the man who flung aside the mere suggestion of total, dictatorial power which might have been his for a nod of the head, not simply because becoming king would be unpatriotic and dishonorable, but "because such a result would have defeated the one great and noble object at which he aimed." It was harder to wait it out, to restore order by muddling through slowly, painfully—but from the people up, not from a dictatorship downward. Far

14. Henry Cabot Lodge, *George Washington*, Vol. I (Boston, Houghton Mifflin Company, 1917), p. 336.

easier would have been martial law and order restored at the head of the willing Army. What is the glory that belongs to Washington alone is that he was keenly aware of the deficiencies of democracy under the Continental Congress, yet had the patience to refuse supreme rule and let this tiny, new seed sprout and break through the earth of freedom.

Washington continued to decry the idea of monarchy and kingship, by letter, in speeches, through continuous support of the philosophy that common men were able to govern themselves, a most radical concept in his time. In his last circular letter to the states on June 8, 1783, the General stressed points he had repeatedly touched upon in his public utterances. He was not unaware, it should be emphasized, of the defects in the Articles of Confederation which governed the young Republic.[15]

> There are four things [*he wrote*] which I humbly conceive are essential to the well-being, I may even venture to say, to the existence of the United States as an independent power.
>
> *First.* An indissoluble Union of States under one Federal head.
>
> *Secondly.* A sacred regard to the public justice.
>
> *Thirdly.* The adoption of a proper peace establishment, and
>
> *Fourthly.* The prevalence of that pacific and friendly disposition among the people of the United States which will induce them to forget their local prejudices and policies, to make those mutual concessions which are requisite to the general prosperity and, in some instances, to sacrifice their individual advantages to the interest of the community.

If anyone else has written a better definition of the responsibilities of individuals in a democracy it has been lost to posterity. These are not the words of a man who wanted to be king, who privately dwelt in marble halls and dreamed of sitting on a throne. This is the philosophy of a true democrat. Had he for a moment seriously entertained tenderness for

15. George Washington BiCentennial Commission Report, Washington, D.C., U. S. Government Printing Office, 1932.

monarchy with his own blood line, the royal American family, he could never have written the concluding portion of the foregoing letter. Thomas Paine or Thomas Jefferson could have done no better.

As late as August 1, 1786—only nine months before the Constitutional Convention—monarchy in America was still raising its ugly head and Washington was still combating it. In a letter which Washington wrote to John Jay on that date, we read:[16]

> Your sentiments, that our affairs are drawing rapidly to a crisis, accord with my own. What the event will be, is also beyond the reach of my foresight. We have errors to correct. We have probably had too good an opinion of human nature in forming our confederation. Experience has taught us, that men will not adopt and carry into execution measures the best calculated for their own good, without the intervention of a coercive power. I do not conceive we can long exist as a nation without having lodged somewhere a power, which will pervade the whole Union in as energetic a manner as the authority of the State governments extend over the several states.
>
> To be fearful of investing Congress, constituted as that body is, with ample authorities for national purposes, appears to me the very climax of popular absurdity and madness.
>
> What astonishing changes a few years are capable of producing! I am told that even respectable characters speak of a Monarchial form of government without horror. From thinking proceeds speaking; thence to acting is often but a single step. But how irrevocable and tremendous! What a triumph for the advocates of despotism to find, that we are incapable of governing ourselves, and that systems founded on the basis of equal liberty are merely ideal and fallacious! Would to God that wise measures may be taken in time to avert the consequences we have but too much reason to apprehend.

By May of 1787, with the opening of the Constitutional Convention, the seed of the first American monarchy had been uprooted completely by the one man who could in all likeli-

16. *Ibid.*

hood have become king.[17] But then, something better and more durable than monarchy was already being built: the totally unique democratic Republic we have in America today. In the creation of that democracy in a republic it was Washington himself, the devout and lonely patriot, who made the firm decision about what the American Presidency was to become: not a hereditary monarch, a constitutional monarchy, a military junta with dictator, nor a colonial despotism under foreign rule and local peers, but the freely elected (and replaceable) Chief Executive of all the people. This above all we owe the first President of the United States.

17. The United States Senate, early in its life, actually voted to refer to George Washington as "His Highness, the President of the United States," but the House voted it down.

Thomas Jefferson

IT WAS one million square miles of the most continuously fertile land in the world, and the President's agents bought it for less than 3¢ an acre. It was a territory obtained without the expenditure of a single life or even one drop of blood. Thirteen states would be carved out of it—larger and wealthier than the original Thirteen Colonies and richer than any comparable stretch of land anywhere in the world. This land gave to a young nation vision of its destiny as a two-ocean world power and guaranteed that the vital port of New Orleans would be permanently American, opening the vast Mississippi-Missouri-Ohio heartland all the way to the sea. From the moment of its purchase, the United States could turn her back on the Atlantic and forget for more than a century Europe's ageless squabbles.

The purchase of this territory was surely the greatest real estate bargain in the history of the world. And when we consider that it was accomplished without the prior consent of a newly elected Congress, most of whose members had just been campaigning (as had Jefferson himself) against the very Constitutional powers that would make it a legal act, the Louisiana Purchase becomes all the more astounding and prophetic.

Though many considered it an un-Constitutional transaction, the Louisiana Purchase was nevertheless immediately recognized in Washington as so rich a bargain that many principles and scruples went quickly overboard in order to justify it. The Senate, which must ratify all treaties, approved the procure-

2

Buys Louisiana – On His Own

ment of Louisiana in less than three days, and Jeffersonian democrats joined hands with their bitterest Tory opponents in ratification and celebration of a magnificent event.

Because of the factors of distance and time, Jefferson had given his representatives in Paris implied carte blanche to bargain for the port of New Orleans and part of Florida, permitting them to bid as high as $2,000,000. To this and this only, Congress had reluctantly assented prior to their departure for Paris. Yet when the opportunity suddenly came, Jefferson's faraway agents struck quite another deal—one that changed the course of our whole history. They spent more in one evening in Paris than the Federal budget then allowed for an entire year, and they spent it without legal precedent of any sort.

Finally, by another incredible twist, history chose John Marshall, Chief Justice of the United States, Jefferson's arch enemy, to provide the constitutionality for the purchase of the Louisiana vastness. If a man called John Marshall had never lived, if another man had been named Chief Justice (which would have suited Jefferson perfectly), Jefferson himself might have been impeached as a traitor and his representatives in Paris declared guilty of high treason. In the end, it was Marshall's liberal interpretation of basic Federal law which vouchsafed Jefferson and the legality of the purchase under "broad powers implied by the Constitution." Indeed, this fundamental conflict of Constitutional philosophies—states' rights and strict construction on Jefferson's side; strong central government and broad, implied powers on Marshall's—underlies the whole fantastic story.

Of all battles for control of the Constitutional destiny and direction of the early Untied States, that between Marshall and Jefferson cannot be outranked. Here two tremendous political philosophies clashed continually in a bloody running war to prove the true meaning of the Constitution and the power of the judiciary. For the first thirty months of Jefferson's first term he scrapped and argued with Marshall, acquiescing only as he approached treasonable disregard of the Chief Justice's decisions giving the Union strong central powers.

In a series of famous decisions early in the life of the Supreme Court, Federal jurisdiction and the ultimate power of the court were molded. The names whirl through early U. S. history like giant snowflakes before a winter storm. There are Marbury v. Madison, the Dartmouth College case, McCulloch v. Maryland, Gibbons v. Ogden, Martin v. Mott, the American Insurance Company v. Canter, and scores of others. Except to those of legal mind, the names are unimportant, but what these legal precedents established should matter terribly to every American.[1] In the end, John Marshall's broad construction of implied powers clearly won, and Thomas Jefferson's "illegal" purchase of the Louisiana Territory was ironically sustained by none other than his greatest political enemy.

This is, then, the amazing story of a strange alliance to legalize the first great stroke of executive power by a President of the United States, an act which fixed forever a pattern of the President as the nation's Chief Executive, and a strong one. From Jefferson's Administration on, a President began to be much more than a European-style figurehead, of use chiefly in ceremonials. He would be the king, the queen, the representation of the flag on the one hand, and the chief executive officer of the majority political party on the other, and many other

1. From sources in the *Harvard Guide to American History* (Cambridge, Mass., The Belknap Press of Harvard University, 1954). See pp. 327–28 for complete bibliography on Louisiana Purchase and John Marshall's decisions affecting it.

things as well. From that moment of history, the Presidency became a lively third of the tripartite Federal government, and
the Supreme Court a judiciary without precedent. And it was
Chief Justice Marshall, whose judicial decisions blessed the
bold stroke of the Louisiana Purchase as a legal act, ex post
facto as something perfectly within the limits of the President's
implied powers.

Any schoolboy knows Thomas Jefferson, yet John Marshall's
name is often found to be obscure. If Americans were asked to
identify John Marshall, only two in ten could do it.[2] Yet here
is a man who was Chief Justice of the United States from 1801
to 1835 when the very status and meaning of the Supreme
Court were in the molding. No period of American history
established more precedents; therefore, no period of American
history meant more to the future pattern of Constitutional law.

Born in a log cabin on the Virginia frontier, John Marshall
spent his boyhood in straitened, primitive surroundings, though
distantly related to the rich Randolphs and Lees through his
mother, as well as to Thomas Jefferson. Marshall served as an
officer in the American Revolution, returning to Virginia law
and politics where he made such a mark that George Washington sought him as Attorney General of the United States, and
later wanted him for American Minister of France. Both of
these posts he turned down. He did, however, represent the
young country in France during the XYZ Affair which concerned America's post-Revolutionary relations with France and
England, and which ended in a weakening of the traditional
French-American friendship.

Marshall's astuteness in uncovering French diplomatic duplicity in the XYZ Affair made him a popular American figure
and he was elected to Congress from Virginia as a Federalist
in 1799. One of a small but loyal unit which continued to support John Adams, Marshall became Adams's Secretary of State
in 1800. A year later, just before Jefferson took office, Marshall
was appointed Chief Justice of the United States. The Senate

2. Statistic from a *New York Herald Tribune* survey of famous American names.

confirmed him, after a battle, most of Jefferson's Democratic-Republicans and the anti-Adams Federalists being justifiably skeptical of Marshall's competence as an interpreter of law for the common man against the traditional rights of the aristocrat.

In thirty-four years of service as Chief Justice, Marshall emerged as the most powerful, famous, and precedent-making jurist in the history of America. He raised the Supreme Court from an anomalous position in the Federal triangle of executive-legislative-judicial to one of majesty, power, and precedent —a balance wheel to be carefully reckoned with. By the breadth and wisdom of his carefully reasoned decisions, and by his broad interpretation of the Federal Constitution—much of this interpretation the first precedents in our law—John Marshall earned the right to be known as the Great Chief Justice.

But Marshall's achievements matched his philosophical-legal quarrels with Presidents Jefferson, Madison, Monroe, Adams, and Jackson, with all of whom he constantly warred. Marshall was a loyal Federalist, a conservative who felt national unity and Federal power essential to the future of the United States of America. This cement took the form of historic interpretations of the Federal Constitution which were, at the time and in the circumstances, considered radical, strange, even un-American. Beyond doubt they established an independent and powerful judiciary.

John Marshall strengthened enormously the guarantee of the security of private property in an age born of the French and American revolutions. Above all, Marshall set forever the precedent that the Supreme Court of the United States had the right to review all legislation challenged as to its constitutionality. If declared un-Constitutional, a law was null and void; Congress and the Chief Executive would simply have to start over again in another direction. This "veto" power over all laws through judicial review had no parallel in other nations; it was an American phenomenon.

Chief Justice Marshall viewed the Constitution as a living instrument which could be broadly interpreted to make legal acts that the original framers could not possibly have foreseen.[3] These "broad, implied powers" enabled future Presidents, among them Roosevelt and Truman, to use virtual dictatorial power in later crises which cried out for quick, decisive action, in F.D.R.'s case the amazing activity that dispelled the blackness of the Depression, in Truman's the "police action" history calls the Korean War.

But broad as these powers were, through John Marshall's interpretation, other powers were quite clearly delegated and specifically reserved in the document he grew to know so well. These were certain powers earmarked, for example, for the Senate, such as ratifying a treaty or trying a President for impeachment; other powers reserved to the states, such as the right of each state to decide its own age qualifications for voting in presidential elections (eighteen in Kentucky and Georgia, nineteen in Alaska, and twenty in Hawaii, but twenty-one in the other forty-six states).

In the famous case of McCulloch v. Maryland, Marshall forever fixed the precedent that the Federal government must be flexible, have room to move around in. The Constitution could, therefore, as Mr. Dooley later said, "follow th' 'liction returns." In other words, it was to be a document broad enough to be adaptable to any age or circumstance.

Inviolability of American contracts was established in the Dartmouth College case. In Gibbons v. Ogden, Marshall ruled in favor of Federal power in interstate commerce at the expense of each state's rights. It was a national matter, he argued, once a vehicle or merchandise had crossed one state line into another, and so it has since remained by Federal precedent.

Marshall generally opposed the doctrine of states' rights when they clashed with Federal rights. The frequently undignified quarrels with Jefferson had one of their earlier detonations in the case of Marbury v. Madison wherein Marshall firmly fixed the right of the Supreme Court to review the constitutionality of legislation, sometimes even down to local laws. Thus, the Supreme Court of the United States ultimately became more powerful than the judiciary of any other democratic

3. E. S. Brown, *Constitutional History of the Louisiana Purchase,* (Berkeley, Calif., University of California Press, 1920), *passim.*

or constitutional monarchial form. It was Marshall's undeniable, unanswerable logic that made this view stick.

John Marshall mixed the honest friendliness of the hearty frontier with the grace of a Virginia gentleman. His writing style was exact, concise, and eminently clear. Each opinion developed from a series of logical sequences deduced from self-evident propositions which no true friend of the common man could deny. He almost never cited legal authority. He simply set precedent himself; and for this, if for nothing else, he must have seemed the devil incarnate to Thomas Jefferson.

Shifting political currents in Europe were creating a new era and new issues as the nineteenth century opened and Jefferson became the people's President. Napoleon was by now master of France, threatening most of Europe, eager to extend his power to the primitive New World which must surely have seemed defenseless to him. The French war with England had faded because the English could not sustain their end of it; the United States of America, now a genuine political unit, was nevertheless tender and impotent, a nation no European militarist yet took seriously.

On October 1, 1800, by the secret treaty of San Ildefonso, Spain was "persuaded" to cede all of the vast Louisiana Territory to France—and Napoleon. The newly elected Jeffersonian Administration had just taken over by the time the news reached Washington early in 1801. Jefferson was alarmed, and wrote to the U. S. Minister in Paris, Robert R. Livingston: "It completely reverses all the political relations of the U. S. and will form a new epoch in our political course."[4] This, as things would turn out, was the understatement of his life.

Quickly, U. S. foreign policy would find itself in a state of political change. France had, of all nations on earth, been America's staunch partner during the Revolution. Lafayette was an unprecedented American hero, the French people our natural friends. Yet, whoever possessed a certain swampy pinpoint on the planet had to be America's natural enemy. That

4. Adrienne Koch, *Jefferson and Madison* (New York, Alfred A. Knopf, Inc., 1950), p. 232.

swampy pinpoint was New Orleans. "There is on the globe one single spot, the possessor which is our natural and habitual enemy. It is New Orleans . . ." Jefferson wrote Livingston.[5]

Nothing could have more radically reversed U. S. foreign policy. For two generations the United States had, as Adrienne Koch so aptly puts it, been "fending off the British monarchy and championing France" and suddenly the administration was faced with "the fear that an unfriendly spirit prevails in the most important individuals of the [French] government towards us."[6] Napoleon could not and did not cotton to republican democracy as represented by Thomas Jefferson. The egotistical Corsican detested liberty, equality, fraternity. He considered himself chosen of God to rule not only the Old World but the New as well.

The fact that Jefferson had been an enthusiastic friend of French radicals and was currently adored by the leading philosophical minds in France did not help the American cause a bit. In a penetrating generalization later at Monticello, Jefferson wisely put Napoleon's distrust of the United States this way: "Bonaparte hates our government because it is a living libel on his."

Talleyrand was quick to point to America as a splendid arena for new Napoleonic glory. In March, 1802, the Peace of Amiens threw open to France and other nations the world's oceans, which had been British-dominated for generations. Twenty years before, this pact would have been hailed in the New World. Now it was regarded with consternation.

These developments deeply worried Jefferson, for no man was more interested in the welfare of the West than he. So long as the outlet for the Mississippi basin had been in the careless, indolent hands of Spain, trouble could be averted. But once leased to the strongest of European countries under a tyrant like Napoleon, and with the high seas open to French ships, the entire United States was in jeopardy.

   5. Ralph Henry Gabriel, *The Pageant of America*, Vol. VIII (New Haven, Yale University Press, 1927), pp. 209–12.
   6. Jefferson to Livingston, October 10, 1802, Writings (Ford), VIII, 173.

The Spanish government quickly closed the port of New Orleans on technical grounds that the United States had failed to apply for an extension of friendly if loose trade privileges provided for in the Pinckney Treaty of 1795. These privileges had never been formally renewed and were by now considered automatic. When Spain acceded to Napoleon and closed the port of New Orleans, which meant French control of the Mississippi basin, the newly opened West became understandably dismayed.

All of the West drained into the Gulf of Mexico. Mushrooming trade along the great Ohio, Missouri, and Mississippi rivers knew but one means of transportation across the great distances in the West and South in those days: water. Jefferson tried to solve the Napoleonic enigma by diplomacy but many in Congress called for war. Jefferson wrote to Livingston in Paris and what he asked Livingston to do was something no President of the United States had yet done or asked a subordinate to carry out. Jefferson was for the first time the Chief Executive of the United States taking a bold new presidential step.

Livingston was to begin at once to sound out Napoleon on American purchase of West Florida and New Orleans. Livingston was to impress the Corsican with our determination to keep the Mississippi open, yet attempt also to gain physical possession of the vital delta. Jefferson's favorite negotiator, the tough, wiry James Monroe, was dispatched to Paris to help Livingston's diplomacy.

From the banks of the Mississippi, Ohio, and Missouri rivers nothing could have seemed more vital than the success of the American negotiation. Into the long reaches of the great prairie basin, the jolting wagons of pioneers had kept pushing the frontier westward in a swelling tide. Settlers seeded their log cabins mile by mile along river fronts and the newly opened roads. The Mississsippi River itself was the ultimate commercial highway and New Orleans its destination.

Napoleon had already begun preparing an expedition to his newly acquired Louisiana; a general of division, three generals of brigade, five battalions of infantry, two companies of artillery, sixteen pieces of cannon, and 3,000 muskets were allotted for this purpose and ordered to Dunkirk for departure to the New World. But, as fast as regiments could be manned and armed and their generals appointed, they were consumed in a fiery furnace called Santo Domingo, a hot little island in the Caribbean that was to mean so much to the future of the United States and the reputation of Thomas Jefferson. This island was known to others as "Hayti"; it was inhabited chiefly by African slaves whom the French found impossible to colonize. The principal reason for this could have been the native leadership of the Haitians by a Negro patriot and martyr, a self-educated slave named François Dominique Toussaint L'Ouverture. This handsome man had joined the Negro rebellion in 1791. He was its organizational genius. Rapidly rising in power, Toussaint L'Ouverture combined forces with the Spanish and, in a series of lightning thrusts, became known by the French as "L'Ouverture," a name he gladly adopted. Though this black knight professed devotion to France, first to the revolution, then to Napoleon, he was perpetually devoted to the freedom of his own people.

In 1801, Toussaint conquered the whole of Santo Domingo, ceded to France by Spain in 1795. Napoleon was forced to send a task force to subdue him; in 1802, the bloody battle between two great military figures was joined in the steaming island jungles of the New World. But Haitian resistance was stubborn and the natives acquired a powerful natural ally, yellow fever. In 1802 alone, 50,000 Frenchmen were lowered into their graves on the island of Santo Domingo, dead of war and fever, with fever the more deadly.[7]

The ultimate success of U. S. negotiations in Paris was undeniably aided by this great black, who was later treacherously seized by Napoleon during an armistice, transported to France, and disposed of in the dreadful dungeon of Fort-de-Joux in the French Jura. As at other junctures in American history, Europe's distresses became America's fortune, and Napoleon

7. Samuel Flagg Bemis, *A Diplomatic History of the United States* (New York, Henry Holt and Company, Inc., 1950), pp. 126–37.

was forcefully persuaded to abandon the strategic Caribbean island on which he had placed such faith as the hub of his attempt at colonization of the New World.

As a result of Napoleon's losses in Haiti, Louisiana was now all but useless to him. England moreover was agitating for another war to unseat the Emperor of France and had strong new allies on the Continent whose eager armies would outman Napoleon's. He had nothing to spare with which to staff or arm fresh expeditions to Santo Domingo, let alone Louisiana.

The scourge of the Continent was increasingly desperate for money. Louisiana now being less than no value to him as real estate, and a costly outpost to boot, it also represented quick money for Napoleon's pocket. Moreover, the Corsican's military instinct told him to shorten his lines before fresh European trouble. At the same time he could restore what had been a most valuable friendship for half a century: American-French rapport.

In Paris, long weeks of perilous ocean travel away from Washington, Livingston was summoned suddenly, in April, 1803, to the French foreign office where François Marquis de Barbé-Marbois, Napoleon's chief negotiator, made him an offer which must have sent blood to his cheeks. Livingston had come pleading for the purchase of New Orleans and possibly West Florida, too. Now Barbé-Marbois officially offered him a quarter of a continent—the whole of the vast Louisiana Territory. Livingston had badgered the Emperor with written and verbal warnings, remonstrances, and arguments for months, intended to prove that the Americans were not empire build-ers, that Napoleon should invite the Americans to protect Louisiana from the Canadians, that Florida and Louisiana consisted largely of barren sand and sunken marshes, that New Orleans was important to the United States only because it sat astride the common mouth of a dozen major rivers west of the Alleghenies. In short, France could care nothing for such remote, desolate places which, to the American West, meant a great deal.

Monroe was not to arrive in Paris until late in April, 1803, and his presentation at the Tuileries was delayed until May 1.

By this time, the French had privately told Livingston they were willing to give up the whole Louisiana Territory, and three weeks had already been spent haggling over a price. The very night of Monroe's presentation, he and Livingston had a postdinner discussion with Marbois, who abruptly made Napoleon's final offer. Knowing that when Bonaparte offered a favor, suitors did well to waste no time in acceptance, Monroe and Livingston hastily whispered together, and a bargain was quickly struck with Marbois for $15,000,000, not all of it in cash. Weeks were required to draw up final treaty papers in two languages, but they were dated back to April 30, 1803.

Throughout this top-level haggling, the American negotiators were at the disadvantage of never being able to make contact with the home office. All they had was Thomas Jefferson's carte blanche, the President's word that what they did, provided it was within reason, would be ratified when they returned to Washington. But was the whole of the Louisiana Territory and the unauthorized sum of $15,000,000 "within reason"? It was a preposterous sum in those days, the equivalent of a large percentage of the entire American public debt and much more than the government had spent during John Adams's final twelve months in office. It was, moreover, an act both Livingston and Monroe inwardly felt to be un-Constitutional, and it had been Jefferson's philosophy which had so persuaded them.

On the republican principles of Jefferson, only the states themselves could authorize incorporation into the union of the United States. Yet this treaty which Jefferson's authorized amanuenses were signing provided that "the inhabitants of the ceded territory shall be incorporated in the Union of the United States, and admitted as soon as possible, according to the principles of the Federal Constitution, to the enjoyment of all the rights, privileges and immunities of citizens of the United States." This, for one thing, expressly violated the President's last-minute instructions.

Embarrassing as these events and embroideries were, Livingston and Monroe knew a fantastic bargain when they saw one, and promptly signed. Jefferson had written Livingston at the height of the negotiations that from the moment of French occupation of New Orleans "we must marry ourselves to the British fleet and nation." Otherwise the little new country called the United States of America would be forever at the mercy of Napoleon Bonaparte. This above all burned in the back of Livingston's mind.

The $15,000,000 was a total price—approximately 80,000,000 gold francs. Of this amount, 20,000,000 francs, or $3,750,000, were to go to American citizens to satisfy wartime claims against France. These claims were largely from merchants from Baltimore to Boston whose goods and ships had been subject to French spoliation and naval action before, during, and after the Revolutionary War. They were a highly sensitive issue along the Atlantic seaboard, and their settlement would help Jefferson sell his bill of goods when the astounding deal became known at home.

News about the purchase reached America at the beginning of the summer of 1803. Jefferson was by turns pleased, shaken, shocked, amazed, and perturbed. The trans-Appalachian people were now assured a trade route and freedom of the River. But acquisition of new territory conflicted with the doctrine of strict construction of the Federal Constitution on which Jefferson and Marshall had locked horns from the day the third President had taken office, sworn in by this same antagonist.

Jefferson did not hesitate. He immediately prepared an amendment to the Constitution to cover the matter. But, apprehension that Napoleon might change his fickle mind, plus pressure from the rising Western frontier, which now saw Jefferson as an incomparable hero, caused the Jeffersonian party to give up amending the Constitution and swing Congress into special session. An "illegal" but prodigious achievement had been accomplished. Now it had to be justified.

No President had yet taken a greater step on his own, and Jefferson knew it. The Louisiana Purchase would fittingly climax the diplomacy of the revolutionary period; Jefferson was acutely aware of its historical importance. While news of the Louisiana Purchase came as a distinct shock to the government at Washington, it also stirred many an American heart, Jefferson's included, by its imaginative greatness.

Jefferson was certain he had no Constitutional authority to purchase territory, and republican discussion confirmed this view.[8] But the stakes were so grand that the President abandoned his reservations. No mention was made of Constitutional anomaly in his message recommending Congressional approval. His party followed obediently the course he outlined. Liberal, broad construction of the Constitution—something which John Marshall's logic had never been able to—had been forced upon Jefferson and his followers by the bare fact of the Louisiana Purchase.

Westerners in Washington closed ranks behind the Administration, happily approving what meant life itself for their constituents. Public approval everywhere was overwhelming as the news galloped across mountain and swamp and river, and this approval echoed back to Capitol Hill. The whole thing flamed the imagination. Americans everywhere could now envision a new nation from the Atlantic to the Pacific and from the Great Lakes to the Gulf, a world power in generations to come.[9]

When the Spanish had abrogated the Pinckney Treaty, they had closed the port of New Orleans to American trade through the simple method of removing the "privilege of deposit" at the mouth of the Mississippi. Privilege of deposit meant giving any citizen of the United States the right of depositing and re-exporting his property or goods duty free at the Spanish-held port of New Orleans. Suspension of this right of deposit had meant personal disaster to settlers along the Ohio, Missouri, and Mississippi rivers because, in the early nineteenth-century wilderness, water was the principal means of transporting goods. The entire valley of the Mississippi from bayou to great

8. Leonard D. White, *The Jeffersonians* (New York, The Macmillan Company, 1951), p. 32.

9. Ray Allen Billington, *Westward Expansion* (New York, The Macmillan Company, 1949), pp. 242–45; see also Edward Channing, *A History of the U. S.*, Vol. IV (New York, The Macmillan Company, 1938), p. 323.

lake, from western Pennsylvania to the Dakotas, therefore, hailed the "Louisiana Procurement," and spoke of Jefferson as a male Joan of Arc.

The President summoned Congress on October 17, 1803, to special session. The Federalists hated Jefferson as they detested no one else in the short history of the country. But these were patriots, and the delicate point of Constitutional law was overwhelmed by actual possession. The fact was already accomplished. This was a rationale. Louisiana *already was* American territory!

Because they had long supported Marshall's view, the Federalists could not oppose the Louisiana Purchase on grounds of strict construction. But they could and did oppose the Louisiana Purchase on grounds of their dislike for the "lordlings of the South," a natural regional distrust of long standing and by no means at an end even today.

The treaty to be approved by the Senate provided for ultimate admission of ceded territory into the union "as a state or states" and this meant a lessening of influences of New England in government as well as the beginning of the end of traditional domination of the Federalists in the halls of Congress.

So the canny Federalists advanced a theory that, although under the Constitution territory could be annexed as a colony, admission of such a territory as a state would require a Constitutional amendment involving the consent of three-fourths of the states.

When this proposition failed and the treaty seemed certain of approval, irreconcilable New Englanders led by Timothy Pickering and Roger Griswold, both of Massachusetts, advocated secession from the United States and the formation of a new union of New England states. But other Federalists like the Adamses, Fisher Ames, and George Cabot discouraged the idea.

Because of Federalist, especially New England, opposition, the Louisiana Purchase treaty was not approved simply by a voice vote. The final tally in the Senate on October 20 was 24 to 7 to ratify the treaty—strictly along party lines. The House gratuitously declared itself in favor of the Louisiana Purchase on October 25, by a vote of 90 to 25—also along party lines, even though it had no jurisdiction in the matter.[10]

But the Constitutional legality of the Louisiana Purchase remained questionable for many years until John Marshall came to Jefferson's moral rescue twenty years after Jefferson had retired to Monticello. France had had no clear title to sell Louisiana: it had been a Napoleonic aggression. Livingston and Monroe had bought what was legally nothing more than "a pretension."[11] Only by propinquity and power was the Louisiana Purchase finally made a fact, and not until Florida and the delta country had been swept clear of "foreigners," first French and Spanish, then the British in the War of 1812. This final act of "propinquity and power" was under the command of a Westerner named Andrew Jackson and it later made him President of the United States.

Albert J. Beveridge's classic *Life of John Marshall* handles Jefferson's acts in the Louisiana procurement with something less than sympathy, but probably comes close to the heart of the material.[12]

The President had been amazed when the news reached him. He did not want Louisiana—nothing was further from his mind than the purchase of it. The immorality of the acquisition affected him not at all; but the inconvenience did. He did not know what to do with Louisiana. Worse still, the treaty of cession required that the people living in that territory should be admitted into the Union, "according to the principles of the Federal Constitution."

So, to his infinite disgust, Jefferson was forced to deal with the Louisiana Purchase by methods as vigorous as any ever advocated by the abhorred Hamilton—methods more autocratic than those which, when done by others, he had savagely denounced as unconstitutional and destructive of liberty. The President doubted whether, under the Constitution, we could acquire, and was sure that we could not govern, Louisiana, and he actually prepared amendments

10. Louis M. Hacker, *The Shaping of the American Tradition,* Vol. I (New York, Columbia University Press, 1947), pp. 320–22.

11. Albert J. Beveridge, *Life of John Marshall,* Vol. III (Boston, Houghton Mifflin Company, 1929), pp. 146-51.

12. *Ibid.*

authorizing the incorporation into the republic of the purchased territory. No such legal mistiness dimmed the eyes of John Marshall who, in time, was to announce as the decision of the Supreme Court that the republic could acquire territory with as much right as any monarchial government.

To add to his perturbations, the high priest of popular rights found himself compelled to abandon his adored phrase, "the consent of the governed," upon which he had so carefully erected the structure of his popularity, and to drive through Congress a form of government over the people of Louisiana without consulting their wishes in the least.

The Jeffersonian doctrine had been that the Union was merely a compact between sovereign States, and that new territory and alien peoples could not be added to it without the consent of all the partners. The Federalists took their stand upon this indefensible ground, and openly threatened the secession at which they had hinted when the Federal Judiciary Act was repealed.

Jefferson was alive to the danger: "Whatever Congress shall think it necessary to do (about Louisiana)," he cautioned one of the republican House Leaders, "should be done with as little debate as possible." A month earlier he had written: "The Constitution has made no provision for our holding foreign territory, still less for incorporating foreign nations into our Union. The Executive . . . have done an act beyond the Constitution."

Therefore, he declared, "the less we say about constitutional difficulties respecting Louisiana the better. . . . What is necessary for surmounting them must be done *sub silentis.*" The great radical favored publicity in affairs of state only when such a course was helpful to his political plans. On other occasions, no autocrat was ever more secretive than Thomas Jefferson. Seemingly, however, the President was concerned only with his influence on the destiny of the world.

At first the Federalist leaders were too dazed to do more than grumble. "The cession of Louisiana . . . is like selling us a ship after she is surrounded by a British Fleet," shrewdly observed George Cabot, when the news was published in Boston.

Though the United States flag was raised over New Orleans on December 20, 1803, the boundaries of the Louisiana Purchase weren't legally settled for years. The French had come to regard the Rio Grande and Iberville rivers as the east and west boundaries of Louisiana, but no such boundaries were set forth in the treaty. Indeed, Talleyrand had vaguely waved his arm and suggested that Livingston himself set them. As with so many facts of history, time, force, and propinquity answered the final questions.

From the Louisiana Purchase, which increased the national domain by 140 per cent, were carved all or part of thirteen new states: Louisiana (which was admitted in 1812), Missouri (1821), Arkansas (1836), Iowa (1846), Minnesota (1858), Kansas (1861), Nebraska (1867), Colorado (1876), North Dakota (1889), South Dakota (1889), Montana (1889), Wyoming (1890), and Oklahoma (1907).

The constitutionality of the procurement, settled in 1828, came about through a side issue,[13] often the way with Supreme Court decisions, in the case of the American Insurance Company *et al.* v. David Canter. In his opinion, Justice Marshall ruled once and for all that the nation had the right, through implied powers of the Constitution which Jefferson had so bitterly contested, to acquire and govern territory.

These were the facts in the historic case, which is Federally catalogued as 1 Peters 511, 1828:

A ship with a cargo of cotton, which had been insured, was wrecked on the coast of Florida after that territory had been ceded to the United States and before it became a state of the Union. The cotton was saved and shipped to Key West where, by order of a local court acting under a territorial law, it was sold at auction to satisfy salvage claims. Part of the cotton was purchased by one David Canter, who shipped it to Charleston, where the insurance companies libeled it—that is, filed a suit of complaint against it. The libelants contended that the Florida court was not competent to order the auction sale because the territorial act was inconsistent with the national Constitution.

---

13. It is interesting and perhaps a bit ironical that this vindication by Marshall came two years after Jefferson's death. He died July 4, 1826, a day which also saw the death of John Adams, his predecessor.

In the U. S. Supreme Court, the question was: "Was the territorial act, under which the local court at Key West ordered the auction sale, valid?"

The answer to the question depended, said Marshall, upon the relation in which Florida stood to the United States. Since the national government could make war and conclude treaties, it followed that it "possesses the power of acquiring territory either by conquest or treaty—ceded territory becomes a part of the nation to which it is annexed but the relations of the inhabitants to each other [do not] undergo any change." Their allegiance was simply transferred—but the law "which regulates the intercourse and general conduct of individuals remains in force until altered by the newly created power of the state." The treaty by which Spain ceded Florida to the United States assured to the people living in that territory "the enjoyment of the privileges, rights and immunities of U. S. citizens." In other words, the power to govern territory flows from the right to acquire it.

The Supreme Court of the United States held that, when the Federal government was expressly authorized in Articles I and II of the Constitution to make war and conclude treaties, it was there given all the powers necessary to carry out either of these functions. That is, in making war it could conquer and occupy enemy territory. In making treaties of peace, it could require the enemy to cede these conquered areas just as fully as it could require a payment of cash indemnity. The power to make war and peace therefore included the authority to do whatever was necessary and proper for war- and peacemaking. This was where, in Marshall's logic, the Federal government got the authority to acquire subject lands and peoples—by implication, the vast Louisiana Purchase.

Jefferson had been overwhelmingly re-elected in 1804 on his newly won popularity in the West, as well as with common, ordinary people everywhere, including those who were bound to emigrate beyond the Eastern mountains. Jefferson had been hailed as our first man of the people and was almost unanimously a hero by the beginning of his second term. Yet, everything he had dreamed and imagined for his country by the amazing purchase of Louisiana Territory might have come to naught without John Marshall's liberal, broad interpretation of the Federal Constitution.

In the end, however, President Jefferson was the man who took the responsibility for the purchase and who made it possible. There could have been no judicial interpretation of an act without the act itself. In giving his representatives in Paris a free hand and his Presidential blessing, in immediately recognizing the greatness of the bargain and its glorious meaning to future Americans, our third President took a giant step, and shouldered the historical consequences, whatever they might be. Henceforth, the President of the United States would be in truth Chief Executive, a person of unprecedented power and leadership in a democratic society. Only a man of great gifts, of soaring imagination, of boundless faith in the ultimate wisdom of the common people, could have made such a terrible, yet wonderful decision. For this reason, with many others, Thomas Jefferson may well have been the most remarkable American.

Andrew Jackson

O N THE DAY of his inauguration, Andrew Jackson solemnly declared that Federal institutions would be better for having civil servants friendly to each incoming administration. He thus took his cue from William Learned Marcy, to whom is attributed the phrase "to the victors belong the spoils," and established the spoils system which is now a tradition in most branches of American government, among them the Presidency. Since the time of Jackson, in fact, no democratic government has allowed as many majority partisan appointments as does ours, nor adhered so firmly to the principle that party members deserve to be rewarded simply because they have been on the winning team.

For more than four decades after Jackson's term of office, dispensation of Federal patronage was strictly by party allegiance, and the inevitable corruption, as well as inefficiency, bred in so partisan a system expanded until it reached staggering proportions under President Grant. Disappointed at the gross disorders in public office, the public demanded a civil service commission and began to get one in 1871; but civil service only modified the partisan chapter begun under Jackson; it did not erase it completely.

Andrew Jackson had been a backwoods child along the borderland of the Carolinas—both states claim him—where he found himself an orphan at the age of fourteen. Born only nine years before the Battles of Lexington and Concord, Jackson

52

3

Invents the Spoils System

nevertheless saw Revolutionary War service and was a prisoner of the British at Camden, South Carolina.

Jackson's father had been an impoverished Scottish linen draper from Ulster County in Northern Ireland. He had come to the Carolinas and cleared the wilderness woods for a farm on which he died while Andrew was still in his mother's womb.[1] With Andrew's birth his mother became housekeeper to a brother-in-law. Andrew Jackson was, consequently, born in hardship, reared in poverty, dressed in linsey-woolsey, and rarely overate. Nervous and frail, sensitive and intelligent, Jackson might well have acquired his inferiority complex and quickness of temper and his awareness of slight from such difficult early circumstances. These also explain his lifelong feeling for the underdog and, probably, his restless ambition. Certainly they explain his feelings when willful political opponents slandered his guiltless wife Rachel, who loved sippin' whisky and a corncob pipe of an evening.

The Revolutionary War not only gave Jackson early war service, but cost him the lives of two brothers and his mother, who died of prison fever while nursing patriots in Charleston. At fourteen, then, Andrew Jackson was a war veteran, an orphan, and the next thing to a neglected public charge.

Politics quickly attracted Jackson, whose Scotch-Irish blood

1. Allan Nevins and Henry Steele Commager, *A Short History of the United States* (New York, The Modern Library, 1945), pp. 170–72.

pulled him that way and also made him a rough man in the
infighting. He became a member of the Tennessee Constitutional Convention and in 1796 was elected the sole member
from his state in the Federal House of Representatives. There
he at once displayed two political characteristics he never lost:
distrust of the rich, the well-born, and all Easterners; and a
profound love of the common man, the plain people with whom
he sympathized heart and soul.[2]

Jackson's distrust of the East can possibly be explained by
the fact that most of the merchants and bankers of his time
lived either along the Atlantic seaboard or in New Orleans.
They paid the producer of the goods in the frontier West
precious little; more often than not a farmer received worth-
less paper for his product and his sweat. This actually happened to Jackson in 1798 when he bought $6,000 worth of
goods in Philadelphia, selling his land to pay for the goods to
a merchant whose notes went unhonored. Jackson was thus
saddled with a huge debt, through no fault of his own, and
never lost his understandable feeling that the East was made
up of cheats and shysters.

Early in life, Andrew married a woman about his own age
by the name of Rachel Donelson Robards; married her, as it
turned out, before she had secured a legal divorce from her
first husband, Lewis Robards. Though Andrew's marriage
ceremony was later repeated, his enemies made much of the
circumstance and, in the end, the well-publicized scandal
broke the man's heart. He bitterly blamed her early death on
the mud and offal plastered on his marriage in the depraved
political campaigns of 1824 and 1828. She was his one and
only romantic friend; he loved her deeply to the day of his
death, fifteen years before the Civil War.

Rachel Robards had first laid eyes on Andrew Jackson when
he knocked at the door of the Donelson stockade on the
Cumberland River near Nashville. Both were young, he an
unmarried lawyer, she a married woman whose husband, Lewis
Robards, drank more Kentucky corn liquor than was good for
him and who had a habit of disappearing from time to time.

2. *Ibid.*

When Robards failed to appear for a longer spell than usual and Rachel faced starvation, she had returned to her family home on the Cumberland. Robards eventually turned up again to sponge off her family, but later disappeared into Kentucky.

When Rachel, a sensuous, dark-haired young matron as yet unstirred by romantic love, first saw Andrew Jackson at the frontier stockade door she was probably taken with his bushy red hair, piercing blue eyes, an overly large mouth and powerful chin, his enormous height, and thin but wiry strength. She told friends she thought he must be six and a half feet tall, at least three heads higher than herself. There was a vibrance about him, a radiance, a glow, a gentle honesty which quickly began to change her sleeping chemistry. There doesn't seem to be any doubt that it was for both strong physical attraction at first sight. From the first, in fact, they were never very far apart until her tragic death on the eve of his inauguration.

Jackson is said to have told her he had been living at inns in Nashville and was sick and tired of the brawling, the drinking, and the greasy food. He wanted a real home to go back to each night, and since her mother took in boarders occasionally (all frontier stockade women did—there was almost nowhere else for a stranger to sleep), Jackson wondered aloud if he might stay with the Donelsons, a request that was readily and happily granted.

After Jackson had taken up happy residence with the Donelsons, Lewis Robards returned from one of his drinking absences in Kentucky. Robards hated the Cumberland Valley and Nashville and made no bones about it, and by now he probably detested his marital responsibilities. Quickly he disappeared once more (he told Rachel he was going to Harrodsburg, Kentucky, for a few days to see his sick mother) and Rachel never saw him again. Soon it became obvious to Nashville that he had deserted her and that their frontier marriage was finished. Jealous of Jackson, seldom sober, a bounder in every definition of the word, Robards persuaded a brother-in-law, one Jack Jouitt, to introduce a bill in the Virginia legislature to grant him a divorce from Rachel

Donelson Robards on grounds of desertion and adultery. The corespondent named was Andrew Jackson.

None of this information had been disclosed to Rachel until the legal procedure was a *fait accompli*. She had not been present to plead her case before the Virginia legislature; she had not even been aware of such a case. Her own feelings on hearing the news must have ranged from anger to consternation, then to fear and relief, and back to anger at such an unmanly thing. Yet, since she had long known that her marriage was over, and doubtless had prayed it would legally end, there was nothing to do but accept the cards as they had been dealt. In frontier America in the last years of the eighteenth century no lone woman could have made the impossible wilderness-trek back to Virginia to tell her side of the divorce proceedings, even had she been aware of them or wished to halt them. Surely her family and the town of Nashville would understand she was better off this way, legally branded as she might be as an adulteress.

In 1791, Jackson and Mrs. Robards took a trip down river to Natchez, Mississippi, where Jackson had wealthy friends. There they were married in the summer of 1791, believing that the legislature of Virginia had granted the jealous "Captain" Robards a legal divorce, though on fraudulent grounds. It was, unfortunately, later learned that the Virginia legislature had merely given Lewis Robards the *right* to file a suit for divorce, not a divorce itself. Frontier ignorance, Robard's carelessness, and the great distances involved had botched the situation. Jackson, himself a lawyer, should have been aware that a legislature normally could not dissolve a marriage but merely permit filing of a bill of divorcement.

Actually, therefore, Rachel had for two years been a bigamist when, in 1793, Lewis Robards got around to the legal act of final separation from her. When Rachel learned of this new disaster to her reputation she became extremely despondent and had to be given sedatives. Jackson, when he heard of it, immediately procured another license and saw that another ceremony was performed. But the barn door had been closed too late. Rachel's reputation was ruined forever, and the defamatory consequences in the presidential elections of 1824 and 1828 led to her early death.

There is no consummate evidence that Rachel was unfaithful or that Jackson was not acting in good faith and in the firm belief that a divorce had been granted to Rachel Robards when first they became man and wife. Soon after, Cumberland secured its freedom from North Carolina and became a legal territory of the Federal government; local events rose to such a pitch of excitement that local gossip seems not to have been published in permanent form, as it might have been in quieter years. We can only guess now; but knowing Jackson's qualities, his firm belief in right and wrong, goodness and sin, righteousness and iniquity, it is hard to believe that he and Rachel Donelson Robards knowingly shared a common-law affair between 1791 and 1793.[3] It simply wasn't in his strait-laced Scotch-Irish nature.

Jackson's friends and supporters often went out of their way to record his sympathy and gentleness with children, which made his childless marriage all the more poignant. Thomas Hart Benton, the great Senator from the new West, never tired of relating how he arrived at Jackson's home one "wet, chilly evening, in February, and came upon him in the twilight, sitting alone before the fire, a lamb and a child between his knees."[4]

> He started a little [*Benton wrote*], called a servant to remove the two innocents to another room, and explained to me how it was. The child had cried because the lamb was out in the cold, and begged him to bring it in—which he had done to please the child, his adopted son, then not two years old. The ferocious man does not do that! and

3. A delightful and accurate historical novel by Irving Stone paints the tragic romance in far greater detail. Called *The President's Lady* (Garden City, Doubleday and Company, Inc., 1959), this fictional account faithfully matches the known facts in the case and is most persuasive of Rachel's innocence as well as Andrew Jackson's.

4. John William Ward, *Andrew Jackson: Symbol for an Age* (New York, Oxford University Press, 1955), p. 197.

though Jackson had his passions and his violence, they were for men and enemies—those who stood up against him—and not for women and children, or the weak and helpless: for all of whom his feelings were those of protection and support.

The child in Benton's story was, moreover, an Indian boy orphaned in one of Jackson's campaigns. It had been found by some Indian women who were about to kill it because its parents had died at the hands of white men. The Indian boy became Jackson's ward and grew up with the implausible name of Lincoyer. The story won the nation more than any of Jackson's victories had done, reflecting, as a contemporary said, "more honour on the heart of the General than the entire glory of the Creek War." This was the child Senator Benton had seen lying down with the lamb between Jackson's knees, dismissed embarrassedly from the room by the General.

Rachel's favorite sister, Jane Hays, wrote at presidential election time with nostalgia for their early Cumberland stockade home and their good times together:

How does my dear Sister Jackson? I cannot take up my bonnet and meet you at Sister Betsy's or Sister Mary's . . . to smoke our pipes, laugh and talk over occurrences of former days, each one taking the words out of the other's mouth. . . . It was a pleasant neighborhood. . . . You will regret leaving it Sister Jackson, and your fine farm and comfortable house, for the City of Washington. . . .

Rachel Jackson couldn't have agreed more with her favorite Sister Hays. Indeed she never lived to experience life in the White House, only uncivilized and unceasing slander. Divorce was bad enough in those days. But to have married a supposedly divorced woman only to find she was a legal adulteress was to give Jackson's opponents a gratuitous political weapon with both edges indecently honed. The issue had first been raised in the lost campaign of 1824 when Henry Clay and John Quincy Adams had managed to deprive Jackson of the Presidency through their so-called "corrupt bargain." Clay's votes had been swung to Adams when there had been found to be no clear majority in the electoral college, though Jackson was high man and undoubtedly the choice of the electorate.

From the "Raleigh Register" of October 12, 1824, had come the following political statement regarding Rachel Jackson's virtue:[5] "I make a solemn appeal to the reflecting part of the community, and beg of them to think and ponder well before they place their tickets in the box, how they can justify it to themselves and posterity to place such a woman as Mrs. Jackson at the head of the female society of the United States."

When the shadow of Andrew Jackson's courtship threatened the forthcoming campaign of 1828 and the common man with it, a testy Jackson wrote to Sam Houston in his own inimitable spelling:[6] "I have lately got an intimation of some of his [Clay's] secrete movements which if I can reach with possitive and responsible proof I will wield to his political and perhaps his actual destruction. he is certainly the bases[t], meanest scoundrel that ever disgraced the image of his god. . . . Even the aged and virtuous female is not free from his . . . slander— but *anough, you know me.* I know how to defend *her.*"

Sam Houston did indeed know his patron, how Jackson had in the past defended his wife's virtuous name in a duel or two, for Houston had trained for a recent duel of his own on the Hermitage grounds under General Jackson's experienced eye. He knew that any hint of adultery regarding Mrs. Jackson meant a challenge in that flamboyant era. Duels were fought by men of honor to maintain honor, a very precious commodity then.

The next person to attack poor Rachel was Charles Hammond, editor of the *Cincinnati Gazette* and a staunch conservative. Wrote Hammond:[7] "Gen. Jackson prevailed upon the wife of Lewis Roberts [sic] to desert her husband and live with himself."

5. Marquis James, *Andrew Jackson, Portrait of a President* (Indianapolis, The Bobbs-Merrill Company, 1940), p. 93.
6. Jackson to Sam Houston, December 15, 1826, Correspondence III, 325.
7. James, *op. cit.,* p. 155.

Then followed a lurid account of the divorce on the shady testimony of a man named McGary who had loosely used the word adultery in the proceedings many years before, ignoring the years the Jacksons had supposed themselves to have been legally married.

But it remained for Adams's conservative mouthpiece, the *National Journal,* to reprint nationally a disreputable handbill written by a candidate for Congress from Jackson's area in Tennessee, one Thomas D. Arnold, proclaiming that Andrew Jackson had spent the principal part of his life "in gambling, in cock-fighting, in horse-racing . . . and to cap all tore from a husband the wife of his bosom."

This now made it official and the country knew the tale. The libel went on: "General Jackson admitted that he boarded at the house of old Mrs. Donelson, and that Roberts [sic] became jealous of him but he omits the cause of that jealousy . . . [namely] that one day Roberts surprised General Jackson and his wife exchanging most delicious kisses. . . ."

The candidate for Congress from Tennessee admitted that in this case Roberts (Robards) acted a coward's part in that he failed to shoot Jackson dead in his tracks. Later, according to Adams's stalwart journal, Jackson neglected to tell that on the voyage to Natchez he and Rachel "slept under the same blanket."[8]

One can well imagine the shock with which such printed words must have struck bluestocking Back Bay of the early 1800s. Having the unprintable suggested about a presidential candidate (and believed as gospel because it appeared in the official Adams journal) damned his political career forever.

Hammond followed with fresh editorial comment in Cincinnati:[9] "Ought a convicted adulteress and her paramour husband to be placed in the highest offices of this free and Christian land?"

Old Hickory by now was fighting to control himself:[10] "How

8. Tennessee State Library, Nashville, quoting a broadside by Thomas D. Arnold, May 24, 1824.

9. James, *op. cit.,* p. 156.

10. Jackson to General John Coffee, June 2, 1828, Correspondence III, 409.

hard it is to keep the cowhide from these villains. I have made many sacrifices for my country—but being unable . . . to punish these slanders of Mrs. J. is a sacrifice too great to be well endured."

But Jackson had put himself in an impossibly frustrating position by accepting the candidacy of President of the United States: an aspirant to the Presidency could no longer fight duels. Burr's fate had proved it politically, if morals and common sense had not. Clay had been close enough to Hammond in Cincinnati to have suppressed the slanders had he wished to do so. Despite his virtuous disclaimers, Clay, the presidential candidate who had made the "corrupt bargain" with Adams and had been paid off as Secretary of State, knew what his man Hammond was about and gave silent consent to the slanders; there is little doubt of it as one looks back through the records.

As for Jackson, he believed to the hour of his death that Secretary of State Clay and President Adams were thoroughly guilty of the whole disgusting libel. (It was not by chance that, when his own two-term Presidency was over, Jackson declared that his two regrets were (1) that he had been unable to shoot Henry Clay, and (2) hang John C. Calhoun, the high priest of nullification.) Jackson was of a very different moral stripe, an instinctive cavalier, a man who felt, like some medieval knight, that women were pure and sacred and shouldn't be brought into the political arena. When a gazette friendly to Jackson came up with a fabrication attributing to Mr. and Mrs. Adams premarital relations similar to those alleged against the Jacksons, Jackson hastily wrote the editor that "female character should never be introduced," except by way of just legal retaliation on the known guilty. In the free-style personal campaigning of those days, Jackson's shining chivalry had few if any parallels.

But Jackson had always been such a gallant knight. His supporters pointed to the way he had defended the beauty of New Orleans womanhood from the savage lust of British soldiery. A Jacksonian partisan asked, during the height of the slanders against Rachel Jackson, how any man who had behaved as Jackson had in New Orleans could feel other than noble about the women of America:[11]

> And you, too, my fair and beloved countrywomen whose first honour is in the gentleness of your nature, will you not unite your sympathies and tears over the grave of that man, who, above all others, was the most devoted friend and admirer, might I not say romantic, that woman ever had?
> Who so prompt to defend and protect her rights, or guard her from injury and insult?
> Who ever cherished or exalted more the purity of the domestic and social virtues, so infinitely more important to human happiness than all others? Whose valour was it that protected our mothers, and wifes, and daughters, from the savage tomahawk, and a licentious soldiery, and one of our finest cities, with its "beauty and booty" from ruthless invaders?
> Whose, but Andrew Jackson's?

Jackson's love of Rachel and his emotional tie with her long after her death were both pronounced and unconcealable. A visitor to the White House soon after inauguration found Jackson crying in his upstairs room:[12] "He was sitting at the little table with his wife's miniature before him, propped up against some books; and between him and the picture lay an open book, which bore the marks of long use. This book, I afterward learned, was *her* prayer book."

The tragedy of Jackson's marital situation is by no means irrelevant to the story of his invention of the spoils system. Indeed, it seems to have been a fundamental cause of his feelings—which stewed in morose anger, then cooled in retribution—and consequent acts as he took the highest office in the land. For his beloved Rachel died at Christmastide, 1828, soon after his election to the Presidency and before his lonely inaugural in March, 1829. He forever attributed her death to her slanderers, and Jackson publicly called Clay and Adams her murderers. The most natural reaction in the world was, then, for the new President of the United States to throw out of

11. Ward, *op. cit.*, p. 194.
12. Nicholas Trist, quoted *ibid.*, p. 197.

office every vestige of Clay-Adamsism, every appointee, every scent of what was emotionally to him a heap of indescribable filth, and undemocratic filth to boot.

Rachel Jackson's maligning and her subsequent death were, above all others, debts her husband never forgot or forgave.[13] Marquis James points out that in the end these slanders appear to have gained the Adams Administration and re-election campaign no advantage with the electorate: such assaults seldom do. The end result was only to "lay waste to the joy of a life, desolating a pious woman whose fortune had been in youth to be beautiful, to marry a bounder, and, existence with him becoming intolerable, to win the heart of Andrew Jackson."

The plan had been to leave Rachel in Tennessee until the inaugural was over and the new administration under way. This wasn't Andrew Jackson's idea, but Rachel's, and seconded heartily by Jackson's high political command. Though the campaign tempest had ceased, Rachel's reappearance among the ladies of social Washington might well have set it off again, and a fretful Rachel knew it when she wrote a letter from Nashville in December of 1828: "I assure you I had rather be a doorkepper [sic] in the house of God than to live in that Palace at Washington." She kept repeating this phrase in other letters and also by mouth to her maid, Hannah.[14]

Suddenly, as Christmas neared, Rachel fell ill with one of those unknown and unmitigated Western fevers common to early winter of that time. Bleed her as they would, the physicians could not seem to revive her health. A few hours before she died she asked the maid Hannah to help her to the chair by the fire and fill her pipe with tobacco (another personal problem to Washington society), whereupon she said to Hannah twice over: "I had rather be a doorkepper in the house of God than to live in that Palace." The following day, December 23, 1828, Rachel Donelson Robards Jackson died, her long flight from fame mercifully over.[15]

Andrew Jackson and she had been inseparable man and wife

13. James, *op. cit.*, p. 158.
14. *Ibid.*
15. *Ibid.*

for thirty-seven years, and from the first he had defended against all men both her virtue and her pipe-smoking. Witnesses to the Tennessee funeral wrote afterward that they wished those who had hastened this mournful scene by their relentless gossip on an unoffending woman could have been brought to view this "saddest spectacle that any present had ever beheld."[16]

At the end of the funeral service President-elect Jackson said aloud: "In the presence of this dear saint I can and do forgive all my enemies. But those vile wretches who have slandered her must look to God for mercy." In such black Gaelic despair, the new President left Tennessee for Washington to organize the first true administration of the common man. Is it any wonder that he clearly and distinctly understood William Learned Marcy when the latter declared "to the victors belong the spoils," or that he adopted the principle as his own?

Four years earlier, Jackson had polled the greatest number of popular votes, almost as many as the rest put together, yet had failed to reach a clear majority in the electoral college. When he heard that Candidate Clay was seeing Candidate Adams he had surmised that "bargains and sales are going on in the monstrous union between Clay and Adams." He was entirely right, for Adams took thirteen states, Jackson seven, and Crawford four in the run-off House vote, with states voting as units. Later, when John Quincy Adams was safely President, certain Adams men had wanted Clay to withdraw his "corrupt bargain" and make a generous gift of his great service to Adams. But Clay, with outward reluctance, had accepted the post of Secretary of State, then traditionally third in line for the Presidency should both President and Vice-President die in office. By now, however, the election of 1828 had wiped away this old debt. Jackson had won landslide endorsement by 178 to 83 in the electoral college and 647,286 to 508,064 in popular vote. Adams had, of course, scored heavily in New England but nowhere else, while Old Hickory's support was by now widely diffused and his enormous popularity with the average

16. *Ibid.*, pp. 128–29.

man, "the common man," was similar to Franklin D. Roosevelt's just over a century later.

So Jackson was coming to power stimulated by better than two-to-one electoral endorsement and provoked to the kind of revenge that only a Scotch-Irish soldier with a trigger temper, a keen sense of right and wrong, as well as strong partisanship for the average man (together with a memory for personal hurts) could bring to the Presidency.

Perhaps it wasn't by chance that Mr. Justice Joseph Story of the Supreme Court, who had wanted Chief Justice Marshall's place when Marshall was succeeded by Taney, later wrote of the Jacksonian democracy: "Though we live under the form of a republic we are in fact under the absolute rule of a single man."[17]

There was, of course, far more in Jackson's background than pique, hurt, the slander of his wife, and a prodigious memory for slights to make him become what he did as President and to espouse the partisan spoils system. The common men who rallied behind Jackson were disappointed with aristocrats as Presidents, men with bloodline, money, and estate. The little people of a growing country, particularly the expanding West, were demanding more equal distribution of wealth and greater responsibility in government. Newly enfranchised masses, especially the foreign-born lately fled from European monarchies and traditional, despotic family power, needed men in office who more accurately represented themselves.

Jackson came from the West, the first President beyond the Eastern mountains. Up to now, all Presidents had been from Virginia or Massachusetts. Washington had come as a Virginia

17. Jefferson had said that in Cabinet meetings all grave and important matters would be put to a vote—"the President counting himself but one." Jefferson had soon repudiated this, of course, since he alone was faced with the consequences of any Cabinet vote. Jackson listened to his Cabinet, then decided for himself, on grounds that he was the Chief Executive and must make any final decision. That was Jackson's bent—to do it himself, on his own, and take whatever consequences arose. Lincoln later found Cabinet meetings so useless he often stayed away from them. A story went about Washington in Lincoln's day that in a Cabinet meeting Lincoln asked for a vote, then said: "Ayes one, Noes seven. The Ayes have it."

gentleman, John Adams a Boston Brahmin, Jefferson a Virginian of wealth and aristocracy despite his political philosophy, Madison and Monroe also Virginians of good family, and John Quincy Adams an aristocrat to his dainty Massachusetts finger tips. But Jackson was a man who had lived on the Western side of the Alleghenies and was, therefore, the common man's first indigenous mouthpiece. Not being endowed as all his predecessors had been, he had had to work hard for a meager living.

Old Hickory, the people's candidate, had had the endorsement of the Workingman's Party in Philadelphia and was also the hero of the Western farmer.[18] He had had overwhelming support in the South, which was largely antiurban in make-up and prejudice. Champion of what John Adams sneeringly called "the *common* people," Jackson personified a new democracy; he was the hero of the "mob" and the "rabble." It was not without purpose that he called his political party Democrats, which label has stuck to this day to his political legatees. For four long years since 1824, Jackson had been able (partly because the Tennessee legislature had formally endorsed him as a presidential candidate) to retire West to campaign, organize, and prepare for 1828. When 1828 had come he was ready, and so were the votes.

One reason Jacksonian votes were readier in 1828 than they had ever been was the sudden mushrooming of suffrage. Homer Carey Hockett, in *Political and Social Growth of the American People*,[19] points out that the stark, crude, self-reliant backwoodsmen of the new Western commonwealth beyond the Alleghenies had written into their young state constitutions the democratic codes of the frontier. One of these codes was enfranchisement of the masses, a rare item in the East.

In early Colonial times voting had been for the most part restricted to white natives who owned property.[20] In many of the Thirteen Colonies a man not only had to own property to

18. Stefan Lorant, *The Presidency* (New York, The Macmillan Company, 1951), p. 108.
19. Homer Carey Hockett, *Political and Social Growth of the American People* (New York, The Macmillan Company, 1946), pp. 524–34.
20. Revolutionary Sources, Pequot Library, Southport, Connecticut.

vote, but he might have to pass other economic and social requirements as well. In still other areas he was barred if he had immigrated; religion was a barrier in some areas; race and color are subtle barriers even now in the South.

Mr. Hockett wisely points out that enfranchisement of whole layers of new white male voters in the West put pressure on the older Eastern states to widen their suffrage too.[21] The trend had been gradually gathering force before Jackson first ran for the Presidency in 1824. When Jackson's common man was defrauded in the Adams-Clay "corrupt bargain" of 1824, a revolution in Eastern suffrage was inevitable. And, instinctively, the new voters of the old states turned to Jackson as a man of the people in preference to the trained statesmen of the old school—an aristocracy somehow responsible for the double cross of democracy in 1824. Politicians did not take long to follow suit, flocking to Jackson's support between 1824 and 1828 as bees to buckwheat. Hockett adds:

> The broadening of the suffrage throughout the Union enfranchised thousands of men who had previously been sheer outsiders in the management of government. Many were undeveloped, untrained in political thinking, apt to follow a magnetic leader irrespective of the policies he advocated. White manhood suffrage introduced a new and incalculable factor into conduct of public affairs.

The crowds that merged in Washington for Jackson's inaugural were beyond anything the aristocrat-led Republic had yet imagined. Daniel Webster said he had never seen such a mob before: "Persons have come from five hundred miles to see General Jackson, and they really seem to think that the country has been rescued from some dreadful danger."

Jackson was staying at Gadsby's, a Washington hostelry overflowing with muddy-booted supporters who roamed the hotel rooms, shook the President-elect's hand, and awaited their reward.

Jackson was a weary figure, in full mourning for his Rachel, his whitening hair carelessly disarranged, but still looking, to

21. Hockett, *op. cit.*, pp. 524–34.

a British visitor, "like a gentleman and a soldier if a sad one." The new President would not allow Henry Clay in his presence, refused to make a courtesy call on the outgoing Adams, and had to be notified by messenger that the White House would be ready for his occupancy on March 4. Adams wrote in his own diary (he meticulously kept each hour) that Jackson eventually requested Adams to put himself to no inconvenience and stay as many days beyond March 4 as the Adams family needed for unhurried packing. Later, however, Jackson apparently feared for the safety of his followers and also the safety of Gadsby's, because of the incredible crush of "common" people there, and he asked Adams if he might go to the White House immediately after the inauguration. Adams left on March 3, refusing to be present at the public triumph of Rachel Donelson Robards Jackson's churlish husband.

In *The Age of Jackson*, Arthur M. Schlesinger, Jr., reports a local source which boasted that the Washington of those days possessed almost a hundred thousand bricks in pavement in an age of generally unpaved road. But whatever bricks there were soon got inundated by the mud of January, February, and early March, 1829.[22] Justice Story termed the Jacksonian throng "King Mob," but others called it "King Mud." Whatever its name, it brought much of this sticky debris unhealthily inside the taverns and hostelries, which made a fortune out of the great bloodless revolution and those who came to drink to it. Eggnog and timber doodles, juleps and slings, sherry cobblers and great drafts of green ale went coursing down throats to ward off winter ills and the effects of King Mud, and to toast the common man who would now be truly king.

Others went to hear and see George Washington Dixon sing in blackface (he would one day popularize "Ol' Zip Coon" as he plunked on a discolored banjo and rolled his white man's eyes for all minstrelsy to imitate). Still others went to see Thomas Jefferson's library which was being placed on public exhibition before being auctioned to pay the debts of Jefferson's recent estate. Those who lived nearby or who preferred

22. Arthur M. Schlesinger, Jr., *The Age of Jackson* (Boston, Little, Brown and Company, 1945), pp. 4–6.

to stay at home had the notorious Peggy O'Neale Eaton to gossip about in whispers over tea. Speaking of promiscuous Peggy, one New York Congressman wrote Governor Van Buren in New York about "using a certain household ——— and then putting it on one's head."²³ The Congressman's omission was undoubtedly "chamber pot."

Besides gossiping and drinking, the political society of that March inauguration also gave serious attention to eating. When Congressmen and Senators (and their hangers-on) sat down to dinner, they began late in the afternoon and continued a very long time. If the menus left for us can be believed, in succession were regularly put down a heavy meat soup, a fish course, turkey, beef smothered in onions, a rack of mutton, ham, pheasant, that jolly new dish "ice cream," jelly, fruit, and a generous flowing of brown and pale sherry, madeira, and champagne. Sometimes the diners toasted the crotchety hero of New Orleans, sometimes the tiny outgoing President, but more often they drank in quaking hope that the Republic would somehow survive the cataclysm that had broken open the past. Daniel Webster said of it all: "My *fear* is stronger than my *hope*."

As they saw the people's President calmly sworn in, black cravat and a plain black suit setting off flowing white hair and a lined, weathered face, the inauguration crowd could scarcely have believed Tory rumors which were greeting the tardy new Secretary of State, Martin Van Buren. These rumors stemmed from John Quincy Adams and his believers who had it that the new administration was feeble unto anarchy and Van Buren had best flee back to Albany and have nothing to do with a political toboggan hell-bent for disaster and destruction. The prolific Adams journal did nothing to deny this possibility.²⁴

23. *Ibid.*
24. It is intriguing to read in the fascinating daily memoirs of John Quincy Adams that, among other things, Adams had heard that Martin Van Buren was the illegitimate son of Aaron Burr. It may also be worth noting that when Van Buren presided over the Senate as Vice-President under Jackson he had so many political enemies he found it necessary to place a brace of pistols on his desk.

The *American Daily Advertiser* reports Jackson's inaugural at the Capitol in the glowing words of one long and giddy sentence:[25]

> The scene was a most beautiful and inspiring spectacle: The building, noble in its size, with its richly sculptured capitals and cornices, and the fine group in the pediment; the massy columns (one for each State in the Union); the far-spreading wings and terraces; the grounds and gates, with the crowd of carriages without; the line of soldiers in the park; the towering flight of steps, covered with members of Congress, officers of the army, foreign ministers, ladies dressed in all the varying hues of fashion; the President; the crowd of heads and of innumerable eyes bent on one spot, all taken together presented to the outward eye an assemblage of images never to be forgotten.

One eyewitness of democracy's first genuine swearing-in was a remarkable woman named Mrs. Anne Royall who had been defrauded of her widow's fortune at fifty-four and had taken to writing to keep body and soul together. Happily for posterity, Mrs. Royall was present and alert when Jackson was sworn in by the venerable Chief Justice John Marshall, who must have had misgivings at least equal to those he had had in swearing in Jefferson. She leaves us this crystal-clear picture of the people's President:[26]

> He was dressed in a blue frock coat, with epaulets, a common hat with a black cockade, and a sword by his side. He is very tall and slender. . . . His person is finely shaped, and his features not handsome but strikingly bold and determined. He is very easy and affable in his manners, and loves a jest. He told one of our party he was "one of the blue hen's chickens." He appears about 50 years of age [he was actually 61]. There is a great deal of dignity about him. He related many hardships endured by his men, in the Army, but never breathed a word of his own. His language is pure and fluent, and he has the appearance of having kept the best of company.

25. Lorant, *op. cit.*, p. 111.
26. Warren S. Tyron, ed., *A Mirror for Americans* (Chicago, The University of Chicago Press, 1952), p. 55.

Mrs. Royall's last phrase undoubtedly refers to aristocratic rumors of the time that Jackson was a murderer (he had killed in duels and in war), a gambler (he had played high-low in Natchez), a drinker (he and Rachel had been known to drink sippin' whisky together of an evening), a bounder (after all, he had been married for four decades to what Boston considered a scarlet woman), and a no-good, illiterate Western thief (he had stolen the Presidency from the wellborn and the traditional, and had sworn he was about to steal their patronage, too). Perhaps Mrs. Royall wished with reason to place on historical record his appearance of having "kept the best of company" as an antidote to gossip.

The new President had walked to The Hill from Gadsby's. After the swearing-in, he mounted his horse and rode down Pennsylvania Avenue to the White House, "that Palace at Washington" which the dying Rachel had so abhorred. He was pursued by a multitude. It was unruly. It was noisy. It was a mob, some on horseback, many roaring with the strength of their whisky, all of them shouting and some even shooting into the air and emitting Indian whoops. As Jackson rode through the White House gates the mob surged after him, a sight without precedent, so horrifying that when Bostonians later heard of it they shuttered their windows.

Filthy country boots—common boots caked with mud and manure—climbed upon damask and velvet, their owners yelling and screaming to colored White House servants bearing great trays of drinks, which went swilling down throats as fast as they appeared.

Justice Story reported: "I never saw such a mixture. The reign of King Mob seemed triumphant." To other guests the sight was reminiscent of the Tuileries and Versailles in bloody, revolting France.

Here was the corpulent epicure, grunting and sweating for breath—the dandy wishing he had no toes—the tight-laced miss, fearing her person might receive some permanently deforming impulse. Several thousands of dollars' worth of art glass and china were broken in the attempt to get at the refreshments; punch, lemonade, and other articles were carried out of the White House in buckets and pails; women fainted; men were seen with bloody noses; and no police had been placed on duty.[27]

The President himself was in real physical danger, just as he had been at Gadsby's. Friends formed a cordon about him, attempting without too much success to protect him from well-wishers and office seekers. Completely worn out from the difficulties of the day and probably as much disgusted, the new President sank into a "listless state of exhaustion" and ducked out a back exit, returning to Gadsby's, where he went to bed. The party soon burst White House seams and was not over when daylight struck the bottle- and body-strewn executive palace yard that President Adams had kept so neat.

John Quincy Adams had not heard the jubilant voice and full-throated whisky roar of "the *common* people" he patronized. Like his father before him, he had already left the town and the ill-matched mob he now utterly detested. The successor's name this time was Jackson, not Jefferson. What John Quincy Adams, a poor President, did not know on the dusty road home that historic night was that the noblest part of his long and devoted public life was yet to come. As a member of Congress from Massachusetts he would return in 1831 to remain in the House until he died on its floor in 1848, a valiant attacker of slavery, a persistent opponent of gag rules, and a devout scientist who helped create the Smithsonian Institution.

No American, however partisan to the democratic cause, should overlook the elemental fact that John Quincy Adams and Andrew Jackson, close contemporaries, lived on what might as well have been different planets. Conservative families like the Adamses could be as patriotically democratic as the lowliest republican cobbler, yet they were, more often than not, highborn gentlefolk whose daily routine was far removed from the do-it-yourself frontier. They had servants, they had leisure and deportment, they were educated, they were endowed, they were "society"—the aristocrats who, under another political system, would have been America's lords,

27. Lorant, *op. cit.*, p. 113.

dukes, earls, and royalty. For all their patriotism—and no American family has a prouder patriotic record—the two President Adamses, father and son, simply and plainly distrusted men like Andrew Jackson, even hated them. They were intellectually willing[28] to give the Jacksons of America equality and freedom under the revered Constitution, which they had helped create, yet were practically unable as yet to call the underprivileged of America their brothers.

Jackson was the people's President and the President of the new West: this was to be a splendid transfusion for the bloodstream of a growing nation. But Jackson shared many faults as well as virtues of the frontier and the lowly born of that rough-living era. He was intolerant and half-educated, and what he did not know he pooh-poohed as rubbish. Like a modern public school graduate who scoffs at private schools as vaguely "un-American," overlooking the good and patronizing the "egghead," frontier Americans blanketed the educated, wealthy upper classes with intolerant hatred and distrust not quite erased to this day.

The new President's first act was to express an ardent desire to free the Federal civil service of incompetence and corruption. Men appointed by Washington, John Adams, and Jefferson still held office, not to mention "corrupt bargain" appointees of the loathed John Quincy Adams. Of corruption Jackson did not find overmuch for it wasn't a corrupt era, but rather new and sparkling and crusading; even so, whatever it was, there was very little money to steal. Of incompetence Jackson found more than he had feared. Most post office and other civil service employees had been at the public trough for a quarter of a century and firmly believed by now that their Federal appointments had been for life.

As Jackson began his Herculean sweeping, one clerk in the Auditor's office slashed his own throat from ear to ear, another in the Department of State went mad. Still others frantically wrote to homes they had long since forgotten, begging

28. To his dying day, old John Adams was believed to be opposed to universal manhood suffrage, though John Quincy, his son, was less rigid in the matter.

employment of any sort, though they had not been sacked nor knew for certain they would be.[29] Whether a man was well suited to a Federal job didn't matter much to Jackson. What mattered was that the man had supported him, cherished his cause, and had detested John Quincy Adams and Henry Clay. Jackson rather oversimplified the requirements of civil service in his rationale: "The duties of all public offices are so plain and simple that men may readily qualify themselves for their performance."

Nevertheless, being an old soldier himself, Jackson was always sympathetic to veterans. An aged postmaster in Albany was about to be sacked; Jackson pounded his fist on the White House table with, "By the Eternal! I will not remove the old man. He carries a pound of British lead in his body!" Any veteran who had lost a leg on the battlefield, even one who had openly supported Clay or Adams, could therefore be safe from dismissal. Jackson said to his patronage officer: "If he lost a leg fighting for his country, that is vote enough for me!" As was to be expected from his blood, background, and impetuous, emotional nature, Andrew Jackson was almost childlike in his defense of men who had served their country in war. They could do no wrong.

Jackson was also the first President to realize the importance of being on cordial terms with the newspapermen of the country. Fifty-six editors of influential papers were appointed to office under Jackson. No doubt they were of powerful assistance to him in securing wide publicity and popular support for his policies, as well as interpreting public opinion at the grass roots and passing it along to the White House.

Under earlier Presidents, public officials had ordinarily continued their tenure during good behavior. This was a sort of unwritten civil service, patterned on the royal courts of Europe where most government officials stayed on the public pay roll until the king died and a new set of sycophants or flunkies were selected to dance attendance, even if they had to neglect their sworn duties to do so. Jackson's first appointments were taken, without exception, from members of his own political

29. Records of the Massachusetts Historical Society, Boston.

faction and he promptly filled all vacancies in the Federal honeycomb with none but Jacksonian partisans.

The triumph of democratic dynamism under Jackson paved the path for the nationalization of the spoils system, long established inside state and local American government. For the first time, there was now no official government aristocracy created largely from the wellborn, the educated, and the endowed. The very concept was repugnant to the common man who had backed Jackson and whose idea of Tory aristocrats frankly approximated blueblooded courtiers of Whitehall and the Tuileries.

Besides, it is clear Andrew Jackson himself felt that the newly enfranchised masses should be given a chance for training in the practical conduct of public affairs. As Franklin P. Adams said it so perfectly a century later, the average man was, to Jackson, "above average" and could be taught to govern himself. If a man believed in democracy at all, he believed that.

Was Jackson's "spoils system" as drastic as old histories would have us think? Undoubtedly not. Arthur M. Schlesinger, Jr., foremost modern authority on Jackson, has stated that tradition considerably exaggerates the extent of Jackson's actual removals.[30] Schlesinger estimates that modern research cuts down Jackson's dismissals during eight years to approximately one fifth to one tenth of all Federal officeholders, "many for good reason."

Jackson ousted or disposed of a not much greater proportion of officeholders than Jefferson had. Yet it is undeniable that Jackson established through his partisan appointment policy the spoils system in national politics. The demand for reform had to be met head on, and a redistribution of Federal offices was the swiftest, shrewdest answer a Western Irishman with good political intuition could possibly have found. The common man had too long been thwarted by aristocratic indifference and Jackson was duty-bound to make the first people's administration in truth a government *of, by,* and *for* those who had finally elected him.

30. Schlesinger, *op. cit.,* p. 47.

Van Buren, the Dutch Jim Farley of his time, had been told by a Pennsylvania politician: "If you wish to keep up the party, you must induce them to believe that it is their interest. Some few may adhere to the party from mere conscientious conviction of doing right but interest is a powerful stimulus to make them act energetically and efficiently."[31]

Redistribution of political posts served urgent political needs. Political rewards had long been used effectively in the colonies and states. They also helped raise funds in the party of the poor workingman. As is true today, the conservative or monied side never needed to look far for large contributions from wealthy adherents. But the party of the common people had few resources save patronage at its disposal. If Jackson's impressive mandate was to mean anything at all it had to be integrated and organized at the roots.

Beyond composing a green political organization of unendowed common men, the spoils system also contributed to the fundamental objective of restoring faith in a Federal government. Mr. Schlesinger says:[32]

In the eyes of the people, the bureaucracy had been corrupted by its vested interests in its own power. Jackson told Congress: "Office is considered as a species of property, and government rather as a means of promoting individual interests than as the instrument created solely for the service of the people."

Jackson believed that official duties could be made "so plain and simple that men of intelligence may readily qualify themselves for their performance." His quick action on this principle meant that the government was no longer "an engine for the support of the few at the expense of the many."

The doctrine of rotation-in-office was thus in a large part conceived as a sincere measure of reform. Many professional reformers so regarded it. Robert Dale Owen hailed it enthusiastically in his radical New York sheet, the *Free Enquirer*, and Jeremy Bentham, the great English reformer,

31. *Ibid.*, p. 46.   32. *Ibid.*

confided to Jackson, as one liberal to another, that he had held the doctrine of rotation himself since 1821.

In a larger context, which contemporary Americans could only have dimly apprehended, rotation-in-office possessed another significance. The history of government has been characterized by the decay of old ruling classes and the rise of more vigorous and intelligent ones to replace them. This process had already begun in America. The "natural aristocracy" of Richard Hildreth—the class composed of merchant, banker, planter, lawyer and clergyman—had started to decline after the War of 1812. The rise of the military hero, a new "natural" aristocrat, hastened the time for a general breaking-up of the old governing elite. In extreme cases one ruling order succeeds another by violent revolution, but a democracy which preserves equality of opportunity may escape so drastic a solution. The spoils system, whatever its faults, at least destroyed peaceably the monopoly of offices by a class which could not govern, and brought to power a fresh and alert group which had the energy to meet the needs of the day.

A century later, Franklin Delano Roosevelt proved anew this truth by destroying the traditional monopoly of those he termed "economic royalists" and substituting laws made by officeholders and policymakers from every walk of life, income, race, creed, color, and religion, many of whom had been previously barred by a "gentleman's agreement" among members of this economic royalty. Fresh ideas, fresh talent, fresh enthusiasm immediately surged through the circulation of political blood in the 1930s, as they had in the 1830s, and reforms whose advocacy had beaten Greeley and Bryan (and hurt T.R. and Wilson with intelligent, influential families) became law almost overnight. The people were once again running the works, in Carl Sandburg's phrase, as the people had first run them after the bloodless Jacksonian revolution.

Until recent years [says Mr. Schlesinger], the study of the spoils system has been marred by a tendency to substitute moral disapproval for an understanding of causes and necessities. There can be small doubt today that, whatever evils it brought into American life, its historical function was to narrow the gap between the people and the government— to expand popular participation in the workings of democracy. For Jackson it was an essential step in the gradual formulation of a program for democratic America.[33]

After Andrew Jackson, Presidents of the United States found the office immeasurably more powerful because they now possessed that most persuasive of authorities: the right to hire and fire. This victor's privilege expanded until half a century later when the behavior of General Grant's venal cronies forced the Congress to modify the spoils system in favor of a permanent Federal Civil Service at certain (though by no means all) levels and areas of government.

In spite of modifications, much of Andrew Jackson's rotation policy remains today, to the great benefit of a modern occupant of the White House. The profound frustration most Presidents undergo when their programs and policies either sink into the slough of what Cleveland called "innocuous desuetude" or succumb to downright partisan attack is nevertheless alleviated by the Jacksonian power-precedent of removal and appointment. The American spoils system as it now operates undoubtedly stems from Jackson. And what reader of U. S. history can doubt that its volatile inventor was motivated at least in considerable part by a lifetime devotion to the memory of his slandered, martyred Rachel, the pipe-smoking woman he loved?

33. *Ibid.*, p. 47.

Abraham Lincoln

A TERRIFYING specter had arisen to badger the towering, sad-faced President from the prairie. Devoted since boyhood to the personal freedoms of every man, he was now face to face with the need for a drastic extension of an executive order which would destroy one of the fundamental freedoms of all citizens before the law. What was worse, there was no certainty that he was acting legally—within his Constitutional powers.

Abraham Lincoln had found himself obliged, after the sobering consequences of the military blow to the Northern cause at Bull Run, to modify one of the fundamental precepts of the precious document he had sworn as President to defend.[1] He had had to suspend the traditional writ of *habeas corpus,* a precept of free men, in certain cases necessary to the prosecution of the war and the safety of the Union he would save. Here and there he had had to abrogate free man's fundamental premise since the Magna Charta, but he had done it hesitantly and infrequently, only along the military borders between the Blue and the Gray.

But it was now 1863 and things men would have hesitated to accept in a peaceful democratic society had become less and less important in the glare of the one fundamental fact: this was the most awful war yet fought on the face of the earth

1. "The War of the Rebellion: A Compilation of the Official Records of the Union and Confederate Armies." War Department publication (Washington, D.C., 1902).

4

Suspends Habeas Corpus

and it was not going to be won or lost in a few short weeks. *Habeas corpus,* the safeguard against indefinite imprisonment or detention without due process of law, was of less moment now than the overpowering, overwhelming fact that the United States of America would cease to exist altogether if the President's command failed.

There had been disheartening days indeed for the Union Army. It was now two years of war and there were no victories worthy of the name. Washington itself might be lying in ruins under the Stars and Bars had those triumphant at Bull Run not tried to drink one another under the table in rejoicing. Each day had brought new depressions and disappointments, but to the tall, often depressed, ever-harried President who ate so little at the White House table there was at last a man with a lantern in the darkness. His name was Hooker.

Joe Hooker, blond and good-looking, dashing, not yet fifty years old, a true martial air about him, was the storybook general, spoiling for a fight and brimming with brave words. It was always "when" and never "if"; Richmond was not in dubious assault, it was already fallen. Fearful as Mr. Lincoln was now of optimists and boasters, and aware that Hooker was a brusque man ("this is the most depressing thing about Hooker," he told a friend), the President nevertheless cast his eye upon Hooker's lantern and kept it there as though it were a ray of hope, for there was a certain splendor about Joe Hooker.

It was then that Hooker came to the throne after the unlucky Burnside, the timorous and maladroit McClellan, the beaten McDowell. Forgotten for the moment were the fiasco of Bull Run, the Peninsula campaign, Fredericksburg, and the stinging editorials and cartoons that had followed. This was to be the first move up the ladder out of the muck and mess of slavery, partition, and war. At last the President seemed to have found his General.

By the final week in April, 1863, Fighting Joe Hooker had moved his army to the Rappahannock River and was searching out General Lee. He had not long to wait. Lee, with 63,000 men, rested and waited for the frontal assault near a clearing and a few houses called Chancellorsville, halfway between Richmond and Washington.

On the first of May, Hooker, with what he confidently told Mr. Lincoln was "the finest army on the planet," moved most of this regenerated Army of the Potomac across the Rappahannock, a rain-filled northeast Virginia stream, to crush the rebellion once and for all. A vigilant President had visited this new army and his often wholly funereal demeanor seemed to his associates in Washington to lighten into real hope as the battle was joined.

At about the same time that spring the Federal Navy was attempting to recapture Fort Sumter in Charleston harbor, and a fleet of ironclad men-of-war, fully and carefully prepared for the action, set out to crush this symbol of revolt at the very point of its birth. The nation knew, as the nation always seems to know, of great events in the making. It was one of those electric times; and the pale, thin man in the White House, whose exceeding physical strength was still remembered in the wooded lands of the Kankakee basin, could do nothing but pace sleepless and impotent as he waited for the first dispatches. He needed more than the thrill of a genuine military victory at Chancellorsville or the pride of recapture of beleaguered Fort Sumter. Not Lincoln's damaged ego, nor his stature as President and Commander in Chief of the armed forces, nor his political fortunes alone required shoring up. To Lincoln, a man of principle above all, the two years of disastrous war without a victory had forced him into other painful compromises. A winning Hooker, a victorious Chancellorsville, a recaptured Charleston harbor might make it possible for him to extract one of the tainted thorns which hurt him most—his enforced decision to suspend the inalienable right of *habeas corpus* in limited frontal areas where he had to declare suspension necessary for the public safety.

Now in late April, 1863, almost two years after Bull Run, when apple blossoms burgeoned in unexampled loveliness in the valley of the Shenandoah, the sensitive President who wished above all else to preserve the freedoms of the last best hope of earth awaited news from Chancellorsville and the boastful Hooker, and from the Navy concerning their attempt to recapture Fort Sumter. He had not long to wait.

Communiqués of the victor usually outspeed the report of the defeated, who hangs on to scrape up the crumbs of hope. Long before news came from battlefield and harbor, there were rumors of defeat everywhere in Washington. Reports told how Lee had bluffed with 35,000 men and held a Union force four times its size while General Thomas J. (Stonewall) Jackson was on his way with 28,000 men on a quick long march around Hooker's flank, an encirclement which so crumpled the Union force that Hooker pulled back across the Rappahannock, having used scarcely a third of his troops.

They told how Hooker, who had previously given blow for blow, bluff and hearty, had suddenly traded dashing offensive for overcautiousness and had in fact outdone McClellan in this respect—the McClellan whom Hooker had berated to the President for his tiptoe tactics.

They left little doubt of a Confederate victory far greater and graver than that at Bull Run and confirmed the competence of the rebel generals, even though (unknown to the dispatcher) the incomparable Jackson now lay dying near the shaded bank of a river.

From the sea had also come ugly news. The great shore batteries of Fort Sumter had hurled back the ironclad fleet, sinking or damaging four. Admiral Dupont, who in Lincoln's words was "everlastingly asking for more gunboats, more ironclads and [would] do nothing with any," had emulated Mc-Clellan. Timidity and disaster were the order of the day.

And how did this affect the man who, according to American school histories, never once faltered? Did this lowest muddy ebb of Union fortunes uncover doubts and discouragements yet unplumbed? Without doubt it did, and we have but to examine the record sketchily to see how much suffering this lonely human soul must have endured in the ulcerous, despairing days that spring of 1863.

Chancellorsville's debacle and the naval failure to recapture Fort Sumter meant ominous things in the grand pageantry of Civil War. Years later, when someone asked Hooker what went wrong at Chancellorsville, the culpable general knew a rare moment of humility and remarked, "Well, to tell the truth, I just lost confidence in Joe Hooker."[2] Had he been as forthright immediately after Chancellorsville, Hooker's uninspired leadership might have been partially forgiven by the President of the United States, who had a keen sense of humor and an understandable fondness for candor.

But victory at Chancellorsville was now a bloody fraud and the country knew it; even worse, the President knew that the country knew it. Copperheads were born with Chancellorsville, though spawned at an obscure moment earlier in the war. It was only when the country began to realize failure with the shock of a cold wind on May Day in 1863 that the storm began to break. But break it did by the end of the month.

The Copperheads were the first to sense its proportions. They loaded their guns with this potent ammunition and the noise was enormous. An Ohio Congressman, a Democrat named Clement Vallandigham, spoke out on the floor of the House that the war for the Union "is in your hands a most bloody and costly failure." He advised strongly now as he had hinted before Hooker's defeat and the failure at Fredericksburg that the North should "stop fighting—make an armistice—accept at once friendly foreign mediation."

After Chancellorsville, Vallandigham made such a violent

2. Bruce Catton, *Glory Road* (Garden City, Doubleday and Company, Inc., 1954), p. 230.

and offensive series of speeches against the President personally, and against the government's part in the war, that General Burnside, who was commanding the troops in Ohio, had him arrested and court-martialed. Thereupon most of the Democrats in Washington rose up in loud protest.

Lincoln regretted Burnside's action but supported his own General against the violent agitator. Newspapers of the day and magazines, too, picked up this incident as a firing pin for a broadside of unmitigated, libelous, and often treasonable protest and personal criticism of Lincoln and the administration (which Carl Sandburg believes has no parallel for personal insult in all the depressing story of partisan American politics).

No one loving Abraham Lincoln could wish to believe that he alone held up his head on the black day that the boastful Hooker gave way as all had before him, and Charleston harbor still was rebel. It is Pollyanna stuff, and grossly unfair, to say that Lincoln took it calmly and with a steady eye on the ultimate victory. The record does not show it; the record shows a stricken, brooding human being, dreadfully aware of the shape of things, striding about the room "piteous, broken and so ghostlike," clasping his hands behind him and saying as he walked back and forth: "My God! My God! What will the country say? What will the country say?"

The country as a whole was not at once awake to this fresh and deepest disaster for the Lincoln Administration and the Northern cause. Newspaper headlines then read a good deal like any war communiqués, especially later headlines in the American press during the French and British rout in the World War II Nazi breakthrough at Sedan. They were at first invariably overoptimistic—in fact several papers initially called Hooker's stand a victory, though he retreated the next day.

May First was a day of national fasting. The *New-York Tribune*[3] reported that the Reverend Henry Ward Beecher in Plymouth Church called for thanks to God for the progress of things. On page one of several succeeding issues appeared three- and four-column maps of the territory of the Rappahannock near Fredericksburg, with scarcely a showing of

3. Archives, *New York Herald Tribune.*

Chancellorsville, and the issue of May 2 carried the prominent headline, "The Enemy Confounded," while telling of Hooker's crossing of the river to engage and destroy the enemy once and for all. The issue of May 4 reported: "The Enemy Panic Stricken." And on May 5: "The Enemy in Retreat," with a subsidiary headline: "Concentration of Rebels on Our Right Wing" (what an understatement of Stonewall Jackson's brilliant encircling maneuver!).

But on May 6 the correspondent was not as certain of the completeness of Hooker's "victory" and his dispatch was very forthright. The headlines of the day included: "The Battle Still Unfinished" and "Bad Behavior of the 11th Corps." Next day the lines read: "Nobody Here Knows Anything" and "Loss to Enemy Very Large." On May 8 was reported Hooker's "Successful Recrossing of the River" and "Terrible Repulses of the Enemy." In adjacent columns appeared the first full dispatches from rebel Richmond, where Lee was announcing the greatest victory, with accompanying details which history has borne out. The *Tribune* was one of the few papers in the North to carry this sobering dispatch.

The arrest of Vallandigham had indirectly involved the President's abrogation of the writ of *habeas corpus*. The term *habeas corpus* is Latin for "you may have the body." In law it is a writ directed by a judge to some person who is detaining another person. The writ commands that the body of the person in custody be brought to a specific place at a specific time for a specific hearing. The purpose of the writ of *habeas corpus,* one of the great traditions of free men, is to prevent indefinite imprisonment or detention without due process of law. It is a safeguard against illegal confinement of any sort, particularly effective against dictators, who universally ignore it.

Under Anglo-Saxon tradition a man must be told why he has been arrested and, within a reasonable time, given a hearing. He cannot be held incommunicado and he cannot be held indefinitely without being informed why. If those holding him have no case against him they must, under traditional British-

American codes, let him go free—and not after years of imprisonment, but within hours or, at worst, days. What springs him from indefinite imprisonment without formal charges is the tradition of *habeas corpus*.

The phrase is mentioned as early as the fourteenth century in England. It became part of English law as the Habeas Corpus Act of 1679 and has long been regarded as perhaps the most fundamental legal freedom we possess. British colonists in America were often denied it. Refusal of stubborn colonial judges to issue the writ was among the foremost grievances leading to the Declaration of Independence. The issue is mentioned specifically in the American Constitution, and not by chance: "In all criminal prosecutions, the accused shall enjoy the right to a speedy and public trial, by an impartial jury of the state and district wherein the crime shall have been committed . . . and to be informed of the nature and cause of the accusation."

To implement this freedom, most natural in the making of a free society, it is provided in the Constitution that the privilege of the writ of *habeas corpus* shall not be suspended "unless, when in cases of rebellion or invasion, the public safety may require it."

Mr. Lincoln had, early in the war, authorized General Winfield Scott, the man originally in charge of Federal military operations, to suspend the writ of *habeas corpus* along any military line between Washington and Philadelphia. This order of 1861 quickly brought cries of despotism and military dictatorship against the administration, but Mr. Lincoln did not hesitate to extend it ruthlessly (and did) as he felt the public safety would require.

Before adjourning in August, 1861, Congress had voted, besides the men and munitions to carry on the war, ex post facto justification for Lincoln's suspension of *habeas corpus* and other "illegal" proclamations.

As the President began to tamper with the ancient privilege of the writ of *habeas corpus* many of the guarantees of the Constitution vanished, and Justice Taney, sitting in the circuit court in Baltimore, had handed down the opinion that the

President had no Constitutional power to suspend the writ nor authorize a military officer to do so. Margaret Leech tells the story well:[4]

The venerable judge had become embroiled in the case of John Merryman, confined for treasonable activities in Fort McHenry. The soldiers at the fort would neither yield the person of John Merryman, nor admit the United States marshal to serve an order against their commanding general for contempt. Taney's decision provoked much discussion, but he was an aged man of Southern bias. The conservative Attorney General, Mr. Bates, sustained the President. The majority of loyal men at first accepted the arbitrary arrests as necessary to the nation's struggle for survival, even when in September of 1861 General Dix and General Banks rounded up secessionist legislators of Maryland and clapped them into prison.

One of the most spectacular instances of military rule, exercised under the suspension of *habeas corpus,* was the case of one John Murphy who tried to secure the release of his son James who had enlisted under the legal age of eighteen. A Federal judge in Maryland issued the usual *habeas corpus* just before Lincoln suspended the writ in the District of Columbia. The writ was directed to General Andrew Porter who refused to respect it.

Very quickly, the attorney who had served the writ was himself arrested by General Porter, who was provost marshal, and languished in the guardhouse. Then, the Federal judge who had issued the writ returned home to find an armed sentinel at his door. The authority responsible was capricious Secretary of State William H. Seward, who had boasted that he had but to ring his tiny bell and any man, woman, or child in the Republic could be imprisoned. The ambitious Secretary was hated and feared above all others in the Cabinet for exercising these arbitrary powers as a dictator would. Eventually everyone involved was set free, but not before the Federal Constitution had been not only violated but raped repeatedly.

4. Margaret Leech, *Reveille in Washington* (New York, Harper and Brothers, 1941), pp. 142–44.

Suspects were carried off to military prisons, often secretly, by night. Their houses were searched, their valuables seized. In most cases they were not even informed of the charges against them. They were not permitted to have legal advice, and no expectation of trial by jury mitigated the discomforts of their detention. . . . They could only hope that the pressure of their claims might call them to the State Department's attention, and win them a special examination. Often when this was held, it developed there had been insufficient grounds for the arrest.[5]

On the other hand, there was a remarkable amount of secessionist sympathy in the North, particularly in Washington, Philadelphia, Baltimore, and along the border states. In singular contrast to the arbitrary arrests and dictatorial conduct of Seward and his department, there was unusual leniency in most cases of doubtful Unionists. Often, only in extreme instances were they arrested or imprisoned. Congress had passed a strong bill requiring all Federal employees to take an unusually severe oath to support the Constitution, but many departments had been slack in applying the law because so many Washington employees were of Virginian and other Southern origin.

A departmental mail pouch in the War Department was, for example, freely used by rebel sympathizers for transmission of information to Richmond. It hung in the hall and anyone could without question put notes in and take them out.

On assuming office in 1862 as Secretary of War, Edwin M. Stanton stopped such rebel nonsense—and soon was also given the State Department's jurisdiction over political prisoners, which meant the handling of *habeas corpus*. The most obvious cases of misguided justice under State Department procedures were set free by Stanton at once. Usually there was no record of the charges against them, and Secretary Seward's little bell tinkled no more.

In retrospect, this part of Abraham Lincoln's Administration is difficult for the most pro-Northern sympathizer to swallow, context discounted. More than 13,000 persons were arrested

5. *Ibid.*

by the War Department alone and no one knows how many others were detained on despotic grounds. Military trials in camera and arbitrary arrests developed into a despotic system the like of which our country has never known before or since.

To this day there are few dungeons with a more evil reputation than the Old Capitol Prison on First Street in Washington, where so many victims of the suspension of the writ of *habeas corpus* ate their hearts out, and occasionally were beaten until they died, or sickened out of life on the vile food and filth and disease.

President Lincoln's conduct during the Civil War was conspicuous by the variety and number of his un-Constitutional acts.[6] "Yet every one of them" says historian Woodward, "may be justified on the ground of necessity. The situation clearly demonstrated the Constitutional weakness of the Chief Executive power in a time of emergency. Buchanan was right in declaring that he could find no Constitutional authority for using force against a State that had seceded."

Lincoln had personally suspended the right of *habeas corpus,* though it would appear from the wording of the Constitution that Congress alone has that authority.[7] Certainly Article I, Section 9 is perfectly plain on this point: "The privilege of the writ of habeas corpus shall not be suspended, unless when in cases of rebellion or invasion the public safety may require it."

The implication is clearly *legislative* because Article I of the Constitution has to do solely with the composition, powers, and procedures of the Congress. The Presidency is not mentioned until the first two words of Article II. Therefore, Lincoln's original executive order suspending the writ of *habeas corpus* without Congressional assent was undoubtedly unlawful.

Thousands of Americans were thrown into jail and confined for months without even being informed of the charges against them. Stupid military officers had the power to arrest any

6. W. E. Woodward, *A New American History* (Garden City, Garden City Press, 1938), p. 525.
7. In fairness to Lincoln, it should be explained that Congress was not in session at the time of suspension.

American citizen and put him or her in prison without indictment, warrant, or explanation. As in the case of the Maryland judge, even persons attached to the law were subject to illegal whim. Subordinates even raided newspapers and stopped their publication, once again in defiance of the Federal Constitution, in this instance contrary to the First Amendment.

Did the end justify the means? Let Lincoln himself say it, as he so often did, best of all:

> Soon after the first call for militia, I felt it my duty to authorize the commanding general in proper cases, according to his discretion, to suspend the privilege of the writ of habeas corpus, or, in other words, to arrest and detain, without resort to the ordinary processes and forms of law, such individuals as he might deem dangerous to the public safety. . . . At my verbal request, as well as by the general's own inclination, this authority has been exercised but very sparingly. Nevertheless, the legality and propriety of what has been done under it are questioned; and I have been reminded from a high quarter that one who is sworn to "take care that the laws be faithfully executed" should not himself be one to violate them.
>
> Of course I gave some consideration to the questions of power and propriety before I acted in this matter. The whole of the laws which I have sworn to take care that they be faithfully executed were being resisted, and failing to be executed, in nearly one-third of the States. Must I have allowed them to finally fail of execution, even had it been perfectly clear that by the use of the means necessary to their execution some single law, made in such extreme tenderness of the citizen's liberty, that practically it relieves more of the guilty than the innocent, should, to a very limited extent, be violated?
>
> To state the question more directly, are all the laws but one to go unexecuted, and the Government itself go to pieces, lest that one be violated? Even in such a case I should consider my official oath broken, if I should allow the Government to be overthrown, when I might think the disregarding the single law would tend to preserve it. But in this case I was not, in my own judgment, driven to this ground.

In my opinion, I violated no law. The provision of the Constitution that "The privilege of the writ of habeas corpus shall not be suspended unless when, in cases of rebellion or invasion, the public safety may require it," is equivalent to a provision—is a provision—that such privilege may be suspended when, in cases of rebellion or invasion, the public safety does require it.

I decided that we have a case of rebellion, and that the public safety does require the qualified suspension of the privilege of the writ of habeas corpus, which I authorized to be made. Now it is insisted that Congress, and not the executive, is vested with this power. But the Constitution itself is silent as to which, or who, is to exercise the power; and as the provision plainly was made for a dangerous emergency, I cannot bring myself to believe that the framers of that instrument intended that in every case the danger should run its course until Congress could be called together, the very assembling of which might be prevented, as was intended in this case by the rebellion.

This message was addressed to the Congress on July 4, 1861. The above version was the first draft in which Lincoln wrote as if he might be talking with a friend, using "I" and "my." But by the time the message was delivered to Capitol Hill someone had prevailed on Lincoln to act more like a President, so he modified the personal pronouns and inserted legal jargon.

In whatever form it was persuasive. Congress legitimatized Lincoln's limited executive order in August, 1861, as Congress had legitimatized Jefferson's purchase of Louisiana after the fact, and as it was to do again with President Truman when U. S. troops were sent to aid Korea against Communist aggression.

The President had moved very slowly in abrogating the cherished writ which he, above anyone, instinctively admired as fundamental to a free society. In the spring of 1861 he had authorized limited suspension of *habeas corpus* on a small section of the Florida coast. In the summer of 1861 he had expanded it to the military line north of Philadelphia as far as New-York. In the fall of 1861 he suspended *habeas corpus* for all military personnel in the District of Columbia. He hoped against hope that the war might progress to a point where even these slight trespasses against freedom could be removed.

It wasn't until the disastrous autumn of 1862, however, that Lincoln was compelled to deny the privilege of *habeas corpus* to all persons imprisoned by military order. Slowly the black mantle of defeat was falling on military and civilian alike.

Now in 1863, with Hooker's rout at Chancellorsville and the path wide open for Lee to invade the North (probably at Harrisburg, Pennsylvania), Lincoln considered a final seal on the door of Constitutional freedom. Even the great victory at Gettysburg from July 1 to 4 failed to lift the extreme eventual danger, for no one was then sure that Lee would not try again, perhaps at Philadelphia, Baltimore, or Washington. Gettysburg was a great Federal victory, but a defensive one. It had stopped an invasion. It hadn't won a war.

So in the late summer of 1863 Abraham Lincoln received from Salmon P. Chase, his reluctant Secretary of the Treasury, the following notation:[8]

> You, Mr. President, have believed that you have the power to suspend the writ of habeas corpus without being authorized by Congress and in some cases you have acted on this belief. After much consideration, I have come to the conclusion that your opinion and mine are sanctioned by the Constitution. Whatever doubt there may have been as to your power to suspend the writ, it has been removed by express legislation.

Chase urged the President to make the suspension of *habeas corpus* national in scope, applying to all civilians as well as all military personnel. One reason was that the military draft was making trouble in Northern cities, particularly New-York, and some sort of enforcement had to be legalized. Suspension of *habeas corpus* was as forceful a method as any, for it gave the commanding general in each district the right to clap into jail anyone who refused to be drafted (or pay for a legal substitute) without going to the lengths of protracted court procedure.

8. Carl Sandburg, Vol. II, *Abraham Lincoln, The War Years* (New York, Harcourt, Brace and Company, Inc., 1939), p. 445.

Chase pleaded with the President to make the order suspending the writ a presidential proclamation so bold and clear that it would command public confidence if a collision arose with a state governor or local judge. Lincoln acted at once on the suggestion.

So, on the same day, September 15, 1863, Abraham Lincoln issued the fateful nationwide proclamation as finally drafted by Secretary of State Seward. In what Carl Sandburg aptly describes as "a solemn vocabulary,"[9] it was made known by the President that the privilege of the writ of *habeas corpus* "is suspended *throughout the United States*." This suspension would continue until modified or revoked by a later proclamation. The syllables of the document "produced a sonorous pronouncement" that backed up the provost marshal with all the power at the command of the United States Army and Navy. It would indeed be a sure and useful instrument with which to prosecute the war to a successful end.

Readers of history have often wondered why Lincoln, with Gettysburg and Vicksburg to support him, resorted to universal suspension of *habeas corpus*. But two terrible things lingered in the back of his mind throughout the summer of 1863, combining to make necessary his proclamation suspending the writ of freedom for all Americans.

The first fact was the ghastly pattern of Chancellorsville and the still-to-be-found general who could take charge and end the war. Lincoln could only guess after Vicksburg. It would take the bloody, incredible Wilderness of 1864 and 1865, the bulldog grinding down of Robert E. Lee's once unmatched forces to turn the tide Lincoln still could not be certain of, even after Gettysburg and Vicksburg. The ghost of Joe Hooker and all the other pitifully impotent generals who had boasted and failed continually stalked the reaches of the President's vast mind.

The second fact was draft rioting which broke out in New-York only ten days after the glorious "victory" at Gettysburg. The Union conscription act of March 3, 1863, had provided

9. *Ibid.*

that all able-bodied males between twenty and forty-five were liable to military service. Any draftee who gave the government $300 or furnished an acceptable substitute for a fee was excused. It was a dreadfully defective piece of legislation and the most unpopular in America until the Prohibition Amendment at the end of World War I. It was undemocratic. It placed a premium on wealth, for only the comparatively wealthy of Civil War days could afford to give the government $300, or pay some such sum to another to take one's place. The poor who could not afford these things were clapped into uniform.

From July 13 to 16, 1863, the echoes of glorious Gettysburg still ringing on the front pages, there occurred bloody, large-scale riots in New-York where Governor Horatio Seymour, a Democrat, had publicly declared the conscription act un-Constitutional. The tremendous mob, much of it foreign-born and of the laboring class (which had considerable cause), overpowered the militia and police and seized the Second Avenue armory with its guns and ammunition, setting fire to the building.

Abolitionists and Negroes were singled out for attack in the unreasoning logic of the New-York mob. Southern sympathizers worked overtime everywhere in the city to pour insidious gasoline on the flames. Business ceased. Looting and murder were the order of the day. Tammany ran the town then, as now, and was forced to vote that the city would pay the $300 required for anyone who might be drafted and did not wish to go to war.

Meanwhile, the famous Seventh Regiment of New-York, fresh from the laurels of Gettysburg, was rushed back to Manhattan. With the aid of cadets from West Point, the local police, the militia, and the United States Navy, order was eventually restored. Casualties may have been as high as a thousand people, and damage was certainly in the millions, but no one can ever really know.

Lincoln eventually got Congress to modify the draft act so that the privilege of buying one's way out of service was limited to conscientious objectors. All others had to go when their numbers came up, if they were fit, regardless of wealth, station, influence, or background.

The draft riots deeply impressed the President. Coupled with the perpetually gnawing fear of Joe Hookers by whatever name on his general staff—and there were still plenty of them —it is little wonder that he issued the fateful proclamation of September, 1863, widening suspension of the writ of *habeas corpus* to apply to all American citizens. To a Chief Executive who could write the editor of the *New-York Tribune,* Horace Greeley, that even slavery could be condoned if it meant preservation of the Union, the proclamation of temporary suspension of personal freedom was understandable.

All Presidents feel the greatness of the office, but all Presidents cannot respond to it. That Lincoln knew well the terrible step he was taking when he suspended the precious right of *habeas corpus* no sensible reader of history can for a moment doubt. Nor can there be the slightest question that only great Presidents see ultimate goals and sweep all else aside to achieve them. Taking the grave step he did, the Commander in Chief of the Union he preserved altered irrevocably the concept of the Presidency, increased the precedent of presidential power in a time of national crisis and, however painful to himself, sanctified the highest office the American people have it in their power to bestow.

Chester Arthur

WHEN RUTHERFORD B. HAYES[1] became President of the United States, upsetting Samuel J. Tilden in an election Tilden had rightly won, he wished particularly to show New York that honesty would be his policy, for Tilden had been Governor of New York and every literate American knew that Hayes and the Republicans had stolen the Presidency. Governor Tilden had had a substantial popular majority and, in the original electoral college, a comfortable margin of states as well. But the prevailing post-Civil War Republican machine had so finagled the electoral commission that disputed electoral delegations from Western and Southern states were juggled to make Hayes President of the United States by a single vote.

President Hayes was, therefore, understandably sensitive to charges of corruption and malodorous politics when his salutary new administration spotted smells drifting from the office of the Collector of the New York Custom House. After much self-righteous fanfare, Hayes removed a Republican, one Chester Alan Arthur, the Collector, but left untouched most of the party's pork-barrel underlings. This and other Hayes reforms in the late 1870s were accomplished, however,

1. In 1876, when Rutherford B. Hayes was told that his running mate would be William A. Wheeler, Hayes replied: "And who is William A. Wheeler?" James G. Blaine had had the presidential nomination of 1876 sewed up when suddenly the gas lights failed and the convention was forced to recess on account of darkness. When the delegates reassembled the next day, enthusiasm for Blaine had cooled; thus, Hayes, not Blaine, became President of the United States.

5

Rises to the Occasion

over the violent objection of the New York Republican machine which was led by Roscoe Conkling, Senator from New York and fountainhead of New York Republicanism. The need for civil service reform had been a burning political issue ever since the Grant scandals, but Conkling cared little or nothing for public opinion and reformers made him actively ill. So he broke with Hayes, who had upset Grant's third-term plans, and got his revenge on Hayes at the Republican Convention of 1880.

By that year President Hayes had so alienated Conkling that Hayes had no chance for re-election, and besides he was committed to a single term of office. Moreover, the James G. Blaine wing of the Republican Party, which hated Conkling, hated Hayes even more.[2]

At the convention of 1880, Conklingites characterized themselves as Stalwarts, hewing firmly to the Old Guard and the conservative approach that thought nothing of waving the bloody shirt of Southern insurrection to win an election fifteen years after the Civil War's last gun was silenced. The Blaine faction, on the other hand, was contemptuously referred to as Half-Breeds.

Conkling's Stalwarts came to the convention determined that General Grant should have a third term in spite of the scandals and the incompetence. But such was the temper of the common

2. Peter Levin, *Seven By Chance* (New York, Farrar, Straus and Company, 1948), pp. 146–76.

people that a great resistance began to form against Conkling and Grant and their well-oiled machines.

A total of 378 votes were needed for nomination, and Conkling claimed 300 to 350 for Grant on the first ballot. Blaine's legions claimed 225 to 285. Other nominees were scattered, including John Sherman of Ohio who held 90. It seemed that all the Grant or Blaine managers had to do was bargain proficiently and their man was in, with Grant the favorite to take it.

But the unrelenting stubbornness of the opposition, the arrogance of the autocratic Conkling, the abiding distrust of Blaine, and the obstinacy of Sherman to release a single delegate made it clear even before the convention opened that first-ballot victory was all important.[3]

By the time the balloting opened, Grant had lost fifty delegates to Half-Breed minorities. Blaine's nomination speeches were incredibly bad; the chief nominator not only apologized for Blaine, but got his middle initial wrong. Conkling's oratory wasn't as puerile as Blaine's, being carefully planned and prepared, but it was bitingly sarcastic, which managed to consolidate the alliance against Grant.

Through thirty-three tedious roll calls the two major candidates held without major defection. In the baking heat of a lake-shore summer in Chicago (there were no air-conditioning comforts or loud-speakers to stem the humid chaos), Wisconsin suddenly switched to James A. Garfield, who had placed Sherman in nomination. Garfield jumped to his feet to protest, but was pounded out of order. Blaine and Sherman went immediately over to Garfield, the new hero. On the thirty-fifth ballot Garfield had nearly enough votes, and it was all over on the thirty-sixth, the sudden movement of a new favorite sweeping the day as it has so often in our national conventions, which run on the heady fuel of mob psychology. In the end, 306 Stalwarts still held out for Grant against Garfield, which boded little good for the new candidate in the campaign. Indeed, the convention which had repudiated Presidents Hayes and Grant was quickly made aware by Conkling that the New York Re-

3. *Ibid.*

publican organization, among others, would simply sit on its hands at election time unless the political bosses could now name the vice-presidential candidate.

Garfield hated Conkling with all his being, but he knew, as political leaders from Ohio often knew, that compromise was the best political course and that Garfield and the Republicans would lose the election if Conkling's Stalwarts sabotaged the venture. So the horse-trading began.

First Garfield offered the vice-presidential nomination to Levi P. Morton, a wealthy and respectable Grant man who could help finance as well as lift the social level of the campaign. But Morton was advised that Garfield couldn't win, so he turned down a vice-presidential nomination which would have made him Chief Executive within months of the inauguration. Later Morton did become Vice-President under Benjamin Harrison, and later still Governor of New York.

However unbelievable it would have seemed before the event, the unfrocked Chester Alan Arthur of New York was finally selected to run with Garfield. If Arthur's appointment by party bosses as vice-presidential candidate on the Republican ticket appealed to the practical politician and healed the wounds of the party, it galled not a few others. Though John Sherman publicly endorsed Garfield, he said privately of Arthur: "The nomination is a ridiculous burlesque and I am afraid was inspired by a desire to beat the ticket." To this recondite observation Sherman added that "it was a rather scandalous proceeding."[4]

Lack of enthusiasm for Garfield's running mate was evident in the nation's press, especially among the liberal Republicans. The Democratic press quickly seized upon it, for it gave them plenty of ammunition. Only General W. S. Hancock's incredible political ineptness destroyed this and other initial advantages of a party out of power for twenty increasingly corrupt years.

Few outside New York State knew that Conkling hadn't especially liked the idea of Arthur on the ticket, and believed that Conkling had been instrumental in making the deal. Arthur had never held elective office prior to the election of

4. Archives, Pequot Library, Southport, Connecticut.

1880, but he was patently a Conkling-type politician and had
been so since the end of the Civil War. Moreover, it was undeniable that Arthur had been removed as Collector of the
New York Customs and, guilty or not guilty, his indictment
was fixed in the American mind. (It is said in the newspaper
business that all a man has to have on his record is a headline
reading "Jones Indicted" and Jones is a criminal in the public's
mind for the rest of his days, regardless of his guilt or innocence.)

Chester Arthur's background was far different from what it
appeared to be. There were all sorts of misconceptions about
him, because of his sponsor, his cronies, and his brush with the
Collectorship. Arthur was a gentleman, a man of taste and
breeding, of literary discrimination and polish. He loved
Thackeray and Scott and reread them constantly. His dinner
table conversation was polished, his manners drawing-room
perfect. He wore elegant mutton-chop sideburns which met in
a mustache and his awareness of caste and dress stopped "just
short of foppery," and certainly belied his Baptist minister
father and Vermont origins. It isn't at all surprising that he was
an Episcopalian as an adult, having repudiated the Baptist
faith for one then generally accepted as "more social."

It wasn't by chance that Arthur lived on lower Lexington
Avenue, then the fanciest residence area in Manhattan, had
several servants, married a girl from a fine Virginia family, and
loved good wines and French food. By blood he was fascinated
with politics—Irishmen seem to lean naturally that way. He
was a lawyer, but unsuccessful in the courtroom, preferring
negotiations to briefs or questioning. He didn't cotton to issues,
national or local, but rather liked the manipulation, the game,
the action of man-to-man political give and take. He would
rather let someone else write his speeches—even deliver them
—while he controlled the situation behind the scenes. Mr.
Levin says:[5] "Arthur seldom concerned himself with the *what*
quality of his fascination; the *how* quality consumed too much
of his attention. As a politician he bore the same relationship

5. Levin, *op. cit.*, p. 158.

to a statesman as a mechanic does to a scientist or a printer to a poet."

This, historians feel, explains in large measure Arthur's strange career. Essentially he was a private citizen steadily pursuing a hobby, but he was not a professional in politics. It was his mistress, not his wife. He ultimately became a consummate artist in political control, in what today would be accomplished by incessant phone calling, but was then done mostly by messenger or in person. Just the same, he too was trapped in the quicksand of ambition and, when offered the vice-presidential spot on a major party ticket, simply couldn't refuse. Few American males could, then or now.

Although Arthur wasn't in any way a "clubhouse boy," the journals of his time tarred him with the Conkling brush, much as many deserving Democrats from Manhattan have since been smeared with the transgressions of Tammany Hall. Rather he was a happy, back-slapping, genial gentleman, but he was a gentleman, where Conkling's other associates seldom were.

Arthur had been an obscure second-in-command of the Conkling machine. He now willingly took another second-in-command, the vice-presidential nomination, since in his own words even "a barren nomination would be a great honor," though Conkling had said, "If you wish for my favor and my respect you will contemptuously decline it."[6] Conkling may have wanted the Vice-Presidency for himself. In any case he was a permanent Grant man and a professional politician to whom the nomination of Arthur was just one more essential compromise. Anyway, the pact had been signed. New York nominated Arthur and Ohio seconded him amid the hisses and catcalls of reformers and the silence of the Half-Breeds. Professional politicians had confirmed the arrangement before the first roll call.

The campaign was largely one of silence on the part of the Conkling crowd at first. Garfield needed money for the campaign and New York sat on its hands. Conkling and Arthur

6. Archives, Museum of the City of New York.

literally went fishing, shutting off from Garfield's campaign funds the tremendous resources of Wall Street and the silk-stocking New Yorker. Conkling was simply making certain that his own power would continue in New York, that the Blaine crowd wouldn't try to move in.

Eventually it became so painful to Garfield and his finances that a tour of New York was arranged, ending up at the Fifth Avenue Hotel, which by no coincidence whatsoever turned out to be Conkling's headquarters. Morton and Jay Gould and Chauncey Depew were there to make certain the Republicans would have no money problems. Blaine, Logan, and Sherman were there to promise party unity. Arthur, Governor Cornell, and Tom Platt were present to assure the New York State organization. Only "my Lord Roscoe," as Garfield called him, was absent. He was, however, ready now to work with the party and for Garfield, having received genuine patronage assurances. He and Grant toured Indiana and Ohio in behalf of Garfield. Other Stalwarts were dispatched as apostles.

The "Treaty of Fifth Avenue" may or may not have surrendered all New York patronage to Conkling: Garfield later swore it didn't, though Platt swore it did. The fact is it temporarily settled the feud, at least to Conkling's satisfaction, and Conkling surely felt he had made a bargain: a pledge to deliver New York State in exchange for the state's share of the Federal patronage, in spite of the fact that Conkling had supported Grant.

Maine went Democratic in September, auguring bad omens. But General Hancock, whose nomination had been considered a master stroke by the Democrats, in imitation of the Republicans' successful military candidacies, turned out to be a master botcher and bungler. He said things during the campaign, as many military men have said before and since, that no trained politician ever says. He made enemies by instinct.

Moreover, the Democrats very foolishly forged a letter purporting to show that Garfield favored free immigration of Chinese to the Western states. But the letter was circulated too long before Election Day and was easily disproved by the hour of voting. Even the press sympathetic to a Democratic

President denounced the trick, calling it infamous, and Hancock somehow managed to lose the election by a margin of only four figures, the closest popular presidential vote in the history of the United States. The final tally was:

James A. Garfield (R)	4,454,416
Winfield S. Hancock (D)	4,444,952

Thus, a difference of only 9,464 made Major General James A. Garfield President of the United States and Chester Alan Arthur, Vice-President.

The electoral vote of 214 to 155 was much more decisive, and the Democrats, who had come so close in 1876 with Samuel J. Tilden, only to be swindled out of the election, had fallen for the sixth consecutive election. The upstart new Republicans were still undefeated, a remarkable political achievement for a young party only a generation born.

Garfield had been one of hundreds of politicians Abraham Lincoln's Secretary of War had somehow fitted into uniform.[7] Many of them had been handed officers' commissions outright and Garfield, a Congressman at that time, had high hopes in this direction. Garfield had known, as others knew, the political value of heroism and participation on the winning side. He hoped above hope to get an independent command where he might have the opportunity of associating his name with a great victory. He seemed quite certain he possessed military genius, though he had had little or no training in tactics. But Edwin Stanton, the Secretary of War, was finding it far too difficult to dig up military plums for all the politicians who wanted individual command; so when the assignment came for Garfield it was as Chief of Staff to General Rosecrans of the Army of the Tennessee, primarily an administrative post and no place at all to show off military genius.

When the ill-starred Rosecrans engineered a major Union disaster at Chickamauga he was cashiered, but Garfield, through a minor heroism, which was blown up out of pro-

7. Carl Sandburg, Vol. II, *Abraham Lincoln, The War Years* (New York, Harcourt, Brace and Company, 1939), *passim.*

portion to the truth, emerged a national hero. It won him a major general's stars. Thereupon he promptly returned to politics and his seat in Congress where the two stars were his most valuable stratagem and eventually helped make him President of the United States.

Gradually Garfield inherited the Republican leadership, partly through long tenure, partly through the death of the detestable Thaddeus Stevens (who had persecuted President Johnson), the ascendency of Schuyler Colfax to the Vice-Presidency under General Grant, and James G. Blaine's election from Maine as United States Senator.

When Garfield and Arthur had been elected to the Presidency and Vice-Presidency, Garfield wrote in his journal the second night in the White House: "I love to deal with doctrines and events. The contests of men about men I greatly dislike."

The selection of James G. Blaine as Secretary of State might have been unfortunate for Garfield, for Blaine possessed a strong personality, was sharply and unnecessarily partisan, and was Conkling's mortal enemy. Whether Blaine or Garfield would have been the real President, had Garfield lived, is worthy of conjecture. The struggle to fill his Cabinet and other appointments made Garfield's few months in the White House completely miserable, caught as he was in the wash of dirty politics with Blaine on one side and Conkling's New York cronies on the other. Sometimes there was no way of telling where anybody stood.

Garfield won the first few rounds. He got his appointments through the Senate, including a man opposed to Conkling as the new Collector of New York Customs, as lush a plum as could be imagined in politics in those days, for the Collector in New York kept a percentage of everything he collected in the way of duties and New York was by far the biggest port of entry. Garfield went even further. He had campaigned on a platform of honesty, reform, and civil service legislation, and apparently he meant it. His determination must have given Boss Conkling and others in the Grant camp uneasy nights.

Garfield's first major reforms involved prosecution of the "star route" frauds. A star route was a postal route inaccessible by rail or steamboat. The United States Postal Guide designated such a route with an asterisk, hence the name.

In the days before Rural Free Delivery, star routes were numerous and important, to the West in particular. There was no rail nor water mail route to most Western post offices. The mail got there by stage, rider, or runner. Private contracts for these star routes had, therefore, to be made individually and the bidders were required to be bonded. But the law also provided easy readjustment of these contracts in view of continuously shifting Western populations. A town of 200 might become a city of 2,000 weeks later, then disappear forever. Readjustment of postal contracts was essential to match the shifting tides of population movement.

All star route contracts were let through the Second Assistant Postmaster General, so a great deal depended on that man's integrity. The Second Assistant Postmaster General under Grant had been one Thomas W. Brady, who was, to say the least, not above suspicion. It was suspected that Brady had increased the compensation of many star route postal contractors who thereupon kicked back to Brady or his henchmen. Among these contractors had been a Senator from Arkansas, one Stephen W. Dorsey, a close friend of Brady's. That there had been collusion between these two Irishmen no one, not even Grant, doubted or denied.

All this President Garfield appeared determined to prosecute as part of his pledge of reform. The star route frauds were above half a million dollars. They smelled to high heaven. They were a natural reform field for a man devoted to honest government. But, just as Garfield moved to prosecute, amidst harassing office seekers who sensed a chance of appointment outside Conkling's influence, the President was shot by one of them.

On the second day of July, 1881, Garfield was to have left on a New England holiday trip and Blaine was to have accompanied him. They were deep in conversation as they ambled toward their train through Pennsylvania Station in Washington when a crazy man moved out from the crowd that had gathered to see them off. He fired two shots at point-blank range at the

President, and said something along the order of: "I'm a Stalwart and now Arthur is President!"[8]

For eleven humid weeks the warrior-executive fought for his life. Many times it appeared that he would win the exacting battle. He was only fifty years of age, possessed a strong, army-trained body, and lasted longer than he might have after a year or two of exhausting presidential drain.

Vice-President Arthur was lobbying as usual for Roscoe Conkling in Albany when the news reached the State Capitol of the assassin's attempt. Arthur went into immediate seclusion.

It was well that he did, for the assassin's implications had been damaging in the extreme. It appeared to some that Conkling's Stalwarts had engineered the whole thing, which wasn't true at all. But the public blamed Conkling just the same, and the death of Garfield ruined Conkling forever. An assassin's cry in Pennsylvania Station, Washington, had done in four seconds what the combined forces of decency, reform, and liberalism had failed to do in a lifetime of continuous political assault.

Robert Todd Lincoln, the President's son and Secretary of War in the Garfield Cabinet, reports that never once in the eighty days between Garfield's wounding and his death did the Garfield Cabinet meet to transact official business.[9] When they did occasionally and informally gather at the White House and nightly, later on, at Franklyn Cottage, they talked about nothing but the condition of the President. The business of governing the nation simply went unattended. No one paid the slightest attention to Chester A. Arthur.

In those days, the New York Custom House had more than enough jobs to fill the patronage requirements of the most voracious political machine. In an era when a million dollars was a lot of money, the New York Customs did a $900,000,000 business annually! This was a sum greater than the entire

8. *New York Tribune*, July 3, 1881.
9. Robert Todd Lincoln's Cabinet notes and letters as preserved in the National Archives Building, Washington; see also Bess Furman, *White House Profile* (Indianapolis, The Bobbs-Merrill Company, 1951), pp. 231–37.

Federal budget; it stood to reason that some of the collectors made money on the side and that the man who ran the Custom House was a powerful and practical politician.

Inside the City of New York, Chester Alan Arthur had, therefore, become an acknowledged power in the Republican Party when his appointment as Collector of the Custom House had come from Grant. The Collector did not get a salary; he was paid a percentage of the customs fines he could collect, not to mention anything under the table. In the poorest year of his tenure Arthur had made $35,000 and in the best close to $50,000, an undoubtedly enormous sum in those days, equivalent to a million dollars a year income now, since there were no income taxes then.

Arthur had learned, in 1872, that one of the richest importing firms in the country had been understating its customs values for quite a spell and was liable for $2,000,000 worth of forfeiture and fine. The company settled for a quarter of a million dollars. But, after the fine had been paid, the importer found that his undervaluations hadn't cost the Federal government nearly as much in lost duties as had been suggested in the law suit, yet the quarter million dollars had, by law, already been divided among those who had provided legal advice, Conkling among them, and top officers of the port. This was investigated by Congress and the upshot of the matter was to replace the Collector's percentage income with a fixed salary of $1,000 a month.

All this apparently had had very little to do with Chet Arthur personally, for he was never mentioned in the scandal of what had happened to the quarter-million-dollar settlement, and in 1875 Grant had reappointed him for four more years. Arthur had kept the pay rolls properly filled, which was his function in the Conkling machine, and it is certain that he never allowed the New York Custom House to remain understaffed for long. Indeed, the Republican machine collected a great deal of money from annual contributions by Customs workers hired with this clearly understood. War chests have been so filled by political machines since time began, and in perfect legality, if not always with the noblest motive.

The commission appointed to study Arthur's case had found nothing except the items already mentioned, and little or nothing involving Arthur personally. But the report was very unfriendly, though the law, and not the man, was undoubtedly at fault, and Chet Arthur had gone flying out the front door to great hand-clapping among New York editors and Democrats, who believed anything of a Conkling man.

Arthur, in all the time people witnessed against him, never once took the trouble to defend himself or his record or in any way tried to put the record straight. His seeming diffidence, his habit of playing politics for the game and not its rewards or policies explains a little of the deep mystery about him. He is probably our least-known President and he appears to have wanted it so, for he destroyed practically all his files on retirement.

That no President has ever come to the White House with less training or reason for success than Arthur is to understate the situation grotesquely. Even Harry Truman, forced by circumstance to succeed at a day's notice a brilliant, dynamic President at the very climax of the greatest war in history, had no such albatross as Arthur carried about his fashionably cravatted neck. Among his own followers, Arthur's sudden rise to the greatest office within the gift of the American people caused such shock that one of them said on hearing the awful news: "Chet Arthur, President of the United States! Good God!!"[10]

The country felt precisely this way about it. A calamity of the greatest proportions, the fantastic twist of the wheel of fortune stunned Republicans and nauseated Democrats. Here was an unfrocked politician whose very name meant corruption to many an American and to most of the country's editors. It would be a matter of time only, thought the country, before the Treasury would be subject to such havoc as the United States, now just over a century old, had never imagined possible, not even under the outrageous wickedness of Grant's thieving henchmen.

10. As reported by Levin and others from contemporary sources, none of which identify the shocked follower by name.

If Arthur's honesty and methods as Collector of the New York Custom House were criteria (and the average man had no way of knowing that they were not a true reflection of Arthur's moral standards), the nation was doomed. The ugly word "impeachment" was on many lips. Arthur's incompetence was manifest.

To make it worse, the Garfield assassin's cry kept bouncing around in the minds of those who hoped fervently that postwar Republican corruption had at last been corralled with the defeat of the Stalwarts and the rise of Republican liberalism.

When Chet Arthur, the dandy from New York, came to the White House to inspect it before moving in, he said: "I will not live in a house looking this way. If Congress doesn't make an appropriation, I will go ahead and have it done and pay for it out of my own pocket. I will not live in a house like this."

Just how the White House then looked is described by a Garfield visitor early that year of 1881:

The place is now full of modern abominations in upholstery and garish gilding, and all the rooms look staring, pretentious and Frenchy. The old port-wine colored mahogany sofas and chairs which were in the State Parlours in Lincoln's time were better than anything that has come in their place. At least they were quiet and dignified.

Arthur was true to his word. Between Garfield's death on September 19 and Christmas of that year, President Arthur had the place done over by the artist, Louis Comfort Tiffany, a name which already meant to New Yorkers taste and jewels, gold and elegance.

Every evening President Arthur would leave the granite mansion of his friend, Senator John P. Jones of Nevada, and inspect what had been done in the White House. Twenty-four wagonloads of junky furniture, bric-a-brac, claptrap, and new items Arthur didn't like were removed and sold at auction. Washington society dearly loved the tales of this house cleaning by the dandy new President. One wit said: "Arthur's trap has caught the rat that ate the suit of clothes of President Lincoln."

Arthur would go from room to room altering to his own taste. Colonel H. W. Crook, a member of the White House staff from Lincoln to Teddy Roosevelt, reports that the new President would issue enough orders and tag enough discards to keep the workmen busy all next day.

When the redecorating was all over, Arthur still didn't like it and tried to get Congress to build a new executive mansion across Lafayette Park, where the Hays Adams Hotel is now. But nothing came of it.

Following is Tiffany's own report of some of the proceedings:

> In the East Room, we only did the ceiling, which was done in silver, with a design in various tones of ivory. The Blue Room, or Robin's Egg Room—as it's sometimes called —was decorated in robin's egg blue for the main color, with ornaments in handpressed paper, touched out in ivory, gradually deepening as the ceiling was approached. In the Red Room, the walls were red with a frieze in which the motif was an interlacing of a design embodying both eagles and flags. The ceiling was in old gold. The opalescent glass screen in the hall, which reached from the floor to the ceiling, had also a motif of eagles and flags, interlaced in the Arabian method.

The glass screen, originally designed to give President Arthur and his family privacy, was long a fixture in the White House and the cause of wonder for every visitor who could find no break in a wall of glass in which a door would suddenly open.

President Arthur also put in the first elevator and the first White House plumbing, two bathrooms. Up to then, all the plumbing had been, as they say, outdoors, or, to be more precise, by portable chinaware.

When Mrs. James G. Blaine, wife of the Garfield Secretary of State, dined later in the White House she said, perhaps cattily, that the dinner was "extremely elegant, hardly a trace of the old White House taint being perceptible anywhere, the flowers, the damask, the silver, the attendants, all showing the latest style and an abandon in expense and taste." This mention of "White House taint" was revealing. She and everyone else knew how painful the eighty days of Garfield's lingering had been through the dreadful heat of a Washington summer.

In July, Arthur had been summoned from New York to stand by in Washington while the hero Garfield faded slowly. He had gone at once to the White House to see Mrs. Garfield, and the Cabinet had happened to be there at the time. When the Vice-President had stood at the door of the Cabinet Room, not one of Garfield's choices rose to greet him, nor was he asked in. The Garfield Cabinet simply stared at him like so many cobras upon a mongoose. While he stood at the door of the Cabinet Room another visitor came up and the ice was broken; otherwise, Arthur might well have been left outside without a word. As it was, perfunctory greetings were exchanged, and soon thereafter Garfield improved to such a degree that Arthur returned to New York, only to be sworn in as President suddenly at midnight on September 19, 1881, at his luxurious home on Lexington Avenue.

Here's the way Arthur's latent champion, Elihu Root, saw his plight:[11]

Surely no more lonely and pathetic figure was ever seen assuming the powers of government. He had no people behind him, for Garfield, not he, was the people's choice; he had no party behind him, for the dominant faction of his party hated his name—were enraged by his advancement, and distrusted his motives. He had not even his own faction behind him, for he already knew that discharge of his duties would not accord with the ardent desires of their partisanship, and that disappointment and estrangement lay before him. He was alone. He was bowed down by the weight of fearful responsibility and crushed to earth by the feeling, exaggerated but not unfounded, that he took up his heavy burden surrounded by dislike, suspicion, distrust and condemnation, as an enemy of the martyred Garfield and the beneficiary of his murder. Deep and settled melancholy possessed him; almost despair overwhelmed him. He went to power walking through the valley of the shadow of death and ascended the steps to the throne as one who is accused goes to trial.

11. Elihu Root Papers and manuscript collection, New York Public Library.

So gloomy was the new Chief Executive, in fact, that he took the precaution of sending himself a letter which contained a Presidential Proclamation calling the Senate into special session to elect a President of the United States pro tempore in the event of his own assassination en route to the White House. If he should die, the nation could go on because Chet Arthur had set it up legally with selfless forethought.

On September 22 in the Presidential Room of the Capitol a second swearing-in took place. Garfield's whole antagonistic Cabinet were present. Chief Justice Waite administered the new oath of office with less than enthusiasm.

The new Cabinet was Arthur's first task. One by one he replaced Garfield's men, Secretary of State Blaine being one of the last to go. This shifting of the Chief Executive's official family took the better part of what was left of 1881. What astonished the country most, during this period, was the absence of Roscoe Conkling from any post at all, unofficial or official. Cronies simply weren't being appointed, though Arthur did privately offer his old political boss a seat on the Supreme Court which Conkling haughtily refused. They were never close thereafter.

To the utter amazement of everyone, including the press, the man whose reputation for fraud and corruption smelled worse than any President in United States history suddenly declared himself in favor of civil service reform, got the bills started again in Congress, and eventually signed the great Civil Service Act which put an end to the abuses Grant had allowed to creep into Jackson's spoils system.

In subsequent months, President Arthur refused point blank to fill the New York Custom House (scene of his alleged crimes) with Stalwarts. Senator Conkling, soured on the new President for this and other imagined slights, was soon referring to Chester Alan Arthur as "His Accidency,"[12] and even former President Grant broke with him on grounds that he had repudiated Grant's cronies by ignoring their alleged patronage rights.

12. Archives, Museum of the City of New York.

His own Cabinet came eventually, only one of them being a Garfield holdover—Robert Todd Lincoln.

When the delicate matter of high or low tariffs arose, Arthur anticipated the twentieth century by suggesting reciprocal trade treaties in the New Deal pattern. These never came to pass in his time, but he was on sound footing, and only special interests in gigantic industrial lobbies on The Hill defeated such a far-seeing policy.

President Arthur did, however, manage to set up a Tariff Commission which dealt with an annual surplus of $80,000,000 or more piling up in the Treasury as a result of the continuance of high Civil War tariffs.

He also convinced both houses of Congress that it wasn't good sense or economy to rebuild Civil War battleships; and he was truly the founder of the modern United States Navy which lasted until the age of air. John Spencer Bassett says of him:[13]

> Before he became President, Arthur was a typical partisan of the Conkling group, a friend of the spoilsman and an opponent of reform. Called to the Presidency by the tragedy of July, 1881, he seemed to pass through a transformation and stood out as another kind of man. He took up the reins of office quietly, he managed them with fairness, and he went through the period of his power to the general satisfaction even of the reformers.
>
> The death of a President by the act of a disappointed office seeker called popular attention to the evil effects of the spoils system. Suddenly it became possible to pass a bill of reform. The Pendleton Civil Service Act of 1883 provided for competitive examinations, a Civil Service Commission to supervise the execution of the law, and the elimination of partisan appointments—what was known as the "classified service." By 1883 the number was 13,924, or about one-eleventh of the whole government payroll of the nation.

Although Pendleton was a Democrat, the Pendleton Act had the support of more Republicans than Democrats. By making

13. John Spencer Bassett, *The Pageant of America*, Vol. IX, *Makers of a New Nation* (New Haven, Yale University Press, 1928), pp. 126–27.

it impossible to remove officials without cause, the persons then in office, chiefly Republicans, would be protected if the party lost the next election. The Democrats carried Congress in 1882, and hoped to win the Presidency in 1884 for the first time since the Civil War. Therefore the Democratic Party had threatened to delay the Pendleton Act.

But President Arthur stood fast. He upheld the Civil Service Commission throughout his administration and placed nearly 2,000 employees under the protection of its rules. He laid the groundwork for Grover Cleveland, who completed the job of dignifying Civil Service and modifying what his executive predecessor, Andrew Jackson, had invented.

President Arthur vetoed pork-barrel rivers-and-harbors bills which were promptly passed over his veto, but the people ~~~ the editorial writers in particular began to take to his ho: and courage. He was easily efficient, a good administ who could delegate authority. Soon the antagonism begä fade before his political fairness and personal candor. Wh came time for his re-election many common people liked and many uncommon, too. Mark Twain, for instance, wrc the *Chicago Daily News*:[14] "I am but one of 55,000,000; in the opinion of this one-fifty-five millionth of the cour population, it would be hard to better President Arthur's ministration. But don't decide until you hear from the res

In the White House, Chet Arthur and his family conducted themselves as few other presidential families have: in absolute decorum and taste. When his passion for clothes became a whispering campaign against his renomination, he did not deny, as Mrs. Blaine had charged, that he had ordered twenty-five new coats from his tailor early in 1882 for White House functions. Catty Mrs. Blaine kept insisting, perhaps with self-interest, that all of Arthur's ambitions centered on his stomach and other social aspects of the Presidency, but not on its burdens. He never denied that he found it pleasant to have about him flowers and wine and excellent food, or that it was satisfying to stroll with a lady on one's arm and a quotation from Dickens or Thackeray on one's lips. Nor did he repudiate the

14. Files of the *Chicago Daily News*.

French chef who had served him well in New York and now brought the first really good food to White House tables.

Faultless in dress, immaculately turned out on every occasion, Chester A. Arthur and his famous sideburns were kept in perfect trim by the first genuine fourteen-carat White House valet, another mark against him when re-election came up. He had thought he would win (seeming certain of renomination, as most Presidents had been) on his record alone and the growing editorial praise for his honest term. Yet he was not so honored, one of the few Presidents repudiated by his own party.

Both the Half-Breeds and the Stalwarts had done their best to disown Arthur from the hour of his Presidency. Reformers remained wary to the end of his term because his record simply impelled them to wariness. His demand for civil service reform heartened some, editors especially. But there was always that doubt, as there was to be later with a Vice-President named Richard Nixon. (No matter how much Nixon seemed to have reformed, there was always his alleged record in the Helen Gahagan Douglas Senatorial contest and his rationalizing of liberalism.) With Arthur, the fact that the office had reformed him completely, that he had truly risen to the occasion, was hard to believe even when the public saw it before its own eyes.

The Stalwarts did not like Arthur because he gave them little patronage, and also they were tired of the repudiated Conkling leadership with which they (wrongly) associated the new Arthur. The term "His Accidency" became common talk, which did little to help Arthur's reputation, whatever progress he might make as a human being or Chief Executive.

He employed no bodyguard and walked freely about Washington, to the consternation of the Secret Service. He drove the swankiest dark-green landau in Washington, pulled by mahogany-colored geldings with blankets monogrammed "A." Huge flower orders came weekly from New York to augment the meager White House conservatory output. Every morning he placed a bouquet before the photograph of his dead wife, Ellen Herndon, daughter of the naval hero William Lewis Herndon. She had succumbed suddenly to pneumonia just before his nomination for Vice-President. To this day a stained glass window in her name decorates old St. John's Episcopal Church, directly across from the Hay Adams and within sight of the White House over Lafayette Square.

Naturally, when tales of fancy spending for flowers, elegant food, French chefs, mahogany horses, dandy coats, striped pants, and lush parties were circulated by Blaine's men they somehow became charged to public funds, not private. Mrs. Blaine once said: "If he [James G. Blaine] cannot himself be President, no more can any other Republican without his assent." This was pathetically so, and the "continental liar from the State of Maine" had not the slightest intention of supporting President Arthur in 1884.

Rising young Congressman Joe Cannon, though a fellow party member, put it best when the Republican National Convention of 1884 repudiated the President of the United States. Said Cannon: "Arthur was defeated by his trousers." (In similar fashion had an earlier President who liked lovely things been defeated, though renominated by his own party. Martin Van Buren had lost because he had ordered some gold spoons to raise the tone of the White House table.)

The Forty-seventh Congress had been the first in six years to have Republican majorities in both houses. President Arthur's requests to it had been very simple, and on the whole more along the reform tack than the reactionary. He had asked the Forty-seventh Congress for a tariff revision, for funds to renovate the Navy, for money to create a modern merchant marine, for U. S. troops to deal with the Indians in the new Western territory, for a better presidential succession statute, for reduced excise taxes, a balanced budget with a small surplus, and for a strong civil service law.

To read this presidential message must have been a shock to the American public, for it was plainly the work of a convert to political honesty, decency in office, and an end to some of the nation's fears of the most potentially corrupt administration the country had ever seen. Arthur the politician had departed; Arthur the President had risen to the occasion, and in doing so had molded further the dignity and prestige of the highest elective office in the civilized world.

But at the next biennial election, the Democrats swept the country and early in 1883 took control of the House again: with it went Arthur's last lingering hope of making an enduring record as President of the United States. Between that date and March 4, 1885, the Democrats did very little but hold Congressional investigations designed to bring before the next presidential campaign the stench of unchallenged Republicanism and Stalwart corruption. Arthur had no chance in the circumstances, and the fact that his naturally florid complexion gave constant reminder that he must be a drunkard as well as a political thief did not help his cause. Even the flowers he set daily before his dead wife's picture somehow came in the public mind to be an alliance with one of the Secretary of State's daughters, many years his junior. Now he was a reprobate as well.

Political party control invariably gets settled in the state capitols, usually while the legislature is in session. But the struggle at Albany had left no doubt whatsoever of the stench inside the Republican Party and its undoubted effect on the occupant of the White House, an unfrocked politico from the rocks and crevices of the New York Custom House. It is little wonder that the country gave the Democrats almost two-thirds control of the House in 1883.

It is little wonder, too, that James G. Blaine should emerge as the President's chief rival for control of the Republican Party, for Blaine had little else to do, now that he was an ex-Secretary of State and a thoroughgoing Arthur-Conkling hater. Blaine's every act now involved the nomination for President in 1884. Coming into the convention of 1884, President Arthur stood for nomination on his record, but the reform element combined with Blaine's Half-Breeds and many an old Stalwart now thoroughly disenchanted with Conkling and his Albany odors. So even on the first ballot Arthur was second to Blaine, who won on the fourth.

It is conceivable that Chester Alan Arthur was not only an accident in the Presidency but literally ineligible for the office. In 1884, the year Arthur would have been up for re-election had his own party not disowned him, one A. P. Hinman published a tiny booklet in New York attempting to prove that Arthur had not been born in the United States, as was claimed, but in reality came into the world beyond the Canadian border of Vermont. Hinman's little known book is entitled "How a British Subject Became President of the United States,"[15] undeniably a political tract inspired by the forces of James G. Blaine, who would have done (and did) just about anything to seize the presidential nomination.

The Constitution requires that the President and the Vice-President shall be natural born citizens. Article II reads: "No person except a natural born citizen . . . shall be eligible to the office of President," and the Twelfth Amendment reads: "But no person constitutionally ineligible to the office of President shall be eligible to that of Vice President of the United States."

The question raised by Hinman at the urging of Blaine or Conkling or Sherman (or any one of a dozen jealous politicians of the time) was whether Arthur, being in their eyes Canadian-born, was legally eligible for the office of Vice-President under Article XII of the Amendments. If he was ineligible for Vice-President he was, under the Constitution, ineligible to succeed Garfield.

Hinman's book claimed that Arthur, when nominated for the Vice-Presidency, was, at first, unable to name his birthplace. After diligent search, during what was said to be a fishing trip to Canada immediately following his nomination, Arthur found no existing record of his Canadian birth; so he was, in Hinman's words, "safe in naming some out-of-the-way place in the United States." He chose Fairfield, Vermont, where a deceased brother had been born.

15. A. P. Hinman, "How a British Subject Became President of the United States" (New York, 1884), now in the possession of Theodore Carlson, Wilton, Connecticut.

The encyclopedias and almanacs list the birth date and birth-place of the twenty-first President as October 5, 1830, and either "Vermont" or "Fairfield, Vermont." The fact is that there is no known record of President Arthur's birth, either in Vermont or anywhere else, but that's not surprising. There are no official records of the births of most Americans who were born in the early nineteenth century. Records, when they were kept at all, had a way of disappearing and dissolving in frontier America. Nobody cared, for the most part, anyway. The family knew their child had been born, relatives knew, the town knew, and it didn't make much difference whether an ill-paid, part-time records clerk in northern New England took the trouble to put down a vital statistic for posterity, the clerk being unable to foresee which baby would grow up to be President.

In the month of October, 1830 (when Chester was supposed to have been born), William Arthur, his father, obtained employment as a teacher in Stanbridge, Canada, across the border from Vermont. Mrs. Arthur did not accompany her husband but remained in North Fairfield, Vermont, where a son was born in November, 1830, who was named, according to Mr. Hinman's documents, Chester Abell Arthur in honor of Dr. Chester Abell, a boon companion of William Arthur and who attended Mrs. Arthur's confinement and delivery. The child died in the summer of 1831 at Burlington while Mrs. Arthur was on a visit to friends.

The unofficial prosecutor's charge is, therefore, that Chester Alan Arthur, whenever he was born or where, took his dead brother's birth certificate as his own because he himself was Canadian-born, therefore ineligible to become President of the United States or, for that matter, even Vice-President.

Records indicate that on September 5, 1845, Chester Alan Arthur matriculated at Union College, entering the sophomore class and stating that he was then sixteen years of age. He was graduated in July, 1848. Mr. Hinman's tract claims that this is a true statement of his age and birth. It would place his birth date somewhere in the neighborhood of 1828–1829, at which time Mrs. Arthur did bear a son named William Chester Alan Arthur (Hinman says), but not in North Fairfield, Vermont.

Mrs. Arthur's parents had lived some years at Dunham Flats, Quebec, her childhood home, and she was visiting neighboring Dunham Flats when her eldest son came into the world, if we are to believe Hinman's tract. The exact birth date isn't secure. But the eldest Arthur boy, William (Chester Alan Arthur is said to have dropped this name because it caused confusion with his father), was born either March 16 or 18, 1828; his grandfather remembered saying at the time that William, Jr., was lucky he came a day too early or a day too late, otherwise he would have been called Patrick, having considerable Irish blood.

Later, during Mr. Hinman's exhaustive inquiry on local ground, many friends, relatives, and neighbors remembered the oldest boy, called "Chet," on the sidewalks of Williston, Vermont, being trundled along in a hand cart in 1833 at the age of five, which would square with the birth date. Precisely why the Arthur family, or more exactly Chester A. Arthur, should go to the elaborate trouble of trying to get the public to believe he was his dead brother, Chester Abell Arthur, isn't clear except to verify Hinman's accusation.

Hinman of course claims that Chet Arthur knew he was Canadian-born (of American parents) and, when necessity required it, he simply took the Vermont birth certification of his dead brother whose name his closely resembled.[16]

But Hinman's complicated and thoroughly documented hymn of hate will always appear beside the point. The Constitution words the birth requirement "*natural* born citizen." It doesn't say "*native* born." It may well have meant, in spite of partisan opinions on the subject from time to time, precisely what it has come legally to mean when two American citizens have a child on foreign soil—that the child is truly an American citizen.

So, whether (William) Chester Alan Arthur was delivered at the home of his grandparents in Dunham Flats, Quebec, Canada, on or near St. Patrick's Day, 1828, or in Fairfield, Vermont, on October 5, 1830, may not be terribly important, though a case of this sort has never yet been brought to the

16. *Ibid.*

Supreme Court for final interpretation of the wording of Article II. This fugitive semantic will undoubtedly arise one day when an American child born on foreign soil gets a major party nomination to the Presidency or Vice-Presidency. Arthur's case is closed and nothing the Supreme Court or anyone else can do will alter the fact that, during his lifetime he was, by the people who had elected him, accepted as President of the United States.

What does matter to the office of the Presidency is that a man of undoubted slack reputation and dubious association was thrust by fate into the White House for almost a full four-year term, yet so comported himself that the dignity of the office was exalted. "His Accidency" Chet Arthur rose to the occasion, despite his past and the fears of his constituents, and in so doing molded the Presidency as other Presidents had before him or would do again in the shadows ahead.

Grover Cleveland

THE PRESIDENTIAL election of 1884 between James G. Blaine, the "Plumed Knight" of the Republican Party, and Grover Cleveland, young hero Governor from New York and the Democrats' latest postwar hope, was undoubtedly the dirtiest of all U. S. quadrennials. This is saying a good deal. Andrew Jackson weathered merciless slanders against his beloved wife. Franklin D. Roosevelt was involved in at least two of the vilest slime-throwing campaigns this country's ballot has known. But Blaine-Cleveland outranks them all.

In the first place, the Republican Party early uncovered the fact that Grover Cleveland had undoubtedly sired an illegitimate child in his youth, which Cleveland tacitly admitted. Then the Democrats dug up what American history calls the "Mulligan letters," on the back of one of which the unfortunate Republican candidate had had the witlessness to write "Burn this letter!."

Thereafter the manure flew in Herculean proportions. The "Plumed Knight," coming as he did after the besmirched Grant and the unlucky Arthur, had campaigned for the nomination on reform grounds. But his penchant for gaining payments and commissions from unscrupulous and ambitious promoters who wished to use his political office to insure their favors was thoroughly aired and debated. The Democrats wrote a little jingle still familiar to most school children:

> Blaine, Blaine, James G. Blaine,
> The continental liar from the State of Maine!

6

Dignifies the Presidential Veto

The Republicans, not to be outdone, wrote a ditty of their
own:

> Ma, ma, where's my pa?
> He's goin' to the White House, ha, ha, ha!

Unfortunately for Blaine, the careless recipient of the most
damaging of the Mulligan letters did not fulfill Blaine's request.
Blaine also had appeared at a fabulous millionaire dinner at
Delmonico's, soon known on the Main Street of America as
"Belshazzar's Feast." His unsavory connection with the malefactors of great wealth, as a Roosevelt was later to call them,
damned him with a large segment of the intelligentsia and the
working class, especially the important new foreign-born electorate now flooding U. S. cities.

To make Blaine's case worse, an unthinking Republican
clergyman called the Democratic Party the party of "Rum,
Romanism, and Rebellion." Rebellion was now a generation
dead and the South bitterly resented the bloody shirt being
waved in political debate. "Romanism" offended the enormous
Irish Catholic population of New York City and helped Blaine
lose that pivotal state by only a thousand votes out of hundreds
of thousands. By losing New York, Blaine lost the Presidency.

Cleveland had, to say the least, liked a drink now and then,
and when he tacitly admitted parenthood to an illegitimate
child of the days of his wild oats he had given to the Victorian
households of the time their most powerful political weapon.

Sex just wasn't nice in the late nineteenth century. But his transgression had come to light sufficiently early in the presidential campaign to be explained and discounted. Also, he was painfully honest about his sins. Blaine wasn't, because he couldn't be.

When James G. Blaine had been relieved as Secretary of State under President Arthur and replaced by Frederick Frelinghuysen, a far more conservative statesman, Blaine was given all the time in the world to plan and work for his own presidential nomination in 1884. As Secretary he had been pretty much of a jingoist, and had especially given Great Britain a difficult time, much to the delight of the American press. The country was feeling its oats, it was adolescent, but moving toward manhood; it liked Blaine's bold approach to foreign affairs. Frelinghuysen's unexciting three and a half years gave Blaine, therefore, the best possible ammunition to fire at President Arthur, who would inevitably be Blaine's chief antagonist for the upcoming Republican nomination.

Blaine also began to write a two-volume biographical work called *Twenty Years of Congress* which was sold at private subscription (a great many politically minded men coughed up large checks for their copies) and gave Blaine a greater income between 1881 and 1884 than any other public figure except a President. He made speeches and was paid for them, and he was consulted on legal matters and received fees which went into the campaign fund: object—the 1884 nomination for President.

Blaine lived in a house across the street from the state capitol in Augusta, Maine, and the Republican world beat a path to his door in those three years.[1] President Arthur's stands on various issues were debated on the floor of Congress and in the public press, but they were usually first aired in the Blaine parlor. Arthur, for example, wanted to apply a not inconsiderable surplus to reducing the huge Civil War debt, which ran into the billions, and to replacing obsolete Civil War ships

1. Peter Levin, *Seven by Chance* (New York, Farrar, Straus and Company, 1948), p. 174.

with new designs. Blaine went back to Henry Clay's theory of distributing excess tax receipts to the several states. He was against lowering those wartime tariffs which were flooding the Treasury with an embarrassment of riches.

Blaine never talked issues for long, however. The candid conversation almost always switched to personalities and 1884. John Alexander Logan[2] seems to have been promised the vice-presidential nomination for assuring he could deliver Illinois at the convention and the subsequent election. Tom Platt, who had been caught in a hotel bed with a lady of easy virtue and had as a result lost out in New York, came back on the Republican scene by waving a banner for Maine's Blaine, the "Plumed Knight."

By summer, 1884, therefore, the upshot of the matter was that Arthur had lost any chance of renomination. Coming to the convention on his amazing record for progressive administration, Arthur could nevertheless not quite match the more practical mathematics of one of the most carefully laid, long-term campaigns for a Republican presidential nomination. No other matches it in U. S. history except Thomas E. Dewey's incessant campaigning between 1936 and 1948.

No hour of a day went by without some action being taken, usually in Augusta, with that end in view. Arthur had, it is true, Southern delegations which could be bought overnight, and he did fairly well with Republican businessmen and the banking interests, who had been amazed at his clean White House record. A few Stalwarts backed him still, but Grant had become embittered at Arthur's independence and unwillingness to favor the former President-hero's cronies.[3]

The reform crowd, hypocritical as always, repudiated Arthur despite his splendid conversion. A public letter reminded the

2. James G. Blaine and John Alexander Logan may have been a balanced team politically as the Republican ticket of 1884, but they were bitter personal enemies. One rhyme of the day, in a campaign of doggerel, put their partnership this way:
We never speak as we pass by
Me to Blaine—nor Blaine to I.
3. Levin, *op. cit.,* p. 175.

party that "Guiteau [Garfield's assassin] was the original Arthur man."[4] Two top reform Senators from New England had been turned down on collectorship appointments when Arthur had put a nonpolitician into the port of Boston, and he had vetoed a juicy rivers and harbors bill smelling to heaven of pork. These reformers had been aided and abetted by a wild-eyed young man with a pince-nez on a string, a bristling mustache, energy to burn, and a noisy high voice which he used at top volume while standing upon a chair. This young man's name was Theodore Roosevelt, Jr. He came from New York, was son of the man who had once been selected to replace Chester Alan Arthur as Collector of the New York Custom House. All of these reform politicians, young Roosevelt included, descended upon Arthur, without overmuch reason considering his administrative marks, and gave the nomination nod to James G. Blaine.

President Arthur, therefore, had no chance. He played with a stacked deck. After the second ballot, Arthur's support fell rapidly away; on the fourth it was all Blaine, much to the disgust of Grant's and Conkling's Stalwarts and the just newspaper editors of the day. Arthur, loyal organization man to his buffed finger tips, gracefully gave in, made a speech offering his unquestioned support of the new nominee, and congratulated Blaine before the multitude. It was Blaine's shining hour, and Mrs. Blaine's too. Few political wives, except perhaps Florence Harding and Mary Todd Lincoln, have been as ambitious for their husbands. And Harriet Stanwood Blaine might well have been First Lady had it not been for the diabolically damaging Mulligan letters.

James Gillespie Blaine, seven years Cleveland's senior, was himself only fifty-four when nominated for President. This made it one of the youngest elections in American history up to that time, and Cleveland one of the youngest Presidents, at forty-seven. Blaine was a Pennsylvanian by birth and had studied law while teaching at the Pennsylvania Institute for the Blind. When he was twenty-four, he had gone to Augusta,

4. *Ibid.*

Maine, where he became an influential editor by buying an interest in the *Kennebec Journal*. When the Republican Party arose from the ashes of Whiggism, Blaine helped organize it in Maine and was delegate to the first Republican National Convention just before the Civil War. He remained Republican leader of Maine most of his life.

At thirty-three, he was elected to the House of Representatives where he stayed until 1876; his last six years he was Speaker of the House. In the House he became a close friend of James A. Garfield of Ohio and other Westerners whose support he would need if he were to run for national office, his lifelong ambition. Opposing Grant on more than one issue, Blaine could not help become the mortal enemy of Roscoe Conkling of New York, who thought Grant should have not only two but three terms as President and detested anyone who spoke otherwise. Conkling's Stalwarts were, therefore, natural political opponents of Blaine's Half-Breeds, a name contemptuously bestowed upon them by Grant's followers, meaning that they were neither Republicans nor Democrats, but mongrel politicians.

With the assassination of Garfield and the assumption of Arthur (and assumption is as good a word as any, in the circumstances), the Republican Party had become more and more divided against itself. One of the reasons for its difficulties was the 1884 presidential nomination of James G. Blaine, who was Garfield's Secretary of State and later became Benjamin Harrison's also. (History reports with the accuracy of 20–20 hindsight that Blaine was an excellent Secretary of State, one of the very few really top Secretaries of State in the history of American foreign relations. But he proved to be a highly vulnerable candidate for President.)

The chief reasons for his remarkable vulnerability were the "Mulligan letters," but of course there was more to it than that. The flaw lay in Blaine's very nature. Ambition seared him, gnawed at his vitals, made him (and Mrs. Blaine) vindictive and stupidly arrogant when they should have been humble and compassionate. The voters were not fooled.

These letters were so called because one James Mulligan of Boston had kept some books for Warren Fisher, Jr., of the Little Rock & Fort Smith Railroad, and still held much of Blaine's correspondence. The letters Mulligan possessed and eventually publicized made it painfully clear to the public that Blaine, after having granted favors for the railroad, called railroad officials' attention to his favors and soon after received the privilege of selling the road's bonds for a secret and generous commission.

The selection of Blaine, with his dubious railroad fees, his private belief that the spoils system was infinitely superior to Civil Service, his propensity for waving the bloody shirt, sent many Republican liberals, editors, and independents out of the party and into the arms of Cleveland. Carl Schurz bolted, Henry Ward Beecher bolted. President Eliot and most of the Harvard faculty publicly condemned the author of the Mulligan letters and supported Cleveland.

Old and less sensational Mulligan letters had already been surveyed and discounted through Congressional hearings. When the Democratic hierarchy went back to them at the outset of the 1884 campaign, many thought it a mistake to revive so dead a horse. But the animal was far from dead. New Mulligan letters were soon made public from the apparently inexhaustible files of the Little Rock line. Blaine's disclaimer in the *Kennebec Journal,* wherein he stated that there wasn't a word in these letters not entirely consistent with the "most scrupulous integrity and honor," didn't cut ice with discerning voters, though many a Republican editor either suppressed the letters or gave misleading summaries of their contents.

One Blaine letter had a particularly stunning effect. For greater secrecy, the letter had been mailed to the Parker House in Boston and Blaine had then telegraphed an old business associate to pick it up there, though he knew full well that the associate lived at the Commonwealth Hotel. The letter enclosed the draft of a letter Blaine wanted the associate to write and sign, exonerating Blaine. Then Blaine signed his own warrant: "Regard this letter as strictly confidential. Do not show it to anyone." And on the back were the words: "Burn this letter!"

Reformers fell upon the letter with joy and delight.[5] Carl Schurz, his keen German mind functioning at top performance, gave a series of speeches as unrelenting and merciless as the logic of Blaine's misdeeds. There wasn't the slightest doubt by the time he had finished that Blaine had used his Speakership to multiply his own railroad interests and had profited handsomely from them.

One speech Schurz made in Brooklyn on August 5, 1884, was so searching and sarcastically logical that Blaine was forced to sue him for libel, but, of course, the suit never came to trial. The *Nation* and *Harper's Weekly* followed Schurz's lead, and soon the country's intellectuals were almost wholly in Cleveland's camp, and a winning camp it proved to be.

Grover Cleveland's first name was Stephen; Grover was his middle name. He was born in Caldwell, New Jersey, the son of a poorly paid Presbyterian minister, and once considered the ministry as his own career. Law lured him, however, and he practiced it from 1859 to 1881, beginning when he was twenty-two years old. In this period he was assistant district attorney and sheriff. He became Mayor of Buffalo in 1881 and his great reform administration soon attracted national attention in a time when the magic word "reform" was on every conscious voter's tongue, and with good reason.

The New York State Democratic leader, Dan'l Manning, early saw qualities in Grover Cleveland that would make him a fine vote-getter in New York State, for Cleveland had given the City of Buffalo no lick-and-a-promise cleansing, but a drastic reform which had earned Cleveland the title of the "Veto Mayor." Elected Governor of New York, Cleveland kept right on vetoing. He battled Tammany Hall to a standstill, incurring the cheerless wrath of one John Kelly, New York City's Democratic boss. In the subsequent battle for political control of the Democratic delegation in New York State, Cleveland won out. The Democratic delegation to the 1884 National Convention was then Grover Cleveland's.

5. Allan Nevins, *Grover Cleveland, a Study in Courage* (New York, Dodd, Mead and Company, Inc., 1932), pp. 162–65.

Teddy Roosevelt had been trying to reform the municipal government of New York and received Cleveland's full cooperation, though Roosevelt was a Republican and Cleveland a Democrat. This helped Cleveland's popularity with Republican and independent voters whom any Democratic candidate for President had to win over following twenty-four consecutive years of Republican presidential victories. In those days the Democrats were a distinct minority.

Cleveland was, therefore, a national figure by the time the Republicans had assembled to select their presidential candidate. The Republicans did Cleveland, the man whose name was synonymous with reform, quick political service by naming James G. Blaine as their standard-bearer. Cleveland also gained an advantage from the enmity of Tammany Hall, for the "mugwump" or reform element in the Republican Party liked anti-Tammany candidates and would cross party lines to vote for one.

Cleveland's own political cross was the charge of having sired an illegitimate child.[6] Maria Halpin was an obscure young widow from a Pennsylvania family who, leaving two children behind her, moved from Buffalo to Jersey City in 1871 and began work as a collar-maker, then as a drygoods clerk for Flint and Kent, where she eventually came to be given charge of the cloak department. In the years ahead many a story and play would revolve about her prototype: "Nelly, the Beautiful Cloak Model."

Maria Halpin was a pretty widow, pleasant mannered, and spoke a foreign language, French, which gave her a certain social standing in Jersey City despite her occupation and a tendency to alcohol. She attended fashionable St. John's Episcopal Church, and had suitors galore, among them young Cleveland, thirty-seven, one year her senior.

In 1874, on September 14, a son was born to her. She named the child Oscar Cleveland and charged Grover with the pa-

6. The succeeding information is based on exhaustive research by Allan Nevins and others and comes from study of the Buffalo press from 1876 to 1884, of many Cleveland letters, of a carefully prepared Democratic pamphlet, and pertinent files.

ternity. Although, as he wrote to a Boston friend when President, he didn't really know whether the child was his or not, Cleveland made provision for the boy.[7] Those who appeared to know most about the case—and were as neutral as it was possible to be in the circumstances—were of the opinion at the time that Maria Halpin had no real idea who was in fact the father of her child. She had fixed upon Grover Cleveland because he alone of her suitors was then unmarried; she hoped thus to induce him to marry her.

The mother soon began neglecting her offspring and took heavily to drink. Eventually she was taken to the Providence Asylum, an institution for the mentally deficient run by the Sisters of Charity. Meanwhile, her boy was committed by the Overseer of the Poor to the Protestant Orphan Asylum on Main Street, Jersey City. When the mother had regained her sanity she attempted to get her child back by kidnaping him on April 28, 1876, from the orphanage. But the law soon intervened. The boy was finally committed to the orphanage at the usual board rate of $5.00 a week, which Cleveland paid, and eventually adopted formally by one of the best families in western New York, becoming a distinguished professional man under another name never revealed to Cleveland or the outside world.

Cleveland gave Mrs. Halpin money to start her own business in Niagara Falls, but she quickly disappeared. Twenty years later, during Cleveland's second term as President, she threatened the President in two letters. One asked for money; the other threatened to publish facts in her possession. Neither letter produced action on Cleveland's part, for he must have been heartily sick of her by now. In Alexander Hamilton's candid words after his own affair with Mrs. Reynolds: "I have paid pretty dearly for my folly." Similarly, Cleveland had acted a man's part, as had Hamilton, denying nothing and making no attempt to evade a responsibility which could not certainly be his in the circumstances.

When the flabbergasted Democratic Party heard this accusation against its presidential standard-bearer on July 21, 1884, Cleveland was asked by letter what the party should do. Cleve-

7. Cleveland Papers.

land's reply is probably the best measure of the man. He simply said: "Tell the truth."

It was a common-sense decision, for from the truth he had very little to be afraid. Had the scandal been disclosed during the convention in Chicago there is little doubt that Cleveland would not have been nominated. No modern presidential candidate could survive such a tag—in Cleveland's time the scandal was, if anything, harder on a candidate because of hypocritical Victorian sex standards.

Had the illegitimacy issue been brought to light in the last weeks of the campaign, Cleveland would undoubtedly have lost the election.[8] There would have been no time to discount the story and explain it by telling the true facts. As it was, the period from July to November was sufficiently long to enable Grover Cleveland to survive his culpability in personal relations, whereas Blaine's delinquency in public life came too late for sufficient rebuttal, if indeed there ever was an opportunity for one.

Cleveland's campaign was cleverly handled by William C. Whitney, a brilliant Wall Street attorney and financier. Whitney's greatness lay in his combining reform with practical politics—he wasn't afraid to go out and buy blocs of votes with promises to minorities. Thomas A. Hendricks of Indiana gave the ticket balance. Cleveland, a naturally friendly man, helped enormously by his candor in the illegitimate child accusation and his patent honesty as reform Mayor of Buffalo and Governor of New York.

Cleveland was physically unimpressive, short and dumpy, unduly plump; but somehow he gave the public a portrait of power and immovably honest stolidity.[9] He was heavy-handed

---

8. Nevins, *op. cit.*, pp. 164–68.

9. Ike Hoover writes in *Forty-two Years in the White House* (Boston, Houghton Mifflin Company, 1934), p. 13: "President Cleveland, naturally a hard-working individual, seemed to be the most laborious of all the Presidents under whom I served [he served under ten]. Breakfast at nine, lunch at one-thirty, dinner at seven-thirty, were almost the only breaks in his day. It appeared as if the President for some reason worked much harder to accomplish the same results than other men who have occupied the office. He dictated but little, preferring to write practically everything with his own hand. It was no uncommon thing for him to

and unimaginative and literally found honesty to be the best policy. Sometimes this led to ticklish situations where bad timing and refusal to compromise hurt him; yet he seemed to make up for this among the independent voters, who were always attracted to his candor and straightforwardness.

It may not have been sound philosophy nor always sound politics to run a presidential campaign this way, but as the newspapers said, "it was magnificent."[10] In his public relations, Cleveland's honesty often appeared as "stubbornness, tactlessness, suspiciousness, and irritability, but these qualities were attractive to those citizens who were tired of the specious gloss of the 'Plumed Knight.' "[11]

One Boston newspaperman (Cleveland had long been a favorite of the newspapermen because of his candor) probably was keeping Cleveland's converted Harvard audience in mind when he wrote the following endorsement for his Republican paper, the *Boston Advertiser*:

> Cleveland is stout, has a well-fed look, is indeed a good liver, has the air of a man who has made up his mind just how he ought to behave in any position where he may find himself. He is getting bald; he is getting gray—though his white hair does not show conspicuously, since his complexion is sandy. He dresses well, carries himself well, talks well upon any subject with which he is familiar, and upon subjects with which he is not familiar he does not venture to talk at all. He has the happy faculty of being able to refuse a request without giving offence. It has been my fortune to see him several times during the past winter upon business in connection with some of the State institutions. He has impressed me always as one heartily desirous of getting at the bottom of any matter he may have in hand, and of acting wisely in it.

---

remain in his office until two or three o'clock in the morning, diligently laboring on some important document. On various occasions he was known to remain there the entire night working on a message to Congress or something of the sort he considered unusually urgent."

10. Leland D. Baldwin, *The Adult's American History* (West Rindge, New Hampshire, Richard R. Smith, Inc., 1955), p. 349.

11. *Ibid.*

Partly through candor and apparent rudeness, Cleveland was to lose re-election in 1888, only to win back the Presidency in 1892 on his third try, the only President we've had whose two terms were not consecutive. Indeed, Cleveland's growth and development are plain in the differences between Cleveland as President from 1884 to 1888 and Cleveland as President from 1892 to 1896. In the first term he regarded the Presidency, as did most of his contemporaries, as a policeman's beat, with the social forces about him entirely free to battle among themselves. In his second term he used government as a creative social force.

The Republican Party had, quite naturally, dominated American politics since the Civil War because the Democratic Party was identified, not without some justice, as the party of slavery, disunion, and defeat. The waving of the bloody shirt of war and rebellion was by itself nearly sufficient to elect and re-elect for President one Republican candidate after another between Lincoln and Arthur. One whole generation was born and grew to manhood without knowing a Democrat in the White House. In reverse, a whole generation was to be conceived and grow to manhood between 1932 and 1952 without the experience of a Republican President. As at the end of the New Deal-Fair Deal chain of undefeated Democrats, corruption from too many consecutive years in office and overconfidence linked arms to defeat the Republicans of the mid-eighties. No political party could be entrenched for a whole generation and not show the consequences inside its organization. The Republicans of the 1880s were no exception, any more than were the Democrats seventy-two years later.

James Buchanan had been the last Democrat to win the Presidency, in 1856. He was perhaps our weakest President. He had done nothing at all in four dreadful years of increasingly critical debate and political inaction over slavery. Like Pilate, Buchanan had washed his hands of the unsavory affair and looked the other way. This had given the Republican Party its reason for being: within a short span of two years, 1858 to 1860, the upstart Republicans had come from a gleam in the founders' eyes to the White House, there to stay through six consecutive quadrennial elections covering twenty-four years.

Lincoln, of course, had been its first hero. His martyred memory helped the Republican cause more than any other single factor in the continuous re-election of Republicans as President. His name was political magic for the Republican Party and still is.

Lincoln had beaten General George B. McClellan when time came for re-election, then was shot dead a few weeks after his second inaugural. Vice-President Andrew Johnson was next President and came within a vote of being our only Chief Executive to be impeached. General Grant, a fourteen-carat war hero, could hardly have escaped election and re-election in the next eight years, defeating Horatio Seymour in 1868 and Horace Greeley and a host of other candidates (most of them reform Republicans) in 1872.

Then had come the disgusting Hayes-Tiden election in which the Democratic Governor from New York had not only outpolled the Republican candidate in popular vote, but, if truth were known—and it was never allowed to raise its voice in the electoral college—in the electoral vote by states as well. A rigged (Republican) majority in the investigating commission had finally decided the contest, just before Inauguration Day, 185 to 184, in favor of Rutherford B. Hayes. Governor Tilden, not wishing to rend his country twice in a generation, withdrew, although he and most literate people knew he had been properly elected President, popularly and by states.

The Democrats had, then, not placed a man in the White House in five consecutive tries when General Garfield met General Hancock on the field of political ballot in 1880. But Hancock proved to be the most inept campaigner of the nineteenth century (Alf Landon probably wins it for the twentieth century); somehow, the ground Governor Tilden had gained was relinquished by the Democratic Party. Garfield won easily in the electoral totals 214 to 155, though only 9,464 votes out of almost 9,000,000 separated the two men in total popular vote.

The Cleveland-Blaine campaign of 1884 was, therefore, a

true milestone in American history. Cleveland probably owed his nomination and election in part to the underlying appetite of his day that reform and change were not only essential and overdue, but downright tasty. The preponderance of the intelligentsia were sick of unending Republican victories and corrupt dictatorship. As in 1952, a cry arose from many who would never have voted against their own party except as a gesture toward a true two-party system, healthy for the American body politic. And while both candidates in 1884 were involved with scandal in the filthiest of all our political extravaganzas, this overwhelming desire for a change undoubtedly was the prevailing factor.

Precious little high-level campaigning was done on either side, in the circumstances. An emotional binge, it would have been worse had radio and television been available then. As it was, each voter read of the campaign's progress, its speeches, accusations, charges, countercharges, political proposals, and promises only in the newspaper of his own political choice (there were a Democratic paper and a Republican paper in just about every city in the land in those days) and nowhere else, except perhaps in *Harper's Weekly* or a similar organ tuned to national issues.

The party platforms, as usual, read about the same, but liberal Republicans, led by the influential *Harper's*, supported Cleveland when the tart new Mulligan letters were made public. Cleveland was, moreover, thoroughly supported by conservative businessmen for he was, to some, "sounder" than Blaine. In the words of a business journal of the time it really didn't matter which man won because "a good President cannot make the country; a bad President cannot ordinarily mar it."[12]

With "Rum, Romanism, and Rebellion" ringing in their unwashed ears, just enough Irish Catholics in New York City swung to Cleveland to give him electoral victory. The total popular vote was:

12. W. M. Gewehr, ed., *American Civilization: A History of the United States* (New York, McGraw-Hill Book Company, Inc., 1957), p. 314.

Grover Cleveland (D)   4,874,986
James G. Blaine (R)   4,851,981

Yet this margin, small as it was, was far greater than the 9,000 by which Garfield had beaten Hancock; it meant true resurgence of the Democratic Party and the two-party system of American government, the first such emergence in a quarter of a century. In the electoral college, Cleveland won by 219 to 182, entirely chargeable to New York State which went Democratic by a thousand votes, undoubtedly Irish Catholic in majority.

The revolt of liberals in the Republican Party, known to historians as "mugwumps," the defeat of Blaine by a handful of votes in pivotal New York State, and the first election of a Democratic President in twenty-four years meant that the demoralizing shadow of the Civil War was passing, that it was no longer good politics to depend on the bloody shirt and a genuine handicap to be against reform.

Cleveland had been a notable reformer in New York State. But when he had become the first Democrat to take over the White House since James Buchanan, he was faced with a plainly voracious political party, a party which had had no administrative political patronage for a generation. Ravenous for jobs, spoilsmen badgered Cleveland almost beyond endurance. During the campaign, a Republican Senator had taunted Cleveland, "You cannot serve both God and the Democrats at the same time"; now that appointments had to be made he would do his best, which was very good indeed, to make the Republican a liar.

Cleveland quickly appointed two former Confederates to his Cabinet, which rankled the G.A.R., as a wartime enemy might rankle with the American Legion today, though the American Legion has never held a shadow of the power the Grand Army of the Republic and its veterans wielded in post-Civil War years. To irritate the heroes of blue still further, the new President tried to return captured Confederate battle flags. There was also the almost daily matter of veterans' bonuses, and it was here that Cleveland dignified the power of the veto.[13] The veto is one of the oldest of democratic checks and balances. It consists of an action by the Chief Executive in withholding his approval of a law already passed by the legislative branch. In a sense the United States Supreme Court maintains its own veto in the form of judgment as to the Constitutionality of any law, but only in the case of the Chief Executive is this nullifying action called precisely "veto."

Article I, Section 7 of the Constitution gives the President of the United States veto power, but it is a qualified or limited veto, not as absolute as monarchs and dictators have known it in history. From them there has been no recourse in the legislative branch; from the presidential veto there is. For he may be overridden and the vetoed act become the law of the land through a two-thirds vote of both houses of Congress. The veto doesn't apply to proposed Constitutional Amendments, questions of adjournment, or concurrent resolutions.

Veto power goes back to Roman law and the word is in the Roman language; veto literally means "I forbid" in Latin. England still has a royal veto on its law books, but no British monarch has used his or her veto power over acts of Parliament since Queen Anne in 1707. Most countries don't allow their chief executives as much say in legislation as Americans do, and the veto is a potent weapon, indeed sometimes the only weapon a President has when one or both houses of Congress has a majority of the opposing party. President Eisenhower, for example, used his veto successfully hundreds of times and wasn't overridden until his seventh year in office, despite huge Democratic majorities.

Edward S. Corwin points out in *The President—Office and Powers*[14] that the early talent Americans revealed for conjuring up Constitutional limitations and balances moved like a bee to buckwheat toward the veto power. It meant for those who framed the Constitution yet another weapon for making certain that no one power—legislative, judicial, executive in

13. Horace Samuel Merrill, *Bourbon Leader: Grover Cleveland and the Democratic Party* (Boston, Little, Brown and Company, 1957), pp. 41–42.

14. Edward S. Corwin, *The President—Office and Powers* (New York, New York University Press, 1940), pp. 337–46.

particular—could take control of the country at any time in any situation without a check from one or both of the other two powers. Corwin writes: "The veto was solely a self-defensive weapon of the President; it was the means furnished the President for carrying out his oath to 'preserve, protect and defend the Constitution' and was not validly usable for any other purpose."

To give the President even more power through the veto, the framers of the Constitution worded this passage to make it read that the President would have ten days from presentation rather than passage of a bill in which to disapprove of it. This would make it possible for a President, even in the days of slow travel and faulty communications, to move about the country, indeed to roam the world without fear that the legislative would put over something in his absence. Through careful wording of the veto section, presentation and not passage became an added check on uncontrolled legislative domination and power.

Furthermore, as Corwin points out, by withholding their signatures from bills passed by both houses, the presiding officers of those bodies can lengthen the period between actual passage of a measure and its presentation to an absent President, so that on his return he will not be swamped with such measures. With this Constitutional precedent, Franklin D. Roosevelt signed a bill on July 13, 1936, no less than twenty-three days after the adjournment of the Congress.

For years, Presidents have urged that Congress make Constitutional provision for itemized veto of bills, but nothing along this line has gotten very far in an organization dedicated to helping the members' political problems through legislative logrolling. If a President could veto item by item he could reduce or eliminate specific sections—particularly in appropriation bills with extraneous riders—without destroying the good features he felt should be enacted into law. The Senate has always been the roadblock against giving the President item veto power, for the Senate insists that the reform would require a Constitutional Amendment, two-thirds of both houses and three-fourths of the states assenting within a given period.

This has, so far, been too much for such a controversial measure, which nevertheless makes sense in rapid, complicated modern legislation and life.

The President's veto can almost certainly be ascribed to the framers' fears that without it the executive third of our government would soon sink into nonexistence.[15] Almost to the hour of its final adjournment, the Constitutional Convention shifted back and forth between requiring two-thirds and three-quarters vote in both houses for overriding a veto. Those who wished it to be three-quarters felt that the executive was already too greatly weakened and needed shoring up. Those who wished the overriding to take place at two-thirds sought to limit the presidential power over the direct voice of the people—their legislature; and two-thirds was closer to a majority of one than was three-quarters, ordinarily a difficult number to obtain in any serious legislative vote.

In any case, Presidents used the veto sparingly at first, more and more as the years and precedent stabilized fears of dominant executive power. The pocket veto, by which a President can postpone veto until after adjournment, thereby stifling any overriding vote, was one ruse soon learned at the other end of Pennsylvania Avenue from The Hill.

Cleveland's first brush with the power of veto had come when he was Governor of New York. Cleveland's veto of Teddy Roosevelt's tenure of office bill had caused some eyebrow raising in New York State, as well it might. The bill had been aimed at ridding the New York City government of Hubert O. Thompson, whose corrupt conduct as Commissioner of Public Works had aroused public and editorial condemnation regardless of party. Even the Democratic *New York Times* wanted Cleveland to sign the bill, which authorized the next elected Mayor of New York to appoint a fresh public works commissioner before Thompson's term expired. But Cleveland vetoed the bill a week before the legislature adjourned. He called it the most carelessly written legislation ever sent to him for signature. Cleveland went on so in his veto message

15. *Ibid.*, p. 338.

that the state could well say it thought "he protested too much."

Reformers were disappointed in him and said so. They were, naturally, deeply interested in what motivated Cleveland's veto and they hadn't far to look. For Cleveland's veto of the Theodore Roosevelt reform measure abruptly ended a break between Cleveland and Tammany Hall, indeed patched it so well that Hubert Thompson's power to select Tammany delegates to the 1884 Democratic National Convention appeared to be a decisive factor. There's not the slightest question that Cleveland was highly delegate-conscious at this time and that he had already been approached at top level with the White House in view. Teddy Roosevelt was among many who screamed that Cleveland's veto action had more to do with ambition than an innate feeling for reform.

It was as President of the United States that the power of the veto began to appeal to Cleveland as a weapon for the public good.[16] Presidential vetoes in that era required a lion's courage, for veterans' pensions and patronage had long been whips and powerful ones in the hands of the Republican Party and the Grand Army of the Republic. The Republicans had been bent on demonstrating that they and they alone were the only true friends of Civil War veterans. They had campaigned long and lustily that the advent of a Democrat in the White House would mean the beginning of the end of veterans' pork-barrel pension bills and bonuses. When Cleveland therefore failed to ask the Congress for the usual pension largess, the G.A.R. and their Republican allies screamed from the new West to Maine and from Michigan to Maryland.

Cleveland had adopted a system of applying the principle of veteran's preference in removals and appointments only to disabled G.A.R.s. (Naturally, no Confederate veteran had the slightest chance of government aid in those days.) Suddenly

16. Carl Schurz, a maverick Republican liberal and confirmed mugwump, became one of Cleveland's Cabinet and stated later that Cleveland chided him with these words: "What's the use of being elected and re-elected if you don't stand for something?"

a flood of private pension bills drowned the House and Senate hoppers—and Cleveland vetoed almost every one of them. Cleveland now pleaded that the pension system be made fairer, more honest, more efficient, and more up-to-date. The G.A.R. would have none of it and appeared outraged. Veterans had been at the public teat for a whole generation and they weren't going to lose their hold easily on such a succulent and nourishing breast.

As the accumulating battle between Cleveland and the G.A.R. spread to new veterans for whom private pension bills had been arranged in every Northern state, Cleveland's veto messages became more and more sarcastic.[17] His irritability increased. His language hardened, became caustic. He placed himself on more than one occasion in the untenable political situation of being an economic enemy of men who had saved the Union. When Cleveland had to point out that many a Congressman was voting for bills based on fraudulent claims, and in doing so used sarcastic and searing language, the wrath of Democratic and Republican political bosses alike descended in white tongues of flame upon the first Democratic President since the Civil War.

Early in 1887, a long-pending bill actually offered pensions to *all* disabled veterans who had served for three months in the Union cause and had no known friends or relatives to support them. Congress passed the bill quickly and without much care in the wording. Old age was to be regarded as disability; other nonmilitary causes were sufficient to qualify for a life pension. Known as the "pauper's bill," this amazing measure went so far as to include the dependent parents of soldiers who had died in the service of the North.[18]

Cleveland took a deep breath and promptly vetoed the parody. His veto was the very mark of a courageous, candid man. It was wrong, he argued in his veto message, to place mere charity cases on the Federal pay roll. He reminded the Congress what such a precedent would eventually mean to the United States Treasury. If dependent parents of dead veterans

17. Merrill, *op. cit.*, pp. 106–34.
18. *Ibid.*, pp. 105–7.

were now accepted, their brothers, sisters, cousins, and aunts might be included in the next bill. Pretty soon every family north of the Mason-Dixon Line would be on the Federal pay roll, and that was something the "businessman's President" couldn't swallow. The veto's logic stuck.

The political losses Cleveland sustained among Civil War veterans and their puppet politicians from this and other veto messages were more than made up for by citizens who shared Cleveland's acute indignation at dishonesty and corruption in government. But Cleveland failed to get through the Congress a decent substitute pension bill, and in this his own temper was a factor. The pension problem remained when he left the Presidency. Where he might have treaded gingerly in his relations with The Hill and the G.A.R., powerful voices in the America of the late 1800s, Cleveland seemed forever to jump squarely with both feet into the heart of the wasp's nest of Civil War memories and sentiment.

Grover Cleveland vetoed more bills than any President before him. But most of the bills he vetoed were for private pensions in which each man or group of men up for pension constituted an individual bill, repeated *ad nauseam*. Cleveland promptly upbraided and vetoed each bad bill as it came to his groaning desk.

Actually, Franklin D. Roosevelt vetoed the greatest number and variety of measures of any President.[19] It was calculated at Roosevelt's death that he and Cleveland were, between them, responsible for two-thirds of all the vetoes cast since Washington first employed the presidential veto power in 1792.[20]

Arthur M. Schlesinger, Jr., suspects that Franklin Roosevelt

19. Dwight D. Eisenhower later was to give the veto new armor through his amazing power to make vetoes stick. In his first six years as President, Eisenhower was never once overridden by the required two-thirds vote of both houses of Congress, though they were usually Democrat-controlled. In 1959, when his record was finally broken, it had to be on pork-barrel legislation, the sort of local self-interest bill which had plagued Grover Cleveland and caused him to dignify the veto as a presidential prerogative.

20. Arthur M. Schlesinger, Jr., *The Coming of the New Deal* (Boston, Houghton Mifflin Company, 1959), p. 555.

later used the veto purposefully to enforce respect for the President's policies and titular position.[21] It seemed sometimes as though Roosevelt were casting about for bills to veto simply to flex his executive muscles and show his power. Cleveland, however, never invoked the veto in this way. He was far too candid and direct. He was incapable of dissembling or of puckishness. He dignified the veto as a presidential instrument, using its unique power to maintain fiscal integrity against an almost insane, emotional veterans' lobby which was, beyond doubt, the most venal and powerful legislative minority ever to haunt the cloakrooms of The Hill.

Indeed, President Cleveland vetoed 301 bills in his first term, almost all of them private pension bills. Allan Nevins says that the general evil of giving every needy ex-soldier pensions, and quite a few not so needy, was tolerated by "that immense good nature which is rather an American vice than a virtue."[22]

Almost a quarter of a million pensioners had already been placed on the public pay roll, but this number began to decline as veterans died off with greater rapidity. To check this decline, the veterans' lobby had then pushed through Congress the famous "arrears of pensions" act which President Hayes had cheerfully signed. This act was intended to do justice to veterans who had incurred illnesses as a result of war injuries or whose wounds had eventually caused them disability.

President Hayes had been a thoroughgoing, even willing, veterans' man. President Cleveland felt as deeply as the next for ill, wounded, disabled veterans in real want—he signed 1,453 private pension bills in his first four years as President! But an obvious racket was wrong and dishonesty something so repugnant to this first postwar Democrat that he simply could not bring himself to hoodwink or bankrupt America. Dr. Nevins reports as follows:[23]

> There were thousands of "invalid" pensioners who were robust and able-bodied. There were other thousands pen-

21. *Ibid.*
22. Nevins, *op. cit.*, p. 326.
23. *Ibid.*, 326–32.

sioned for diseases really incurred in civilian life. There were "dependent relatives" who were quite independent, and "widows" who had long ago remarried. There were still more glaring cases of successful fraud by swindlers who impersonated dead pensioners and continued to receive their checks. The system had been at fault in three principal ways. The evidence upon which pensions were granted was *ex parte*, being furnished by comrades and neighbors, the examining surgeons were local physicians, often glad to help a friend and bring more money into the community; and the gauge of a pensioner's disability was his unfitness to do manual labor without regard to his mental capacity or private income.

It was Cleveland's object to call sharp attention to the carelessness of the system; and in a special veto message of May 8, 1886, he unlimbered his artillery against the most careless feature of all—the host of special pension bills which Congress had fallen into the habit of passing without any real consideration. He complained that Congress had recently sent him in one day 240 special bills, of which 198 covered claims already rejected by the Pensions Bureau. Any veteran whose claim was too silly or impudent to get past the pension authorities was at liberty to take it to his Representative or Senator. The resulting bills became thick as autumn leaves in Vallombrosa. The House had set aside Friday evenings for enacting them with a jubilant whoop, while the Senate, in a single field-day (April 21, 1886) voted some four hundred of them. As Cleveland said, many of them were the result of nominal sessions held for their express consideration and attended by a small minority of the members of the respective houses.

The principle involved was simple: The nation had in its Pensions Bureau a virtual pensions court, hearing cases fairly and interpreting the laws in a liberal spirit. Congress was setting itself up as a rival pensions court, and reversing hundreds of decisions made by the proper tribunal. It is not too much to say that three out of four of the special bills were flagrantly bad. The President's method of dealing with them was to send back measure after measure with brief and sarcastic messages of exposure. He approved many —several times as many as he rejected; but by the middle of August, 1886, he had penned more than a hundred vetoes. He thus fixed the eyes of the country upon a gross perversion of Congressional energy, which combined robbery of the Treasury with a vicious time-wasting habit of attention to special and local bills. As he pointed out, Congress should either rely upon the Pensions Bureau, or reorganize it to make it reliable. If it really constituted itself a supreme court to deal with claims, in justice to the veterans it would have to attend to *all* that were offered. Indeed, the number of private bills was increasing by leaps and bounds; Representative Warner showed that in about six months 4,127 pension bills had been introduced in the House, and a larger number in the Senate—enough if given ten minutes apiece, to consume four months of Congressional time. No earlier President had ever vetoed one of these bills! Cleveland signed far more than he vetoed, and far more than any previous President had ever signed; but he took a stand against the enactment of an indiscriminate and unconsidered mass of legislation.

His brief, pointed veto messages were so good that it was a pity he weakened their effect by occasional gibes or ridicule. It was easy to find objects for his humor. One claimant explained that he had been registered "at home" and had set out on horseback *intending* to complete his enlistment, that on the way his horse had fallen on his left ankle and that he was thus entitled to a cripple's pension. A widow whose husband had been killed by a fall from a ladder in 1881 traced this to a slight flesh-wound in the calf in 1865! A Louisville policeman demanded a pension for the death of his son ten months after desertion from the army. A similar claim was made by the family of a Pennsylvanian who, after deserting, had been drowned in a canal six miles from home. An Illinois soldier who had been captured and released on parole had been injured at his home in 1863 by the explosion of a Fourth of July cannon, and now in 1886 asked for a special pension. The widow of a captain who had died in 1883 from cerebral apoplexy swore that it was the result of a hernia contracted in 1863. One gallant private claimed that a disease of the eyes had resulted from army diarrhea.

To nonsense like this, Grover Cleveland applied the unsparing veto as an instrument of permanent executive policy. He did so without apology and without regret. By the end of his first term, Cleveland had made enough enemies through private pension bill vetoes alone to assure his defeat for reelection. The recipe was simple: Stir in natural four-year defection of once loyal voters, hard times, native anti-Democratic sentiment still current as a result of war, and the President's inability to tell anything but the unvarnished truth, and you have a formula unlikely to return anyone to the White House.

But Benjamin Harrison, who beat Cleveland in their first encounter, created enemies and hard times of his own between 1888 and 1892; Cleveland was then returned to office, whereupon he continued to veto whatever he believed to be not in the public good.

Indeed, many an encyclopedia and history book refer to Cleveland as "The Veto President," not because he used the veto more often than any other Chief Executive, but because he dramatized and realized its potential. Cleveland pioneered massive use of the veto as had no other President before him. He had visualized in the veto a powerful force in the constant changes of executive-judicial-legislative power balance. He had made the veto an instrument of national policy. He had, through sheer honesty and blunt resolve, implemented and dignified it, given it a luster it had not had before, and in doing so strengthened the powers and the office of President of the United States.

Theodore Roosevelt

MANY words in many languages define many different kinds of trade restraint or other arrangement involving monopolistic practices in the market place. In continental Europe, the word frequently used is of French-German origin, "cartel." To most Americans this translates as "monopoly." And "monopoly" has often been called "trust" in the philosophical writings of those who have sought to prove that monopolistic practices contribute to the discomfort of the common man and are contrary to the general welfare. All three words, "cartel," "monopoly," and "trust," are akin and, to historians, practically interchangeable.

There are two types of trusts in the classic definition: horizontal and vertical trusts. While both have to do with unnatural monopolies, each has its own distinct shape, size, and structure. A horizontal trust is a combination of corporations or businesses engaged in the same line or product; a vertical trust is an organization which, within itself, controls everything necessary to its own line of operation from raw material and transportation to final packaging. In the United States, both kinds of trusts are illegal when in restraint of trade.

Competing drug firms manufacturing a new medicine will charge $4.50 for it, though it may have cost them $0.23 to process and package. The government conducts an inquiry, charging they are a horizontal trust. They have agreed among themselves to fix the price in restraint of free competitive trade to the detriment of the public. They have done so, of course,

7

Trust-Busts Changes in the Presidency

to insure their profits, prevent price-cutting, and maintain a solid front against what they consider unnecessary competitive risk.

Automobile companies, on the other hand, are often sued as vertical trusts, since many of them not only own the ores and other raw materials from which they produce their autos but manufacture their own steel, operate their own railroads, and make the end product these railroads haul to market.

The original Standard Oil Company, for example, was once a sprawling trust which almost completely controlled the supply, manufacture, and distribution of petroleum products in vast areas of the United States. Standard Oil in John D. Rockefeller's heyday induced various stockholders in supply enterprises to assign their stock to a common board of trustees for which they received dividend-bearing trust certificates in exchange. The oil trustees were thus able to manage what should have been competing supplier firms, fix prices at both wholesale and retail levels, throttle competition at its supply source, dictate freight rates, control profits, and otherwise perform in the classic vein of the "combination in restraint of trade."

The Sherman Anti-Trust Act, passed by Congress in 1890, has often been invoked in similar cases because it makes illegal any attempt to monopolize an industry or to restrain the normal competitive capitalistic system to the detriment of the general welfare. Nowadays there is no one Standard Oil Company. There are Standard Oil of Ohio, Standard Oil of Indiana,

Standard Oil of California, Standard Oil of New Jersey, etc. Each is a separate company and, broken up, Standard Oil now has nowhere near the unholy restraining power, the huge monopoly once within the grasp of its trustees and officers.

Why are monopolies bad for the public? Simply because the human beings who operate them profit exorbitantly at the public's expense and prices stay artificially high. There is no free flow of competition which, in capitalism, is the life of trade. When the supply of a finished product or raw material is controlled so that its purchasers cannot buy it anywhere else and are forced to meet the arbitrary terms of sale laid down by the restraining combination, the result is monopoly.

Except for temporary monopolies in times of stress, such as war, none of the non-Marxist nations will long tolerate monopolies or trusts or cartels under the democratic political system. Laws are quickly passed to relieve the public. In communist countries, of course, everything is monopolistic: the government controls, prices, distributes, and withholds at its own discretion and for its own purposes, in spite of the fact that Karl Marx's foremost philosophical enemy was the monopolist who was, he said, chief of the workingman's devils.

The Sherman Anti-Trust Act took its name from Senator John Sherman of Ohio. Monkey business in high places in the mushrooming mergers of the late nineteenth century caused the act to be passed. Increasingly the public opposed unbridled impudence in its royalty type economic structure. In an era devoted to long overdue reform in politics, it was most natural to regard industrial combinations and mergers in restraint of free trade as an evil thing. So the public acted.

Demand for restrictive legislation against trusts, cartels, and monopolies rose to such a pitch by Cleveland's time that it became a political issue no major candidate could avoid, though many tried. In 1890 an antitrust measure finally passed both houses of Congress and was signed by President Benjamin Harrison (grandson of President William Henry Harrison, the hero of Tippecanoe). The act was a simple one; it was based on the Constitutional power of Congress to regulate interstate commerce.

The Sherman act declared illegal every combination, cartel, monopoly, trust, contract, or conspiracy in restraint of trade, either interstate or foreign. The act set up a fine of $5,000 and imprisonment for one year as maximum penalties for violation. But, in the first decade of its life, the Sherman Anti-Trust Act had the wind taken out of its sails by the Supreme Court, which watered down its powers and jurisdiction, chiefly through its decision in the E. C. Knight Company case of 1895.

What the act needed, in the long run, was not legal wording or interpretation but a man who believed trusts, combinations, mergers, cartels, monopolies, contracts, and conspiracies in restraint of trade to be truly against the public interest, and to do something about same. That man became President of the United States quite by accident on September 14, 1901, at the age of forty-two. To understand why he was an accidental President and what his accession meant to the prosecution of monopolistic trusts, one has to go back to the renomination of William McKinley, ardent friend of business and the status quo.

McKinley's love of unbridled capitalism and faith in it has no parallel among modern American Presidents. Usually a President has displayed somewhere a feeling for the industrial underdog, the downtrodden workingman, the man who "labors so others may profit." But not the twenty-fifth President of the United States. He supported every manufacturers' measure proposed by his backers, among whom was the powerful capitalist-politician Marcus A. Hanna, from McKinley's state of Ohio.

Not only did McKinley endorse the gold standard and abhor free silver but he championed a protective tariff so high that foreign trade began to dwindle dangerously. Isolationist and conservative by nature, McKinley became nevertheless a war President, if the Spanish-American affair can be called one.

Hanna had wangled the Ohio Governorship for McKinley, an undistinguished Republican Congressman. In 1895, Hanna began to move toward McKinley's presidential nomination. Through as adroit and skillful a campaign as any ever handled in U. S. politics, Hanna made McKinley not only candidate but President. He easily defeated William Jennings Bryan, the Democrat, regarded by his time as a radical, labor's champion, and no friend of the economic royalist.

McKinley's first term was placid, except for the Spanish-American disturbance, which was confined to the year 1898 and two memorable events: the sinking of the battleship *Maine*, and the dramatic charge up San Juan Hill. America remembered the *Maine* and glorified its victorious war President who was thereupon assured of renomination. But the reform element of the Republican Party was progressively lukewarm and the 1900 ticket needed a liberal reformer to win back those postwar recalcitrants who disliked McKinley's big-business bias. That man was Theodore Roosevelt. By nominating him for Vice-President, the Mark Hanna-"Boss" Platt combine thought they had shelved Teddy Roosevelt forever and deprived him of the Governor's chair at Albany. They reckoned with everything but fate.

Teddy Roosevelt had become a national war hero, partly because he was supposed to have led the heroic charge up San Juan Hill, which is at least debatable. At any rate, Teddy Roosevelt came back home a candidate for everything. He had had a splendid record in the New York State legislature from 1881 to 1884. Then he had backed James G. Blaine and lost his own reform following. Disgusted with politics and the effete East, Theodore Roosevelt had gone West where he failed as a rancher but learned much of value to him later as Chief Executive of a nation progressively aware of its frontier. His political repudiation and the deaths of his beloved wife and mother within the same twenty-four-hour period had very nearly broken his health. The West restored it.

T.R. came back from Dakota Territory in 1886 and inevitably plunged at once into politics. He was defeated for Mayor of New York but the Republican Party was beginning to notice him again, and in 1889 President Harrison appointed him to the Civil Service Commission, where he stayed for six years. Civil Service as this country knows it today owes much to Teddy Roosevelt's vigor and honesty in that office.

From 1895 to 1897, T.R. was head of the civilian board

which ran the New York City Police Department. Few politicians ever rubbed more crooked ward heelers the wrong way or made more personal enemies in the name of reform, for T.R. vigorously and continuously called a spade a spade. But his name was beginning to shine, his reputation to widen, his word to count for something when, in 1897, President McKinley appointed him Assistant Secretary of the Navy, a post his presidential cousin Franklin also held at a later date.

When the war with Spain broke out, Teddy Roosevelt resigned to organize with Leonard Wood the volunteer regiment known to history as the Rough Riders. No such glamorous cavalry troop had galloped across the American mind since J.E.B. Stuart's, and Stuart had been an unspeakable Rebel.

T.R. was, therefore, a genuine, fourteen-carat popular hero by war's end. It was inevitable that he should be a foremost candidate for the Republican nomination for Governor of his home state, New York, a fact which galled Thomas C. ("Boss") Platt and disturbed the sleep of many another entrenched Republican politician. So Platt, after consultation with Mark Hanna and, of course, William McKinley, made an apparently clever move. He began beating the drums for Teddy Roosevelt as McKinley's running mate on the next national ticket. The vice-presidential nomination had buried political hopes before. It seemed a sure-fire scheme for ridding New York of one of its most pesky and successful reform politicians, a type "Boss" Platt loathed.

Teddy Roosevelt tells in his own words the first inklings he had had that some liberals in the Republican Party genuinely wished him to be Governor of New York:[1]

It was Mr. L. E. Quigg [an independent Republican leader] who called on me at Montauk Point to sound me about the Governorship; Mr. Platt being by no means enthusiastic over Mr. Quigg's mission, largely because he disapproved of the Spanish War and of my part in bringing it about. Mr. Quigg saw me in my tent [at headquarters of the First Volunteer Cavalry—the Rough Riders] . . . and

1. *The Autobiography of Theodore Roosevelt,* Centennial Edition (New York, Charles Scribner's Sons, 1958), pp. 147–69.

spoke very frankly to me, stating that he earnestly desired to see me nominated and believed that the great body of Republican voters in the State so desired, but that the organization and the State Convention would finally do what Senator Platt desired. He said that county leaders were already coming to Senator Platt, hinting at a close election, expressing doubt of Governor Black's availability for re-election, and asking why it would not be a good thing to nominate me; that now that I had returned to the United States this would go on more and more all the time, and that he [Quigg] did not wish that these men should be discouraged and be sent back to their localities to suppress a rising sentiment in my favor.

For this reason he said that he wanted from me a plain statement as to whether or not I wanted the nomination, and as to what would be my attitude toward the organization in the event of my nomination and election, whether or not I would "make war" on Mr. Platt and his friends, or whether I would confer with them and with the organization leaders generally, and give fair consideration to their point of view as to party policy and public interest. He said he had not come to make me any offer of the nomination, and had no authority to do so, nor to get any pledges or promises. He simply wanted a frank definition of my attitude toward existing party conditions.

To this I replied that I should like to be nominated, and if nominated would promise to throw myself into the campaign with all possible energy. I said that I should not make war on Mr. Platt or anybody else if war could be avoided; that what I wanted was to be Governor and not a faction leader; that I certainly would confer with organization men, as with everybody else who seemed to me to have knowledge of and interest in public affairs, and that as to Mr. Platt and the organization leaders, I would do so in the sincere hope that there might always result harmony of opinion and purpose; but that while I would try to get on well with the organization, the organization must with equal sincerity strive to do what I regarded as essential for the public good; and that in every case, after full consideration of what everybody had to say who might possess real knowledge of the matter, I should have to act finally as my own judgment and conscience dictated and administer the State government as I thought it ought to be administered.

The Republican Committeemen soon realized they needed a man of T.R.'s courage and drive to win the 1898 Governorship and, accordingly, their leaders were in what T.R. himself called "a chastened mood" and ready to accept any candidate with whom they thought they had a chance of winning.[2] Senator Platt finally picked T.R. He was, said Roosevelt later, entirely frank in the matter, making no pretense that he liked him, but deferring to the judgment of those who insisted that Teddy was the only man who could win the election. His judgment was confirmed when T.R. squeaked through by only 18,000 votes over Augustus Van Wyck.

There had always been considerable opposition to the Republican machine and "Boss" Platt but, as T.R. pointed out in his autobiography,[3] reform leadership was "apt to be found only among those whom Abraham Lincoln called the 'silk-stockings.'" Much as reform excited the leadership of the silk-stocking districts, it seemed in those times to result in derision among the plain people approximately equal to their anger or dislike of machine politics. Teddy Roosevelt puts it very nicely:[4]

> When reformers of this type attempted to oppose Mr. Platt, they usually put up either some rather inefficient, well-meaning person, who bathed every day, and didn't steal, but whose only good point was "respectability," and who knew nothing of the great fundamental questions looming before us; or else they put up some big business man or corporation lawyer who was wedded to the gross wrong and injustice of our economic system, and who neither by personality nor by programme gave the ordinary plain people any belief that there was promise of vital good to them in the change.

T.R. was silk-stocking, all right; but he was much more. Of a prosperous and distinguished family, T.R. had been edu-

2. *Ibid.*, p. 147.
3. *Ibid.*, p. 151.
4. *Ibid.*

cated by private tutors, graduated from Harvard, and had studied law at Columbia. Every move he made was made with hyperglandular vigor and self-righteous sureness. He was barely forty when the nation hailed him for his war exploits and elected him Governor of New York. Indeed, his egotism shone through every page he wrote and Mr. Dooley said of him that his widely read story of the Rough Riders lacked a subtitle: "Alone In Cuba."

But self-confident and silk-stockinged as he undeniably was, Teddy Roosevelt was made up of other qualities more important to the offices he held and the people he served. He was a thoroughgoing democrat; he possessed deep religious feeling for the underdog, social or economic. Roosevelt was above all things impetuous. In the popular mind, the boyish, boisterous quality of T.R.'s outbursts "gave the appearance of sheer energy turned loose without benefit of sober thought."[5]

This explosion of boundless vitality was likely to attract attention, but his impulsive and emotional nature wasn't likely to wean sober businessmen to his standard. Yet the businessmen were wrong. T.R. was no temperamental schoolgirl; his own moral standards were far above the standards of his day, and he was absolutely appalled at the amoral atmosphere in which public and private business were transacted. Honest to the core, T.R. believed others should be honest, too—not honest in the traditional business sense, but completely, openly, painfully honest. Honest in the Lincoln tradition of walking miles to return a 6¢ overcharge; honest to a point where his admirers, long tired of the novelty of a moral issue and perhaps even threatened with inconvenience or financial loss, could say with feeling that he had gone too far in his exuberant, egotistical crusades. Once embarked, T.R. never turned back, continuing the hammer blows against evil until the plague spot was fully eradicated.[6]

Henry F. Pringle, one of Teddy Roosevelt's most successful and perceptive biographers, points out that his military repu-

5. Peter R. Levin, *Seven By Chance* (New York, Farrar, Straus and Company, 1948), p. 179.
6. *Ibid.*

tation never impressed Army men.[7] One reason for this was an unforgettable picture of a tactician who measured his battle successes by the length of the casualty lists. As in much of T.R.'s scholarship and learning, his references and reasons were often spotty and his conclusions warped through monumental bias and self-righteousness. He preferred to prove a thesis, to rationalize his own stand, rather than lead up to logical conclusions. This professional military men simply couldn't abide; and of all the weaknesses of Theodore Roosevelt (and he had more than his share for a man constantly in the limelight) rationalization was undeniably the most flagrant and unappetizing. Yet the very breadth of his interests, the scope of his vision, his catholicity of taste, and the general warmth with which he approached anything or anyone somehow helped his time and history to forgive his flaws. Deeper concentration, Peter Levin feels, in any one subject, "may well have cost him his amazing touch."[8] This is undeniably and perceptively accurate. Indeed, the wideness of T.R.'s fabulous horizon is matched in the Presidency only by Jefferson and T.R.'s young cousin, Franklin.

T.R.'s very appearance set off deeply grounded loyalties and hatreds. There were those close to him who glowed under his compliments and would swear he loved them and all the world. Yet there were always those for whom his personality was an antagonizing red flag. Though T.R., to his perpetual credit, admitted that he possessed only an ordinary mind encased in an endlessly energetic body, his sententiousness appalled many sober people, liberals and conservatives alike. These became his perpetual adversaries, citizens he could never convert, even to the best of purposes. Levin writes:[9]

To them, the crackling epithets and pithy sentences were infuriating. His famous teeth and the drooping moustache—useful in producing a wide grin or an expression of ferocious anger—were hostilely thought the mask of a poseur. The

7. Henry F. Pringle, *Theodore Roosevelt, a Biography* (New York, Harcourt, Brace and Company, 1931), *passim*.
8. Levin, *op. cit.*, p. 181.
9. *Ibid.*, p. 182.

furious gestures merely emphasized an absence of constructive thinking and the man's incredible narrowmindedness. And Roosevelt's part in the creation of these hatreds was considerable. His opponents were never to be reconciliated; they were to be damned. Implacably he went after them; a mistaken opinion became an arrant sin; a criticism or a rejection a personal affront. In "malefactors of great wealth," in "muckrakers," in "reformers," and in "anarchists" he found little to commend. Their disagreement with him or with his methods he answered with all the picturesqueness of his vocabulary.

For such a man, close-mouthed conservatives like "Boss" Platt and Mark Hanna could come to have only fear and contempt—fear that their neat little apple carts would suddenly be dumped over, contempt for self-righteous ego and infuriating temperament. It was not long after T.R. became Governor that Platt wholeheartedly regretted what he had reluctantly agreed to. As fear and contempt turned in the boss's mind to outrageous anger at the new Governor, smoke-filled meetings began to take place with the national election of 1900 ever higher on the agenda. Some means simply must be found to rid New York State of the menace of Colonel Roosevelt. The Vice-Presidency seemed a logical sidetrack.

Two years of sorrow had followed T.R.'s election to Albany. The Governor rapped the knuckles of New York City traction interests that "Boss" Platt adored; the Governor held a tight rein on political patronage; the Governor opened salvo after salvo at corruptions so close to home that Platt and his cronies could scarcely bear to open the morning papers. Something creative simply had to be done, particularly in view of the fact that T.R. soon told Platt he wanted a second two-year term in 1900 and would pursue it with all his considerable energy. Re-election would inevitably put Governor Roosevelt, as chief of the country's most populous and prosperous state, directly in line to succeed President McKinley in 1904.

Platt persisted; it was too great a poker pot to give up. And little by little the ambitious Colonel began to take seriously what had originally been in Platt's Machiavellian mind only a clever maneuver to sidetrack a dangerous and unappetizing Republican hero. Roosevelt at first told friends that he couldn't see himself presiding over the Senate and keeping his opinions to himself, as he would have to do, except in case of a tie. John Hay, now head of the Department of State, and a warm friend of T.R., offered sensible advice: he told the Governor that no Vice-President had ever been "elected by violence." But if T.R. didn't go after the vice-presidential spot under McKinley he might find himself in the position of being drafted by the bosses and beholden to them. Platt might manipulate the convention delegates and put T.R. on the ticket in spite of himself, knowing the loyal Colonel would never refuse to serve his country if nominated and elected.

Something else made the energetic young Governor take the vice-presidential gambit seriously. Platt still had immense power among those who would nominate the Republican candidate for Governor in 1900. If Platt dictated his own candidate for the Governorship, T.R.'s elective career was probably at an end. Positions on government pay rolls he might still secure—he might even be appointed Secretary of the Navy as a sop from Platt. But the Presidency was not an appointive office though it was in those days a hand-picked nomination, and those who picked and chose were men like "Boss" Platt. When they had chosen, on both sides, the people voted, but the people voted only on presidential candidates the professional bosses had picked to oppose one another.

Soon, fewer and fewer disclaimers came from Albany as to a place on the national ticket. Mark Hanna may have wanted to succeed McKinley himself, but in any case he relished king-making more. When he learned of Platt's maneuver to place T.R. in the Vice-Presidency and thus remove him not only from Albany but as a threat in 1904 (the Vice-Presidency was more of a political sidetrack in those days than it is now), Hanna cried out prophetically, "Don't any of you realize that there is only one life between that madman and the Presidency? What harm can he do as Governor of New York compared to the damage he will do as President if McKinley should die?"

Although Hanna was reluctant and wary, he gave in finally, and the Republican Convention of 1900 screamed itself out for the Rough Rider, the vital and outspoken Colonel who appealed to commoner and patrician alike but who made an almost equal number apprehensive. There was no middle ground with Teddy Roosevelt—he had the sort of personality you either loved or despised. It was, moreover, in violent contrast to President McKinley's.

Everywhere Theodore Roosevelt went during the presidential campaign—and he made more political speeches than any vice-presidential candidate had ever made before—Republicans flocked to hear him rip and tear at William Jennings Bryan for the Great Commoner's "doctrines of anarchy." McKinley, by contrast, scarcely made a speech. He simply issued solemn bulletins from Canton, Ohio, or from the White House, the prototype of the front-porch campaign.

On November 6, 1900, T.R.'s magic showed in the ballot; Bryan proved even less popular than he had been in 1896. McKinley picked up almost a quarter of a million votes while Bryan lost more than 100,000 in the popular total. McKinley had won by 271 to 176 in the electoral college four years previously. With T.R. his running mate, McKinley's electoral majority swelled to 292 to 155.

If anything about the hyperconservative inauguration on March 4, 1901, could be called sensational it was the volume of publicity that a Vice-President of the United States was being accorded for the first time. T.R. felt he had made a wise decision in leaving New York, and "Boss" Platt privately congratulated himself for having conjured it up. Albany was his once again.

To imagine the impetuous T.R. sitting still hour after hour, as all Vice-Presidents must do as presiding officers of the United States Senate, strains and taxes the imagination. Certainly it would have irked Roosevelt beyond endurance had he continued for long in the unfamiliar sedentary role. He confided in family and friends that he might take a job in a nearby university teaching history to pass the time when the Senate was not in session. It simply wasn't done in those days for a Vice-President to be as active politically or ceremonially as Richard M. Nixon in his two terms under Eisenhower.

T.R. also considered studying more law so he might have some profession if his star grew dim. By midsummer 1901, with fewer than six months of the Vice-Presidency behind him, he seems to have kept his sanity and hope only because certain newspaper editors wished to maintain his name in the public eye, with a view to 1904 when McKinley would not be eligible again. A series of American speaking tours was suggested, and Teddy Roosevelt leaped to the lure like a trout to a royal coachman. He never had time to fulfill the tour. For, on September 6, President McKinley absorbed his fatal wound while speaking in Buffalo. A week and a day later McKinley was dead,[10] gracefully accepting his fate by a faltering recital of "Nearer My God to Thee." Platt's best laid plans had exploded in his face.

A brash political youngster was now, suddenly, at forty-two, President of the United States, our youngest White House incumbent. William Allen White recalls in his *Autobiography*[11] that what seemed most worrisome to the new President was not the sudden burden of office, which he absorbed as though born to it, but the depressing thought that, even if re-elected in 1904, over Hanna's certain opposition, he would be barely fifty-one when he would have to retire from the Presidency. As things worked out he had a right to fret. Meddlesome by nature, T.R.'s years of "retirement" never kept him far from the national spotlight and gravely affected the lives of William Howard Taft and Woodrow Wilson, among uncountable others.

Up to now, Teddy Roosevelt had been a sort of brash political joke, amusing to some, nauseating to others. Now, older and more stable figures—Elihu Root, John Hay, and Mark Hanna—did not know precisely what to call him in private and ended up using "Theodore," "Teddy," and occasionally

10. Leon Czolgosz was executed on October 29 for McKinley's murder, and the Secret Service was at last given a fair chance at keeping safe the most precious man in the United States government.

11. William Allen White, *Autobiography* (New York, The Macmillan Company, 1946), p. 339.

"Mr. President" if a third person was around. Mark Hanna swallowed his suspicions and his pride, his dread fear that the talkative cowboy would unthinkingly turn the world upside down. Indeed, Hanna gently suggested to the upstart President that he go slow, take things easy for a while, not only for his own political sake but for the sake of a country shocked to the core at the third presidential assassination in thirty-six years. Conservatives seconded Hanna. Listen to everyone, make no snap judgments, be certain when you finally move—this, Hanna told the young man, made more sense than any other course of action. Roosevelt gratefully received every conservative leader in both houses of Congress, at his own invitation.

Nothing in the first messages to Congress suggested that President Roosevelt was further to the left than McKinley had been.[12] Indeed, conservatives on the whole were relieved and foresaw seven more years of "McKinleyism": high tariffs, corporation mergers, standpat legislation, accumulation of enormous wealth by the select industrial few, no new tax measures, hard money, little or no reform. The American public didn't seem to care much. It was relieved that no great sociological crises were imminent and was fascinated by the strenuous new occupant of the White House whose athletic feats, epigrammatic language, youthful vigor, and political color were a vaudeville show in themselves.

Just when or why Teddy Roosevelt became the trust buster we know him to be historically cannot be pinpointed to an hour or a day. All that can be accurately determined is the date of his first essay into the battle against the economic royalist, soon after J. P. Morgan had the Northern Securities Company incorporated in November, 1901, for purposes of ending the competition between the Great Northern, Burlington, and Northern Pacific Railroads.

Why did Teddy Roosevelt attack as he did? To begin with, he found Washington, Jackson, and Lincoln stimulating Presidents, men who had used the Presidency as a tool, who had been creative in legislation, not constantly operating in the

12. Theodore Roosevelt Papers.

passive voice. Washington had leaned toward Alexander Hamilton's theory of a strong central government and, while refusing monarchy for himself, strongly endorsed the view that the President of the United States *was* the President of the United States, not simply a social figurehead but the representation of the flag, the Republic, and the people as well as chief executive officer of prevailing political opinion. In no other large country, T.R. knew, were all of these functions wrapped up in a single office. The British had their kings and queens *and* a Prime Minister besides. The French had a Premier as well as a President. In the American Presidency alone both offices were combined into a single personality.

Teddy Roosevelt heartily disliked the memory of Thomas Jefferson, in spite of the Virginian's belief in the common man. Of Jefferson, T.R. once said that his worship as founder of the Democratic Party was a "discredit to my country." Besides, Jefferson's doctrine of local and state's rights (repudiated when he purchased Louisiana on his own) was anathema to a vital, strenuous forty-three-year-old now beginning to enjoy every moment of power.

Jackson fascinated Teddy Roosevelt, perhaps because Jackson was the most outrageous President before him. Nothing could be innately wrong with wielding enormous personal power if that power were directed to the good of plain people. A President was no office boy to Congress, but a "steward of the people," responsible directly to them since they had personally voted the President into office. It mattered not that not one American had cast a ballot in 1900 for Theodore Roosevelt as President of the United States. Now that he was President he meant to use his enormous vitality in behalf of the plain people: creatively, actively, powerfully, as Lincoln had done. The precedent of the founder of the Republican Party was for T.R. more than enough to go on. The people simply had to have a champion and the President had to be that man. There was no other in the plain man's corner.

Men often admire other men they wish they were. Qualities in one man which appeal to another often parallel the capabilities, background, hopes, and potential of the admirer. So it was with Teddy Roosevelt: a vigorous human being, he admired vigor and creativity. He could not possibly have hero-worshiped the do-nothing James Buchanan, yet was hopelessly attracted to the forceful Jackson and the strongly moral Lincoln. Egotistical and self-assured, Theodore Roosevelt found things admirable in Napoleon which Thomas Jefferson had not.

If Mark Hanna or those conservatives in business and industry whose fears had been quieted had known that all this was still very much a part of the Roosevelt personality, their faith in the future would surely have been shaken. Though President Roosevelt had promised faithfully to continue "absolutely unbroken" McKinley's policies and disposition of the Presidency, the economic royalty of his time should have hesitated to believe such a metamorphosis. Little in T.R.'s past as civic reformer, naval administrator, soldier, or Governor could have deluded any logical person for long that spots would change with a new oath of office. Big business was used to getting its own way. Truly it was the royalty of the economy. And, as so often happens to royalty of any sort, continuous power was not only corrupting but self-deluding.

Levin feels that Theodore Roosevelt's reputation for radicalism is overblown.[13] His trust-busting, his friendliness with organized labor, his fight to conserve the nation's natural resources, the reactionary nature of his enemies, his forthright and picturesque speech and manner, his running again for President as an independent Bull Mooser in 1912 have created a legend that is false, for T.R. was close to the middle of the road in almost every act as President. But what was the middle of the road to the people and Theodore Roosevelt in 1901 was dangerously radical nonsense to the contemporary industrial monopolist who had, until then, escaped much of the punishing social legislation long a legal fact in Europe. Levin goes on:[14]

> Exactly when he took cognizance of the progressivism that was boiling beneath the McKinley prosperity is difficult to determine. Before his ascent to the White House he had

13. Levin, *op. cit.*, p. 217.
14. *Ibid.*

displayed leanings toward reform and the correction of some of capitalism's grosser abuses; but he had always been pulled back to the Republican line when party leaders waxed less enthusiastic than did he. The Presidency, however, had made him leader of his party. Where a young assemblyman could be forced to subside and an unruly Governor shelved in the Vice-Presidency, a Chief Executive could not be fought by his nominal backers with impunity.

Conservatives were as yet unaffected by an almost universal journalistic assault on big business and monopoly. Although the Sherman Anti-Trust Act had languished on the statute books for a decade, almost totally abandoned by Presidents Harrison and McKinley, its effectiveness had been further reduced as a result of the Supreme Court's 1895 rulings. In this context it is not surprising that when T.R. opened fire on J.P. Morgan's railroad consolidation in November, 1901, big business was shocked to the core. Morgan tried to negotiate in Washington but his mission failed. Theodore Roosevelt had charted the ship of state on a new and vital mission: the busting of trusts inimical to the interests of the plain people. This venture was formalized in St. Paul, Minnesota, on March 10, 1902, when suit was filed against the merger by the Federal attorney for the Minnesota district.

President Roosevelt was quickly assailed by once friendly businessmen and political conservatives. He was now a Judas, a disrespecter of adjudicated law, turncoat, and hypocrite. There was no choice in his vigorous soul but to take his crusade to the people, and take it he did. He made one speech after another, pleading in every section of the land for support to his crusade. How many millions heard him no sensible man could guess—and it is well to remember that the loudspeaker, radio, and television were still in the future. Speeches to multitudes were strenuous physical facts in T.R.'s strenuous time.

The President made three points plain everywhere he spoke: he was overwhelmingly in favor of capitalism and free-enterprise economics; he was not opposed to corporations but he held them accountable to government; and again and again

he made the point of distinction between good business practice and bad, men who kept the public good in mind and evil
men who damned the public. Had the phrase "malefactors of
great wealth" been coined he would surely have used it. T.R.
didn't think of it until 1907.

The common man came to hear him everywhere. He was
cheered to the echo by liberals heartsick at America's humiliat-
ing disregard of the trust evil. Labor unions made him their
champion. To many a working man in the era of the twelve-to-
fourteen-hour day, bad wages, dangerous machinery, nauseating child labor, and bleak old age, here was a genuine Messiah.

Union League clubs shuddered as they listened to his logic,
couched in more moderate terms on Chestnut Street than in
Union Square. It was said at the time that the President used
the White House only to come back to for fresh linen. Newspaper writing verged on hysteria, divided between those who
foresaw anarchy and Bolshevism and those who hailed the
prophet of long overdue enlightenment.

The Northern Securities Company case took more than two
years to make its frustrated way through the labyrinth of lower
Federal courts. On March 14, 1904, it reached the decisive
stage in the Supreme Court. Four of the eminent justices ruled
that the Sherman Anti-Trust Act had been enacted to forbid
all combinations in restraint of trade, whether reasonable or
unreasonable. One justice argued that those who wrote the
law had had in mind only unreasonable combinations, but he
voted to order the Northern Securities Company dissolved because he found it unreasonably in restraint of trade. A witticism
of the time had it that Teddy had won his case 4¾ to 4¼. It is
an interesting sidelight that Oliver Wendell Holmes, long regarded as one of our most liberal justices, voted for J. P.
Morgan and Big Business against the President in a highly
sarcastic dissenting opinion.

But the President was satisfied, as well he might have been.
His wide-ranging speaking tour was now justified. He had
championed the cause of the common man and been cheered
to the rafters by him, and he and the people had won. The
narrowness of the vote meant nothing in view of the court's

vindication of presidential executive power. In many ways T.R. was to regard this as "one of the great achievements" of his first term,[15] one of the few understatements Theodore Roosevelt ever uttered.

President Roosevelt had asked for a Department of Commerce and Labor. Congress had overlooked his request until a vice-president of Standard Oil made the mistake of lobbying against the idea by sending incriminating telegrams to The Hill instead of the usual verbal persuasions. T.R. smelled his chance, called in the press, informed them of the telegraphic barrage, and arbitrarily changed the sender to John D. Rockefeller, whose name alone was enough to inflame the trust-conscious public. Within a week T.R. had his new Department of Commerce and Labor and, most important, a Bureau of Corporations with unprecedented powers of Federal inquiry and investigations.

It has been said of the Roosevelt Presidents that they and all their tribe had an extra gland. It has also been said that they were born with political antennae which gave them unerring instincts when to act and also when not to act. Theodore Roosevelt, having proved the first statement by his limitless and energetic demonstration of presidential power, now set out to prove the second. He became suddenly aware of the presidential campaign of 1904 and its financial requirements.

Until after his re-election, T.R. made no major moves to implement the trust information his new Secretary of Commerce and Labor, George B. Cortelyou, had been piling up for almost two years. Only when the political war chests had been filled by placated industrialists and corporations and T.R. had become President in his own right did he return to the battleground on which he was to say that even the most powerful men in the United States were held accountable before the law.

The new Department of Commerce and Labor was at first a very inoffensive body.[16] Any investigations and inquisitions so feared by big business were not to begin until after Election

15. Theodore Roosevelt Papers.
16. Pringle, *op. cit.*, p. 342.

Day—T.R. saw to that with unerring instinct. No doubt can exist, says Henry Pringle, that Theodore Roosevelt, as the 1904 convention drew near, was playing politics in his own behalf.[17] Expediency dictated some of his appointments and he was trimming sail on the trust-busting tack for months before the convention.

T.R. cleverly ignored Mark Hanna's growing signs of cordiality, finally writing his son Ted: "Senator Hanna . . . has been intoxicated by the thought that perhaps he could be nominated himself, or at least dictate the nomination."[18]

The President was progressively unkind to the aging Hanna, whom he detested politically and who was in an increasingly difficult position as to 1904. Roosevelt said in May, 1903, in the state of Washington: "I have not asked any man for his support. I have had nothing whatever to do with raising the issue as to my endorsement. Sooner or later it was bound to arise, and, inasmuch as it has now arisen, of course those who favor my administration and nomination will endorse them, and those who do not will oppose them."

Through the spring of 1903, Roosevelt kept making it appear that Hanna opposed his nomination; step by step Hanna had to retreat from the point of one who had opposed T.R.'s re-election and perhaps even wanted the nomination for himself to a humiliated supporter of a second term. Happily for the Republicans, the two men came together before the year 1904 began, for Hanna, who was by now sixty-six, became seriously ill in February and died on the 15th of that month. The honeyed obituary notices published in Republican papers had little to say about Mark Hanna's traditional wickedness, of his dalliance with despotic wealth, of the corruption often laid to his door in the raising of campaign funds. Even T.R. penned a fond obituary notice, pointing out how Hanna had supported him without question after McKinley had died. "He was a big man in every way," T.R. wrote.[19]

The renomination of Theodore Roosevelt had now been

17. *Ibid., passim.*
18. Theodore Roosevelt Papers.
19. *Ibid.*

made certain but his re-election had not. Being President, T.R. could not in those days go on the stump. This tradition has long since been shattered by another Roosevelt, but it was then ironbound. The *New York World* destroyed the campaign's lethargy with an eight-column editorial signed by Joseph Pulitzer on October 1 complaining that in the year and a half of its existence the Bureau of Corporations of the new Department of Commerce and Labor had done absolutely nothing and, by a funny coincidence, Mr. Cortelyou, the department head, was the new Republican National Chairman succeeding Hanna. Pulitzer suggested that the big corporations pouring money into the Republican campaign assumed they were buying protection from Mr. Cortelyou's inquiries. It was too pat, said Pulitzer: the sudden cessation of trust-busting simultaneous with a perfect flood of big corporation funds to be placed at the disposal of the man the President had picked to break up monopolies, mergers, cartels, trusts, and other combinations in restraint of trade against the public weal.

Oddly enough, Alton B. Parker, the Democratic candidate, did nothing with Pulitzer's editorial charges for more than a month. Naturally, T.R. didn't acknowledge them, since Parker hesitated. But when Parker made the mistake on November 3 of baldly calling the corporation donations "blackmail," made in return for silence in regard to damaging facts collected in the trust and merger surveys of the Bureau of Corporations, the President was quick to reply. Parker had lost the election then and there, if indeed he'd ever had a chance of winning, which is doubtful. Roosevelt said:[20]

That contributions have been made . . . is not the question at issue. . . . Mr. Parker's accusations against Mr. Cortelyou and me are monstrous. If true they would brand both of us forever with infamy; and inasmuch as they are false, heavy must be the condemnation of the man making them. . . . The assertion that Mr. Cortelyou had any knowledge, gained while in an official position, whereby he was enabled to secure and did secure any contributions from any corporation is a falsehood. The assertion that there has been any

20. Presidential Addresses, Vol. III, pp. 97–100.

blackmail, direct or indirect, by Mr. Cortelyou or by me is a falsehood. The assertion that there has been made any pledge or promise or that there has been any understanding as to future immunities or benefits, in recognition of any contribution from any source, is a wicked falsehood.

Since everyone knew and believed in T.R.'s explicit honesty, painfully blunt at times but a beacon in the wilderness of political hypocrisy and cant, and since the complete and unequivocal denial rang true with the known facts and the character of both T.R. and Cortelyou, Parker issued no further communications. It had been an ill-starred venture and the Democrats did not thank Pulitzer for it. Indeed, the famous publisher was in the political doghouse as a result of a truthful editorial.

The President was elected on November 8 to his own first four-year term; now he was at last in truth the people's choice. He swamped the Democrats by 336 to 140 in the electoral college and by a popular majority of more than two and a half million, most decisive of all Republican victories up to that time. Pringle points out that "in his ecstasy of joy . . . he issued a statement that was to cause him poignant regret" in the years to come: "On the 4th of March next I shall have served three and a half years and this . . . constitutes my first term. The wise custom which limits the President to two terms regards the substance and not the form; and under no circum-stances will I be a candidate for or accept another nomination."[21]

But Pulitzer had had a point, as it turned out. T.R. had indeed been trimming sail on the trust tack with election storm clouds on the horizon. There was a gift of $125,000 from Standard Oil, $48,000 from New York Life Insurance Company, and equivalent amounts from Mutual and Equitable. E. H. Harriman, the railroad baron, had donated $50,000 and collected $100,000 more for T.R.'s campaign funds. In fact, it became public knowledge later that almost three-fourths of the $2,-195,000 collected for Theodore Roosevelt's 1904 campaign had come from corporations. J. P. Morgan had personally given

21. *New York World*, November 9, 1904.

$150,000, all of it in cash, while Edward T. Stotesbury, whose bank in Philadelphia had close connections with Morgan's, had collected $165,795.60 for the campaign. The New York, New Haven and Hartford Railroad had come through with $50,000; General Electric with $3,000; James Hazen Hyde with $25,000; H. C. Frick with $50,000; James Speyer with $25,000; James Stillman with $10,000. The list was endless. It also involved the worst investment any of these shrewd industrial and banking giants ever made. For, the day before his inauguration, T.R. is supposed to have declared: "Tomorrow I shall come into my office in my own right. Then watch out for me!"[22]

T.R.'s message to the new Congress was utterly innocuous in regard to trust-busting and merger-dissolving. There were reassuring platitudes and a suggestion that Congress supervise insurance company transactions, then a developing scandal which was to bring the not inconsiderable talents of Charles Evans Hughes to the forefront. It remained for an address before a dinner of the Union League Club in Philadelphia for T.R. to show the shape of things to come. The wealthy and substantial men of banking and industry who attended must have been shaken out of their brandy-and-cigars lethargy to hear the following quotation from the man whose successful campaign they had just financed:

> . . . the great development of industrialism means that there must be an increase in the supervision exercised by the Government over business-enterprise. . . . Such men as the members of this club should lead in the effort to secure proper supervision. . . . Neither this people nor any other free people will permanently tolerate the use of the vast power conferred by vast wealth . . . without lodging somewhere in the Government the still higher power of seeing that this power is used for and not against the interests of the people as a whole.

The newly elected President went on that the business of the United States was by now conducted in a way the founders of the nation could not possibly have anticipated, that all business transacted anywhere by a large corporation was in truth

22. *New York World,* March 5, 1905.

interstate and that the Federal government, not helpless state governments, would have to step in to control same. As for the venal railroads, they must be particularly policed by the national government. T.R. went on:

. . . in temperate, resolute fashion there must be lodged in some tribunal the power over rates, and especially over rebates . . . which will protect alike the railroad and the shipper on an equal footing. . . . We do not intend that this Republic shall ever fail as those republics of olden times failed, in which there finally came to be a government by classes, which resulted either in the poor plundering the rich, or in the rich . . . exploiting the poor.[23]

The *New York World* immediately remarked:[24]

. . . an open—almost a defiant—challenge to the railway interests that opposed Federal regulation of rates and to the Republican leaders that have aligned themselves with the great corporate interests. . . . The President's speech shows that he has no intention of compromising with the corporate influences in his party.

The annual message to Congress was less than two months cold, yet the fearful specter of broad-scale Federal intervention in private business was being raised anew by a man the Union League clubs of America had helped elect with their not inconsiderable influence and considerable monies. When William Jennings Bryan, anathema to any Union Leaguer, praised the speech as "perfectly sound," the gage was cast for keeps.

The Sherman Anti-Trust Act had been validated by Roosevelt's victory in the Northern Securities case, but T.R. felt, with justice, that the law still wasn't adequate to protect the public against the unlimited power of the corporation octopus. One idea cropped up from a rereading of Bryan during a prior presidential campaign: Federal licensing of corporations. Elihu Root advised Roosevelt not to do it because, said Root, licensing involved evils "far greater than its benefits." T.R. listened

23. Presidential Addresses, Vol. III, pp. 217–24.
24. *New York World*, January 31, 1905.

to many another proposal for strengthening his antimonopoly forces but always came back to the sensible remedy he had proposed first as Governor of New York. The best corporation policy, he said again, lay in generous publicity of capitalization, earnings, and interlocking directorships.

At Chautauqua, New York, on August 11, 1905, T.R. put it this way:[25]

> I believe that all corporations engaged in interstate commerce should be under the supervision of the national Government. . . . It may be that we shall . . . require all corporations to produce proof . . . that they are not parties to . . . any violation of the anti-trust law and that . . . [they] shall agree, with a penalty of forfeiture of their right to engage in such commerce, to furnish any evidence of any kind as to their trade between the States whenever so required.

To understand this point of view it is necessary to understand Theodore Roosevelt's fundamental precept that the Federal government was sovereign and the President of the United States master of the ship. This viewpoint had by no means been shared by all other Presidents and in taking so strong a stand on it Theodore Roosevelt irrevocably changed the conception and powers of the Presidency. When in his message to Congress in December, 1905, T.R. said that U. S. corporations were "subjects without a sovereign" he added that a national license law might be a solution. By 1907 he was advocating such a statute because, as he put it, it wasn't a matter of destroying the free enterprise capitalistic system but simply "looking facts in the face."[26]

To be accurate, Theodore Roosevelt did not personally bust many trusts. What he did was to set in motion the machinery for trust-busting, to create a climate in which mergers and monopolies contravening the public welfare could be dissolved and Federal laws enacted through which the common man might be protected from the evils of illegal combination. It is true that suits were begun against the tobacco and packing

25. Presidential Addresses, Vol. IV, pp. 451–52.
26. Theodore Roosevelt Papers.

trusts, and the New York Central Railroad was fined for giving huge rebates to the American Sugar Refining Company in restraint of free trade. But it wasn't until William Howard Taft was President of the United States that the Federal government was able to order the American Tobacco Company and Standard Oil Company finally dissolved.

T.R.'s title as "trust buster" was, he would have been the first to admit, a technical misnomer. Taft instituted forty-five proceedings leading to indictments under the Sherman Anti-Trust Act; Roosevelt instituted only twenty-five. But, says Pringle, "the significance of Roosevelt's corporation activities lay in what he *said* rather than what he *did*."[27]

This is undeniably accurate. What Roosevelt accomplished was to progress against the "malefactors of great wealth"[28] in order to head off the average man's unrest and uneasiness and forestall something he detested worse than his hatred for the economic royalist: socialism.

He could complain to his friend Taft in 1906: "I do not like the special conditions at present . . . the dull, purblind folly of the very rich men; their greed and arrogance . . . and the corruption in business and politics . . . [tending] to produce a very unhealthy condition of excitement and irritation in the popular mind, which shows itself in the great increase in the Socialistic propaganda."[29] The at-home policies of President Roosevelt's second term were based chiefly on this growing fear which, time and again, he voiced in letters and speeches boiling down to the proposition that, in his opinion, the growth of the "Socialistic party is far more ominous than any Populist or similar movement in times past."

It is to T.R.'s eternal credit that he, a patrician, realized with genius undeniably intuitive that there were evils in an unfettered free enterprise capitalistic system then taken for granted in the United States and that, if these evils were not rooted out, the system itself might succumb and American democratic society with it. But Roosevelt's gifts for publicity

27. Pringle, *op. cit.*, p. 427.
28. Presidential Addresses, Vol. VI, pp. 1351–66.
29. Letter from T.R. to Taft, March 15, 1906.

and his flair for arousing the average man to insist that something be done to correct an evil were unfortunately not matched by sound knowledge of economics. Like his Presidential cousin Franklin, economics and business details bored him. He lived and worked in a world of ideas, morals, philosophy, ego, and politics. He and F.D.R. had to learn their economics lessons in the White House, painfully but, in the end, well enough. To contemporaries, Theodore Roosevelt's abysmal lack of business training and intelligence in matters economic verged on ignorance.

Yet smart men of his time—Speaker Cannon and Senators Allison, Aldrich, Spooner, Foraker, and many more who knew their Adam Smith to the least comma—had fewer forebodings of class war than did T.R., to whom such an event was not only possible but perhaps imminent. On the other hand he could not, he knew by instinct, go too far. If he did he might cause a business slump (the panic of 1907 made a terrific impression on him) which would end in the dread Socialism he feared more than he hated the monopolist and merger-man. If he went so far as to alienate his own party he might turn over the reins of government when he retired in 1909 to the Democrats, an event which in his mind came near the top of the worst imaginable dangers to the country.

Of Theodore Roosevelt's economic service to the average American, his war against railroad monopoly, illegal rebates, fixed rate charges, corruption, interlocking directorates, and public-be-damned philosophy in high places was, in the end, the most valuable and lasting.

The Interstate Commerce Commission received new powers through the controversial Hepburn Act of 1906, a forward step which would never have become law without Roosevelt's direct intervention and driving energy. By the Hepburn Act, the ICC now had jurisdiction over express, Pullman operations, storage, refrigeration, pipe lines, widened ratemaking, and all other items covered by the tenuous phrase "transportation across state lines." Rates theoretically had been a function of ICC. Now its police powers were strengthened to enforce its edicts. Honest accounting required under the new regulations ended in honest rate and rebate practices, to the glory and advantage of the average consumer, who for the first time had an energetic advocate in the White House.

By Inauguration Day, 1909, when his friend William Howard Taft succeeded him (only to become his political enemy by 1912), Theodore Roosevelt had set the stage for trust-busting.

In doing so, T.R. had irrevocably altered the tradition of President of the United States and brought to the office a new and deep-rooted precedent that the occupant of the White House was to be thenceforward the people's champion and lobbyist, since they had no other. It was mandatory in Teddy Roosevelt's view that he be truly the Chief Executive in all matters, including that once forbidden land, the business-industrial world and its relationships with the public. Through the Federal government's first serious regulation and intervention under T.R., the immunity which economic royalists had perpetually taken for granted would never be the same again. A man who led a strenuous life had been in the White House and he expected his successors to emulate him.

Woodrow Wilson

THE TEACHING profession does not as a rule participate actively in American politics. Contrary to prevailing opinion, people who teach are apt to be extremely practical people: they have to be to exist on the money they earn. The reason for their political nonparticipation, therefore, isn't impracticability or woolly-headedness, or disinterest in the real world about them, or a taste for the theoretical in preference to the pragmatic. What they traditionally lack are two fundamental elements every man must possess in almost unlimited quantity if he is to run for public office: time and money. The teaching profession rarely has a sufficiency of either.

Thomas Woodrow Wilson[1] was one of the rare exceptions, a university professor who possessed neither the time nor the money to run for public office, yet ran so successfully that he became Governor of New Jersey and President of the United States. As though to prove the rule, Wilson as Governor and President pushed through reforms in each body politic that were not only long overdue but seemed miracles of accomplishment. It was as though, having achieved the impossible by getting elected at all, the brilliant Princetonian could continue

1. When Ike Hoover, one of the chief ushers in the White House, went to Princeton to arrange for removal of the President's effects to Washington, he noted that Wilson had autographed his own books in various ways: Thomas W. Wilson, Thomas Woodrow Wilson, T. W. Wilson, T. Woodrow Wilson, and Woodrow Wilson, as though, at various times, he hadn't made up his mind which by-line to use for which purpose.

8

Ignores the Senate and Loses His Dream

performing miracles indefinitely in an arena seldom if ever assailed by those who teach and theorize.

Yet, in the end, when the miracle dissolved, Woodrow Wilson had only himself and his extraordinary individualism to blame. He had done it on his own, without unlimited funds and with only the time he could set aside from constant teaching or writing. He had done it, in Trenton and Washington, without overmuch help from the professional politician. In the end, his dream of a League of Nations was shattered because, having been kissed by fortune throughout an amazing voyage, he fell to depending upon himself and fortune alone. He ignored those who sought to advise him, repudiating the democratic muddling-through he should have known existed at all levels of political procedure and simply could not be ignored. He failed to take a delegation of Senators versed in foreign relations with him to the Paris peace conference. He left a former friend, Henry Cabot Lodge, cooling his heels for hours in an outer room of the White House and, in the end, Lodge, as chairman of the Senate Foreign Relations Committee, dynamited Wilson's precious project.

Had Wilson come up the normal way, through local and state committees, through cloakroom bargains and daily politicking at the precinct level, he would not have ignored the leaders of either political party, particularly Senators in whose hands the ultimate fate of any peace treaty must rest. Yet this is precisely what happened. Ignore them he did and, as the years went on, he became more and more the idealistic recluse who depended less and less on advice and the necessary requirements of political bargaining and more and more on his own (and Colonel House's) intuitive judgment. It cost him his dream.

Wilson was a Virginian, a Princeton graduate and a lawyer first, before moving to Johns Hopkins to teach political science. After winning his Ph.D. there he taught history and political science for a while at Bryn Mawr and Wesleyan University and then at Princeton.

He had already begun to write, in that severe yet beautifully clear and no-nonsense style so characteristic of his work. A volume called *Congressional Government* appeared in the book stalls the year before he took his doctorate in Baltimore. *Division and Reunion, George Washington, A History of the American People* (in five volumes), and *Constitutional Government in the United States* followed from year to year and gave him a wide reputation as an authority on constitutional history, jurisprudence, and political science. By the time he had been at Princeton long enough to be considered for its presidency, Woodrow Wilson was also one of the best known orators in the college. Teddy Roosevelt, no colorless personality himself, had to admit that Wilson made a fine figure on the platform.[2]

Princeton was in those days thoroughly wedded to the Presbyterians who had founded it and Wilson was descended from Presbyterian ministers on both sides. Popular with the students and the more progressive faculty, Woodrow Wilson became in 1902 Princeton's first nonclerical head. He had not been the university's executive officer a semester when controversy engulfed him.

A man of pronounced democratic feelings, keenly conscious of equality, with a Scot's cold logic and Robert Burns's uncompromising philosophy of brotherhood in his bloodstream, Wilson staggered old-line Princetonians by his democratic sentiments and acts. To the horror of traditionalist alumni and reactionary faculty, the new president set off salvo after salvo

2. Theodore Roosevelt Papers.

against an age of snobs and the very core of educational snobbery, the wealthy Princeton clubs. Dean Andrew F. West
quickly and forcefully opposed his democratization of the
college, particularly at its social and tutorial levels, and in the
end Dean West won and Wilson lost. But by this time Wilson
was nationally known.

In 1910, soon after Wilson had resigned as head of Princeton, George B. M. Harvey, a New York publisher with Democratic Party interests, came to him and persuaded him to run
for Governor of New Jersey on the Democratic ticket. Supported reluctantly by professional politicians, Wilson amazingly won in a state then traditionally Republican. No sooner
was he seated in his Trenton office than he began upsetting
applecarts again, this time breaking quickly with party leaders.

Governor Wilson's success in battling the entrenched New
Jersey politicians won him increasing attention nationally.
He obtained a direct primary election law, an employer's lia-
bility law, a corrupt practices act, put new life in the state
public utilities commission, and began enforcing social welfare
laws already on the statute books but lying fallow. This sort of
gubernatorial record was bound to push him into the 1912
nomination picture, though Champ Clark was far in front as
the leading Democratic candidate.

Clark had been a lawyer, newspaper editor, and political
leader in Missouri and eventually served his Congressional
District as its Representative for twenty-six years. In 1907 he
had become Democratic leader of the House and, the year
Wilson became Governor of New Jersey, Champ Clark led a
battle to reduce the dictatorial powers of Speaker Joseph G.
Cannon. Clark became Speaker of the House the following
year. With Uncle Joe Cannon's scalp dangling from his belt,
few professional politicians dared oppose Clark for the Democratic presidential nomination at Baltimore in 1912.

But Woodrow Wilson was not a professional: this was part
of his charm with the electorate. Champ Clark fell short of the
required votes on the first ballot and the upstart Wilson began
to gain support from an unusual quarter, William Jennings
Bryan. Bryan himself had run and lost in 1896, 1900, and 1908,

as Democratic standard-bearer (carefully ducking a race with Theodore Roosevelt in 1904). Bryan was still silver-tongued, still represented the voice of the poor and downtrodden, as professional logrollers like Champ Clark never had. During the convention Bryan also came under the influence of a most unusual personality, Colonel Edward Mandell House.

Colonel House came from Houston, Texas, and was a Cornell graduate. He was no United States Army Colonel: his "Colonel" was a Texas state title. Like many another Kentuckian and Texan he wore it proudly all his adult life. Important in Texas politics, Edward M. House's star rose with Woodrow Wilson's. His greatest coup was persuading Bryan to swing his powerful support to the New Jersey Governor in an effort to defeat Champ Clark and Tammany Hall. Wilson became the Democratic candidate, a nomination thought to be of little value early in 1912 because of President Taft's promising prospects for re-election and the Republican Party's traditional predominance. But, as so often happened during his time, Theodore Roosevelt's explosive personality intervened. Roosevelt soon repudiated his own ecstatic postelection declaration of 1904 that he would never run again for the Presidency.

Slamming into his erstwhile friend, William Howard Taft —and all that Taft had, in his opinion, failed to stand for— Roosevelt bolted the regular Republicans and formed the Progressive Party. Taft was nominated as regular Republican candidate. The unprecedented Republican split elected Woodrow Wilson, dark horse amateur, President of the United States.[3] Wilson received 435 electoral votes, Roosevelt 88, and President Taft only 8 (Utah and Vermont). The combined Republican-Progressive vote would have elected a Republican

3. The Democratic Convention of 1912 had been one of the wildest ever. The delegates required forty-six ballots to nominate, and at one point Wilson sent a telegram withdrawing his candidacy. William Gibbs McAdoo, his strategist and son-in-law, tore up the telegram and persuaded the Governor of New Jersey not to quit. Champ Clark, the favorite, finally lost his heavy support and William Jennings Bryan swung his own strength to Wilson, who then won the nomination. Had he had his own way, Wilson would have long since released his delegates.

candidate, 7,604,518 popular votes to Wilson's 6,293,454, although many who might have voted for Wilson cast their ballots for the new Progressive Party and the ever-popular if turncoat Theodore Roosevelt.

As he had done before while chief executive at Princeton and Trenton, Wilson as President wasted no time in shattering precedents in Washington. Reviving a custom dropped after John Adams in 1801, the new President appeared in person before Congress to deliver his State of the Union message. It was stylishly if severely written, as was all Wilson's writing, for he was a professional writer with millions of published words to his credit. He held the new Congress spellbound with his famed oratory. He called for a series of reforms which, during the campaign, he had named the "New Freedom," as his friend Franklin D. Roosevelt was to call his later reforms the "New Deal."

Congress and the country responded wholeheartedly. Here was the first Democratic President since Cleveland and only the second since the Civil War. His program seemed to be a necessary antidote to generations of high-tariff, pro-bourbon legislation. Only T.R. had been an exception, and even the Rough Rider had been a high-tariff Republican working with a business-dominated Republican Congress.

With such a start, the wonder is that Woodrow Wilson's new broom did not sweep all before it. Surely the country was disappointed with President Taft and would have welcomed a prolonged change of direction. But, as his career made painfully obvious, Woodrow Wilson was a political freak, an amateur, an academician. He had never been to a county convention until nominated for Governor. He had never been inside his own state capitol until the day he was sworn in at Trenton. He had never been inside the White House until he came there to live.

What sort of man was this political sport? William Allen White, one of his warmest biographers, says: "Probably no other American ever learned so much politics in 22 months as Woodrow Wilson learned from the Irish of New Jersey be-

tween September, 1910, and the spring of 1912."[4] The fact is
that, as Governor of New Jersey, Wilson had actually turned
over most of his patronage to his two good Irish friends, Joe
Tumulty and James Kerney. Tumulty was his private secretary
and Kerney a newspaper editor who had long advocated his
candidacy. The pair were slightly appalled, yet flattered and,
of course, delighted with a responsibility which gave them remarkable power in Jersey politics at no cost to themselves.
They wrote later that Wilson appeared to care little about the
things that interested organization politicians.

Indeed patronage continued to irk Wilson after he became
President. He considered it a "left-handed job" and practically
farmed out the selection of his first Cabinet. The appointment
of William Jennings Bryan as Secretary of State came against
the instinctive judgment of Mrs. Wilson who distrusted Bryan's
personality, windiness, and intellectual prowess, though she
trusted his goodness. But Bryan had swung to Wilson in the
1912 convention and overturned Champ Clark, and Wilson's
Irish gratitude cottoned to him. Wilson told his wife he
thought he could handle Bryan's wild swings and extravagant
statements.

The President's gross inexperience in the business of national
politics was a terrible handicap. He did not even know the
names of top Congressional leaders, much less their charac-
ters, personalities, positions, or potentialities. His vast indifference to patronage, White believes, and the assumption he
too often made of his university professor's superiority of mind
over others continuously led him into difficulty.

Having written voluminously on the theory of Federal government, particularly the legislative branch, he became, in his
own inimitable way, more of a Premier than a President. That
is, he led Congress along the road to legislation rather than
simply enforcing its acts or remaining aloof from the actual
business of lawmaking. White feels Wilson had legislative
rather than administrative leadership, which probably stemmed
from an amazing ego and an academic background in which,

4. William Allen White, *Woodrow Wilson* (Boston, Houghton Mifflin
Company, 1924), p. 244.

as is natural in university circles, he had rarely if ever been edited by a subordinate student body. Up to the time of the presidency of Princeton it is doubtful if Woodrow Wilson's judgment had ever been severely questioned by anyone. Certainly he had come to be a sort of parochial monarch with absolute authority and little or no reason to consult anyone. Books (and students) didn't talk back. But Washington politicians did.

As Governor of New Jersey, Wilson had been a leader of the legislature and the people—an exalted schoolmaster. When he came to the White House he was forced away from all the dear associations of town and gown, never to return. The man who had said at Princeton "I'll not be president of a country club" wasn't likely to look upon high tariffs and child labor with anything but loathing, but he was also not likely to have the patience or the political skill to get corrective legislation through smoke-filled bargaining. It had to be done, for him, through personal leadership and intervention and appeals to the public. By instinct and personality alone he seems to have won his way in those first fecund, prewar years. The country was, of course, overripe for reforms. This helped his causes.

Wilson often defended Theodore Roosevelt's theory that the Presidency carried with it Congressional leadership. He once said: "Whatever else we may think or say of Theodore Roosevelt, we must admit that he was an aggressive leader. He led Congress—he was not driven by Congress. We may not approve his methods, but we must concede that he made Congress follow him."[5]

A man who had lived in the intellectually fertile, gentle atmosphere of Princeton for twenty-six years, as student, professor, university president, and Governor, could not easily be transplanted to the muck and noise of Pennsylvania Avenue. He had commuted from Princeton to Trenton when he was Governor of New Jersey. He could not commute to Washington or he would surely have done so.

Personal habit sustained him for a time in his transplanta-

5. *Ibid.*, p. 270.

tion. The Wilsons had been openly democratic at Princeton, stopping their horse and surrey along the college roads to pick up a neighbor, a washerwoman with her burden, a carpenter en route home, a messenger on his journey. Since this was impossible in the Presidency, Wilson's democracy took other outward forms after he moved to 1600 Pennsylvania Avenue. He refused to join the Chevy Chase Golf Club, playing when he could on a public course.[6] He went regularly to the Keith Vaudeville house and roared at its common routines.

Wilson and his family often played the piano and sang. The magic of music changed cold White House marble to Princeton fireside for an hour or two each week, and nothing the fastidious new President did for recreation filled the exhausted cup of energy as quickly or perfectly. Wilson sang tenor and sang it very well indeed, if a bit on the Irish side. He was also a magnificent talker, but not to strangers. He liked nothing better than to speculate on great topics and unique ideas, academically of course.

As he began his Presidency, Woodrow Wilson was slightly above medium height and slightly below medium weight, a frail body with large, glowing eyes which sometimes seemed to be shifty, even untrustworthy. His hair was now graying, but it had once been blond, then brown. He walked with a firm step, the very epitome of self-confidence.[7]

But he was forever burdened with the body of a nonathlete, an engine inadequate to the needs of his agile mind, and, of our finest Presidents, Wilson probably required the most sleep. Nine hours in bed was an absolute minimum to make him feel well. He took no exercise besides golf and walking, and at fifty-six his stomach could scarcely keep down what little food Wilson ate. Indeed, he brought with him to the White House a stomach pump which, it is said, he used almost daily.

6. Wilson never attempted proficiency at golf, but regarded it as a chance to get out in the open. He seldom kept score. Good weather or bad was all the same to him. If there was snow on the ground, the President would have his golf balls painted red. He played at all hours, sometimes at five in the morning, but oftener late in the afternoon.

7. White, *op. cit.*, p. 275.

Wilson was an incredibly uxorious man, needing a wife as few other Presidents have needed constant womanly companionship. When Ellen Axson Wilson died on August 6, 1914, it very nearly broke the President. Yet it is not surprising that he married again on December 18, 1915, and his quick second marriage to Mrs. Edith Bolling Galt,[8] a handsome widow, had nothing whatever to do with disloyalty to his dearest Ellen. He needed a woman around as he needed air to breathe, and Mrs. Galt was not only a looker ("She's a looker, and he's a goner," said a friend) but a perfectly matched personality for his. She exuded high spirits, devotion, humor, joy of living, beauty, gaiety.[9]

Wilson had written of Ellen Axson soon after her untimely death: "She was the most radiant creature I have ever known. Something like an aura of light always surrounded her."[10] Of Edith Bolling Galt, the young widow who took her place in his innermost heart, the President might well have written the same words at the end of the nine years they lived together. She and Ellen were essences in the Wilson story though, as William Allen White wrote it, "no man ever can restore a life's companionship which goes."

This is the essential Wilson on whom years later the fate of the peace conference rested. History often shows him as a severely stubborn martinet addicted to a pince-nez, irritable, nervous, loaded with jaw. Yet in truth he was a warmhearted, musically Irish male with more than the average man's love of the touch, companionship, and warmth of the opposite sex, seldom an ogre (until his final illness), and to his close friends, especially women, a dear person. He loved women and women loved him in return. His true nature was in violent

8. Wilson had a private wire installed between his room in the White House and her home, prior to their marriage, and spent hours each day composing letters to her. She received flowers daily, and orchids appear to have had special significance. In those days, Washington flower shops were sometimes hard pressed to find orchids of the color and quantity Woodrow Wilson demanded.

9. Ike Hoover wrote later that President Wilson sent so many love notes to Mrs. Galt that "the Library of Congress was put to a test to find quotations to express his feelings."

10. White, *op. cit.*, p. 284.

contrast to the severity his face and personality seemed to leave as a public impression.

Soon after his inaugural in 1913 Wilson demanded that the tariff be reduced, and Congress responded with a drastic downward revision. Banking desperately needed a kind of flood control system and Wilson supplied it with the Federal Reserve Act and other reforms the same year. In 1915, the La Follette Seamen's Act regulating labor conditions aboard America's merchant marine ended scores of abuses traditional to the mariner. The Federal Farm Loan Act of 1916 provided loans for co-operatives ("Socialism!" screamed the Republican press). The Adamson Act that same year limited railroad workers to an eight-hour day, though most of heavy industry still worked ten to twelve hours daily, often six days a week. The new President also created a body with additional monopoly-curbing powers, the Federal Trade Commission. The FTC immediately began to expose and investigate unfair practices of corporations, especially the claims for their products, a particularly pertinent inquiry in the field of patent medicine ads then flooding even the most respectable newspapers. Another antimonopoly measure was the Clayton Anti-Trust Act which, with existing legislation, was responsible for more than a hundred new antitrust suits.

The new President had, as Governor of New Jersey, instituted the direct primary. He now carried this theory to the nation, asking that United States Senators be elected directly by the people instead of by state legislatures, as the Constitution had always provided. The Seventeenth Amendment was soon passed by the Congress and quickly ratified by the States and, for the first time in American history, Senators were now elected the same way as Congressmen—directly by the people. The Eighteenth Amendment, making Prohibition legal, and the Nineteenth Amendment, by which all U. S. women twenty-one or over received the vote, also were added to the Federal Constitution during Woodrow Wilson's Presidency. It was, indeed, a time of domestic reform and Wilson, the political accident, the reformer.

The United States from 1912 to 1916 was not yet a world

power, but an isolationist adolescent whose chief editorial writers constantly referred to Washington's farewell admonition to beware of foreign entanglements.[11] The nation west of the Alleghenies shuddered at the blood bath which was Europe, and in 1916 the Democrats' campaign slogan for Wilson's re-election was "He Kept Us Out of War." It proved highly successful, though the decision—which rested on the returns from the last Western state to report—was as narrow as it is possible for a presidential election to be.

The vote of California seesawed during election night, with Charles Evans Hughes apparently elected by dawn, Eastern Standard Time. In fact, Hughes went to bed late thinking he was President. A *New York Herald* reporter, hearing that final but unofficial returns had squeaked Wilson in by fewer than 4,000 votes, came to the Hughes house and demanded to see the Republican candidate for a statement. Hughes's son came to the door and said: "The President has retired and cannot be disturbed." "Well," said the newspaperman, "when he wakes up, tell him he ain't President."

Hiram Johnson, as steadfast and bitter an isolationist as ever breathed American air, was ironically responsible for Hughes's defeat in California and Woodrow Wilson's re-election. A fancied slight during the Republican campaign was the pretext, though it is more than likely that Hiram Johnson, himself a frustrated Republican presidential possibility, simply could not stand the thought that a liberal, international-minded New Yorker was likely to be President of the United States, and a war blazing in Europe to boot! So, the man who had "kept us out of war" went back to the White House for four more years: 277 to 254 in the electoral college and, more easily, 9,129,606 to 8,538,221 in popular vote.

But if Hiram Johnson and the *Chicago Tribune* held notions that they had saved the country from foreign entanglements they were to be quickly disillusioned. American public opinion had caught fire against Kaiser Wilhelm. On May 7, 1915, the *Lusitania* had been torpedoed without warning off the Irish coast—1,200 persons, a hundred of them Americans, had died

11. Files of the *Chicago Tribune, passim,* 1912–1916.

frightful deaths. Immediately after re-election, Wilson tried to mediate the European war, but without the slightest success. When Germany renewed unrestricted submarine warfare, and all U. S. ships and passengers were now in jeopardy, Wilson's temper changed, reflecting a swelling tide of American fear and hatred of Germany.

The German announcement of renewed unrestricted U-boat warfare came January 31, 1917, less than three months after Wilson's re-election and only five weeks before his second inaugural. By April 2, 1917, the President was asking the Congress to declare war on Germany to "make the world safe for democracy," and because the "right is more precious than the peace." His ideal was "ultimate peace of the world" and "the liberation of its people." As before, Woodrow Wilson's gift for words and oratory united American opinion behind a principle, an ideal worth fighting for, and on April 6, 1917, the Congress declared that a state of war did indeed exist between the United States and the powers of darkness led by the cocky little Prussian with the stunning mustaches and the withered arm.

William Jennings Bryan had resigned in 1915 as Secretary of State. Bryan had scrupulously favored neutrality and his clashes with Wilson had made him feel politically insecure and uncomfortable. Besides, Bryan had enormous limitations as Secretary of State in charge of the foreign affairs of a country emerging as a world power. Robert Lansing, who replaced him, was more of an internationalist with better grounding in international law. Also, whereas Bryan had been a politician, Lansing, like Wilson, was almost academic in his approach to policy.

The war helped consolidate in Woodrow Wilson a false sense of the rightness of his own intuition and judgment. As a war President, he asked for and received powers of decree untapped since the days of Abraham Lincoln. There had been no major war since Lincoln's time; therefore, no other President had needed dictatorial prerogative nor had Congress offered it. But war goods production, preservation of the sources of raw materials, the draft, the training of millions of amateur soldiers, the taking over of U. S. railroads, the enormous sale of Liberty bonds to finance America's first military venture overseas required ukase. Wilson asked for power and promptly got it.

Emergency war measures in 1917 and 1918 revolutionized U. S. commerce, industry, and private life. The Federal government took over the nation's railroad management and regimented labor, agriculture, and industry as they had never been regimented before. It was America's baptism in total war—and in economic centralization. Both factors left lasting marks and established presidential precedents useful later to Franklin D. Roosevelt. And their effect on the man now in the White House was no less evident. They gave him, quite possibly, delusions that he and he alone could run the country—its domestic difficulties and its foreign policy—without overmuch consultation of anyone. It was an unfortunate intensification of Wilson's very nature and method. Had war not then involved the United States, Wilson's personal-decision system would surely have been exposed to greater and greater editing as his second term wore on. As it was, war and the dictatorial overtones of war affected the President himself to a marked degree.

Less and less did he seek the advice of his Cabinet in matters pertaining to the conduct of the war and its inevitable peace terms. As early as January 8, 1918, not quite a year since war had been declared by the United States, Woodrow Wilson suddenly proposed peace on the basis of fourteen points which had, for the most part, been of his own creation and phraseology. He was no longer simply a national figure; he now had world dimensions, and it is possible they went to his head.

The President's special message to the Congress on January 8, 1918, was thoroughly idealistic, matching his unique private idealism. Yet it had pragmatic overtones. It was intended to tell the Allied political leaders that the United States would have no part of a selfish peace, that the postwar treaty would have to measure up to new democratic liberalism which America's war entry had introduced into world power politics.

The first five of the historically famous "Fourteen Points" were by nature general and idealistically philosophical. They were intended by their author to create in wartorn Europe and untouched America a new moral climate which would unite public opinion behind a democratic peace treaty. They immediately gave Woodrow Wilson a position of pre-eminent moral leadership in whatever peace conference would be held at war's end. Unselfishness, Christian magnanimity toward the conquered, hope for ethnic groups long engulfed in overpowering and antagonistic majorities, freedom for colonial peoples were all at the core of Wilson's idealistic proposals.[12]

The first five points began with an insistence on "open covenants openly arrived at." Here was a thoroughgoing shocker to traditional European diplomacy, conducted since the Roman era behind closed doors and never once in all the intervening centuries "openly arrived at." The New World had for the first time become a conscience to its parents, and the common man in both Old World and New first gasped at its audacity, then applauded its fresh, optimistic viewpoint. Whether the final European peace treaty would in truth be an open covenant openly arrived at was, to say the least, debatable in the context of traditional smoke-filled peace conference procedure. Yet here was a wind fresh enough to rout stale old smells and bring to the diplomacy of the Western world the ozone of true democratic discussion: "open covenants openly arrived at."

Point two was not as startling, yet again a fresh approach to ancient problems: it demanded complete freedom of the seas in peace and war. If this were accepted by the great powers, no longer could a nation declare unrestricted U-boat warfare on helpless, unwarned ships at sea, either belligerent or neutral. Freedom of the seas had been a traditional American cry since the War of 1812 when the British navy had mercilessly halted U. S. ships and kidnaped ("impressed" was then the phrase) American sailors for service on British vessels. Not only was the second point directed at the German U-boats' destruction of anything that floated—without warning and without regard for life or national flag—but it was also aimed at British sea snobbery, and the whole world knew it.

12. Woodrow Wilson Papers, Princeton, New Jersey.

Point three was again a startling proposal in Wilson's time: removal of economic barriers between nations for the freer flow of the world's goods and the economic betterment of mankind. Here was an unmistakable salvo at high tariffs and traditional border duties, which, during Wilson's Administration, had begun to fall in the United States for the first time since the Civil War. The President was talking not only to his military adversaries; he was talking not only to America's allies; he was now talking to America herself. And he had done all this without the advice and consent of the proud Senate whose Constitutional power to ratify encompassed all foreign treaties.

The next point involved reduction of world armaments to a level of simple domestic defensive needs. More startling disarmament proposals had been made at other European peace conferences, but there was one difference: Woodrow Wilson *meant* it! He wanted an end to traditional European armament, particularly armament for offensive war. If offensive armament did not exist, war itself might be made impossible. It was terribly logical in its simplicity and terribly effective at the moral level.

But, of the first five points, the fifth was the most powerful and, to America's allies, the most impertinent. It asked that the claims of colonial peoples be given immediate attention with special regard for local populations. It also asked that rival colonial claims, even prior claims, be redressed where there were clear cases of territorial banditry.

The effect of such an upstart proposal upon the British, the French, the Italians, the Germans, and all other traditional colonial powers can easily be imagined. The British Empire was then intact; it covered a quarter of the world's population and stretched from Australia and Singapore and Hong Kong and India in the East; Canada and Bermuda and the Barbados in the New World; to a dozen spots marked in red on the geography of Africa and the Middle East. Here was the chief executive of a former British colony daring to suggest that its dearest wartime ally painfully but honestly re-examine her vast colonial holdings not always acquired with the consent of the governed and quite often through undeniably naked aggression.

Though subtly pragmatic, the first five of the Fourteen Points reflected the very core of democratic philosophy on which the New World had been founded, unalterably an ingredient of the American Constitution and way of life. But policymakers in Europe were not yet wholly taken with the democratic system. The British had a king, the Germans had a king, the Austro-Hungarians had a king, the Italians had a king; there was nepotic monarchy in Scandinavia, Russia, Spain, Greece, the Netherlands, and Belgium, indeed almost everywhere on the European Continent except France. In such a context, Woodrow Wilson's five-point preamble had a shocking but magnificent popular effect. It gave him, and the freshman United States, undeniable moral leadership for the inevitable peace conference . . . or would have, had Wilson consulted the Senate or the Republican Party or even his own advisers—as Presidents should.

But the fact is that Woodrow Wilson did not have adequate intercourse with either the leaders of the Senate and the House or the Republican and Democratic organizations prior to the dramatic issuance of his unprecedented Fourteen Points. Herbert Hoover writes about it in a footnote to a page of *The Ordeal of Woodrow Wilson:*[13] "Mr. Wilson had no ghost writer. He composed the first draft of his addresses on his own typewriter. He sometimes submitted them to his colleagues for their opinions but he seldom adopted changes in his fundamental ideas."

How much did Colonel House have to do with the Fourteen Points? The Colonel had a tendency to assume latent credit for inspiring Wilson's major speeches, particularly the Fourteen Points address. But Mr. Hoover, who knew them both and knew them well, doesn't accept this claim. He points out that the ideas President Wilson proposed in the Fourteen Points can be found in Professor Wilson's teachings, whereas Colonel House nowhere in his own volumes shows such powers of ex-

13. Herbert Hoover, *The Ordeal of Woodrow Wilson* (New York, McGraw-Hill Book Company, Inc., 1958), footnote to p. 19.

pression, historical background, or philosophical direction. Some of the Fourteen Points, Mr. Hoover reminds us, are echoed expressions of the American Revolution and the Constitution, even to their wording. He goes on: "Colonel House was a useful adviser and a most capable negotiator for the President. But Woodrow Wilson was no Charlie McCarthy."[14]

It might have been better for him had he listened to the considered thoughts of others. Politically, he might even have saved his League of Nations, though the world, America in particular, wasn't yet ready for such a progressive concept of world government. Maybe it still isn't. At any rate, friends like Secretary of State Lansing; Bernard Baruch, Chairman of the War Industries Board; Frank I. Cobb, editor of the *New York World;* Dr. Harry Garfield, Fuel Administrator; and Vance Mc-Cormick, Chairman of the War Trade Board, urged Wilson later not to go to Paris in person, but to send a delegation composed of members of the Congress, the Senate Foreign Relations Committee, the Cabinet, and any other personal representation he might select. Mr. Hoover himself urged the President to think seriously about his decision to head the U. S. delegation personally, for Hoover was convinced that "Mr. Wilson's New World idealism would clash seriously with the Old World concepts of the Allied statesmen, and I feared that the President's dominant voice in creating world opinion would be stilled if he became involved in the inevitable restraints of personal negotiation."[15]

But the headstrong, willful personality traits that had gotten Woodrow Wilson quickly into deep trouble as president of Princeton and had made him, as he went it alone, the very prototype of the amateur politician, dictated that he go in person to any peace conference which might follow the not-yet-ended conflict in Europe.[16] Asking him not to go was like

14. *Ibid.*
15. *Ibid.*, p. 61.
16. Though Wilson is often said to have cared nothing for politics, the fact is that he got through Congress more reform legislation in his first term than had been pushed through that sometimes too deliberative body in the previous century. Wilson accomplished this, however, chiefly through skillful use of public opinion, by going directly to the people.

asking Babe Ruth to tell the manager to send someone else up to bat with the bases full.

The first five and the last of the Fourteen Points were, in the long run, most important because they were chiefly philosophical and outrageously new to European politics. There is no doubt in the minds of his contemporaries that they did much to bring about the effective defeat of the enemy and its disarmament, for his speech of January 8, 1918, and several subsequent addresses, before the peace table had so much as been arranged, firmly established terms of peace with both the Allies and the enemy.

All but one of the remaining nine points were specific sub-divisions of the first five principles. They involved territory held by Russia and future relations with Russia, in the throes of violent Bolshevik revolution; preservation of Belgian sovereignty; settlement of the question of Alsace-Lorraine; re-drawing of Italian boundaries with regard to ethnic minorities; a similar division of Austria-Hungary into its sub-nationalities; the redrawing of Balkan minorities into formally established national states; free navigation through the Dardanelles and drastic reduction of the Turkish empire; the establishment of an independent Poland with access to the sea; and, finally, provision for "a general association of nations."

It was, of course, point fourteen that hurt Wilson most deeply in his own country. In those days of slow communication a man living in Chicago had more than a thousand miles of defendable American soil between him and the Atlantic Ocean, and then the vast ocean beyond to Europe. These thousands of miles of geographical buffer made for natural isolation and violent pro-Americanism. Led by the *Chicago Tribune* and other anti-British, anti-internationalist publications, the parochial, pro-American philosophy of the West could not have been anything but what it was—a predominant emotion of an enormous segment of the American electorate.

When the fourteenth point hit the headlines the gage was cast and the *Chicago Tribune* was only one of many to take immediate issue. Since Wilson had consulted few elected representatives in the House or Senate as to the wording or philo-

sophical merit of his startling proposals, friend and foe alike
were unprepared. In such circumstances, his opposition was
off to an unbeatable headstart.

Reading his books and perusing his startling legislative
record in Trenton and Washington, the objective reporter is
forced to conclude that Woodrow Wilson heartily welcomed
America's abandonment of her traditional isolation through her
first European war, bloody and terrible though it must have
been to the sensitive humanitarian in the White House. The
Chinese have many words with two meanings: one of these is
crisis which is also the word for *opportunity*. Woodrow Wilson
saw in the crisis of America's political adolescence the opportunity for America's political manhood. And to him political
manhood had to include a League of Nations, with America its
standard-bearer in a new and democratic world society.

It is interesting to note that Wilson had long hesitated announcing his Fourteen Points before January 8, 1918, fearing
antagonisms overseas. He was eager to put out his manifesto
before Lloyd George of Britain and Clemenceau of France
could sabotage or forestall it.[17] The timing of the release of
the Fourteen Points called for cables to both governments and
to America's other allies. Then, suddenly, on January 5, as Wilson was discussing the timing of his Fourteen Points speech
with Colonel House, Lloyd George broke the story, so to speak,
with an address on British war aims to a trade union delegation in London. Wilson wasn't notified. It made him furious.
Arthur Walworth writes of it:[18]

> When Wilson learned that Lloyd George had spoken with-
> out consulting him, both his morality and his pride were
> offended. Not only had the prime minister differed in prin-
> ciple by insisting that Germany pay reparations, but by pro-
> posing almost all of the President's Fourteen Points he
> seemed to have pirated the ideas that Wilson had set down
> with great pains. Wilson, the man of literary property,
> seemed to forget the biblical truth that his father had

17. Arthur Walworth, *Woodrow Wilson* (New York, Longmans,
Green and Company, 1958), p. 150.

18. *Ibid.*, p. 151.

preached but had often overlooked—that no servant of the Lord had light of his own, but merely bore witness to the "heavenly light." The ambition to seize the pulpit of peace for himself and to give leadership to his own people in serving the world still burned strongly in the prophet in the White House. He was no more inclined than he had been at the age of thirty to be any man's follower in a matter on which he felt that he had qualified himself to speak.

Wilson had thought that it would in consequence be impossible for him to make his Fourteen Points public, but Colonel House argued that Lloyd George had simply cleared the air and made it the more necessary to speak.

This explains in part why Wilson appeared to be so precipitous in his famous pronunciamento. It is possible that, had Lloyd George not spoken in London on January 5, Wilson might have consulted more Republican leaders, more Democratic members of the Foreign Relations Committee, more political figures in both houses and parties before making his Fourteen Points, which might, in consequence, have been edited and altered. But when the Prime Minister threatened to steal his thunder, Woodrow Wilson the man could wait no longer. It wasn't in his nature to take back seats, particularly in the field of idealistic statesmanship. Yet, while the isolationist press either snubbed his utterances or decried them, their immediate practical effect in Europe and in America was slight, though their historical significance was immense.

Theodore Roosevelt soon went to war against the Fourteen Points, for he realized at once that they constituted a campaign document of incalculable importance. Congress was up for re-election in November, 1918; the Republicans eventually won majorities in both houses. That Wilson's Fourteen Points influenced the Congressional vote of isolationist mid-America there cannot from the record be the slightest doubt.

Wilson said in October that a Republican victory would be interpreted on the other side of the water as a "repudiation of my leadership."[19] Theodore Roosevelt immediately sent tele-

19. *Ibid.*, p. 202.

grams to influential Senators urging that the Senate declare itself against adopting the Fourteen Points and even wrote to Senator Henry Cabot Lodge: "I am glad that Wilson has come out in the open. I fear Judas most when he can cloak his activities behind treacherous make-believe of nonpartisanship."[20] The old Republican warrior then made several public speeches in which he charged that Wilson was placing support for himself above loyalty to the nation, that this was not "the President's personal war," a topic on which T.R., of all then living statesmen, was the undoubted expert. The Fourteen Points even united Roosevelt and Taft, who made a joint statement on the evils of partisanship in the prosecution of any military campaign and the disloyalty of any President who would do such a wicked thing.

Unknown to the Allied side, the German General Staff had on August 14, 1918, confessed to their Kaiser that the fatherland's cause was forlorn, that the Austrians were on the verge of suing for a separate peace, that even the departure of Russia from the Allied ranks (because of the Bolshevik revolution) could not long forestall the end. Morale grew so low in the German army that by September General von Hindenburg voiced the opinion that the need for peace negotiation was "immediate."

Colonel House was dispatched by Wilson to Europe as soon as these facts had become obvious even to the Allies, and the good Colonel went about the Continent making personal friendships, soothing suspicions, allaying fears, sensing currents of ambition, greed, jealousy, and aggrandizement that flowed among Allied statesmen.

In Europe it immediately became obvious to Colonel House that the Fourteen Points, when laid before the Allied premiers for discussion, could not be pulled through by diplomatic trading alone.[21] Lloyd George had already stated serious reservations to two of the fourteen; Clemenceau was about to disclose France's objections to others. So Colonel House—whose

20. *Ibid.,* p. 203.
21. *Ibid.,* p. 181.

shrewd Texas statesmanship usually inhibited such bluntness—
did what he seldom did in public life. He stated baldly to his
friend Clemenceau that, if the Allied leaders in Europe ob-
jected wholeheartedly to Wilson's principles, he would immediately advise the President to lay all the facts before the
American Congress in a hearing open to the press and ask
whether the American people should continue to fight for old
European peace terms or make a separate peace with the
Kaiser.[22]

The effect on Wilson's allied counterparts was electric and
delighted Wilson who cabled House: "I am proud of the way
you are handling things." The effect on Germany was equally
potent, for it soon became public knowledge that Wilson's
liberal approach to peace now had brought the offensive to
the Western side. Although the Allies would eventually have
been able to liquidate or erode the German military force, still
incredibly formidable after four years of butchery, the President's Fourteen Points quickly vitiated much of the German
will to persevere.[23]

On October 6, 1918, with the reluctant consent of the Junkers
generals, a new German chancellery dispatched a note to the
President accepting the Fourteen Points as a basis for peace
negotiations and privately suggesting an armistice. In the exchange that followed, the President struck a posture charitable
enough to lead the Germans on, yet force them to total surrender.[24] With each new response in the exchange, Woodrow
Wilson's world stature rose; the old cliché of European power
politics shuddered from the idealistic dreamer's New World
assault. As the British had gagged at freedom of the seas and
the French at the absence of reparations payments, the entire
European diplomatic community was taken aback at the
audacity of an upstart American practically negotiating single-
handed an armistice with the detestable Hun. Yet this approximated the truth; and when, on November 11, the Armistice

22. *Ibid.*, p. 195.
23. John Morton Blum, *Woodrow Wilson and the Politics of
Morality* (Boston, Little Brown and Company, 1956), p. 149.
24. *Ibid.*

was announced by the Western powers, they pledged to make
a peace based on those selfsame Fourteen Points, with the reservations noted.

During the war, the coalition which was the Democratic
Party (it has sometimes been a preposterous and precarious
coalition in U. S. history) had begun to crumble and eventually
to fall apart completely. The liberal dynamite of 1912 was
gone, the progressivism of 1916 had all but vanished, the middle class groaned under high war taxes, the Midwestern farmer
thought he was getting too little for his wheat, the cities missed
their beer and detested the draft, the intellectual fussed about
Wilson's disappointing performance in civil liberties, the Republicans under Will Hays were beginning to close ranks, and
wheatless, meatless, sugarless days were becoming downright
distasteful in a spoiled young nation that had never had to
worry for long about overflowing food and comfort since the
Civil War, which few living could remember. Families without
men around were yet another irritating thorn.

But worst of all for the Democratic Party was the personality habit pattern of the President. A political egotist, a
"loner," an idealist, habitually willful, more than ever impatient
with local politics and the insipidly stupid but necessary protocol, Wilson had publicly stated with gross inaccuracy and
condescension that politics was adjourned. The Republican
Congressional victory of November, 1918, and its subsequent
assault on Wilson's foreign policy changed the President's
mind. He had refused to campaign, to endorse Democratic
candidates from coast to coast with his prestige and personality
at a time when he thought other items more important. He
could not now have made a worse mistake. He was becoming
partisan too late.

The Republicans immediately began to assault his entire
foreign policy on grounds that he alone would be responsible
for a "peace without victory." This sentiment, echoed of course
in London, Paris, and Rome, which were understandably
thirsty for revenge and total triumph, had the effect at home
of questioning Wilson's entire political leadership, domestic as

well as foreign. Teddy Roosevelt demanded that peace be dictated to the defeated through "hammering guns . . . not clicking typewriters." Democrats in Congress soon picked up the refrain; next the Cabinet; then the Democratic National Committee; finally the press of the nation joined in the "hate Germany" obsession.

The President tried his best to make a concession to understandable war's-end emotions by increasing the severity of his notes to Berlin, yet he never asked for the unconditional, prostrate surrender with staggering reparations and total dismemberment of Germany that frightened Democrats demanded. To his credit he did not give in or temporize. His splendid purpose, his exquisite idealism, his hope for a world made safe for democracy which must now surely germinate in the kingdoms of Europe never for an instant wavered at a time when a lesser man might well have caved in. He could write: "God has in His good pleasure given us peace. It has not come as a mere cessation of arms, a mere relief from the strain and tragedy of war. It has come as a great triumph for right." He had believed from the day of his first faith in man's ability to govern himself that Christian democracy was a viable principle by which to live, not a welcome mat to be taken in with the first few drops of rain. He had believed in it in the beginning; he believed it still without compromise.

John Morton Blum says a penetrating and remarkable thing about the Wilson mind of 1918–1919:[25]

> Fixed on its notable end, the one-track mind sensed less and less its growing isolation. Election Day in 1918 left no impression. Increasingly thereafter conscience made a coward of resilience. The pace, already faltering, was broken. The President went one way; his Congress, his constituency, indeed his world, another, until he stood at last alone.

With the Armistice signed, Wilson faced twin tasks more difficult than any he had ever faced before, and with less physical strength and political backing to sustain him.[26] First

25. Blum, *op. cit.*, p. 158.
26. Col. Edmund W. Starling wrote, with the late Thomas Sugrue, a book about life in the White House, where Starling was on the security

he must cope with America's wartime allies, nations deci-
mated, tortured, hurt by and angry at an aggressive, brutal
enemy of four bloody years of interminable trench warfare.
Whatever he might be able to do with the crafty old statesmen
of ancient and now victorious states he would then have to get
somehow ratified by a two-thirds vote of the United States
Senate, now in Republican hands.

When he said that the war had been won solely by the
inspiration of democratic ideas he was talking errant nonsense,
so far as Britain and France were concerned. Nor would the
rest of the Western world agree with him that there was "a
great wind of moral force moving through the world, and every
man who opposes . . . that wind will go down in disgrace."
This was patronizing gibberish to men like Lloyd George,
Clemenceau, Orlando, and the traditional governments they
reflected.

A man capable of saying wonderfully naïve things on the
eve of a world peace conference would also be capable of
amazing pragmatic error; and Wilson was capable of both.
He chose neither a member of the United States Senate, without whose consent no treaty could be ratified, nor any active
member of the opposition party to accompany him to Paris.
He would brook no slightest dissent, mild as it might be, from
his master plan. He could not forgive Theodore Roosevelt nor
the Republicans for attacking his foreign policy during the
recent campaign. He began to believe that the peace conference to which he was moving in person was peculiarly his own
and had little or no relationship with anything or anyone else.
It is perhaps not too much to say that his public statements
of 1918–1919 suggest an aberration that he had invented democracy and wanted no one else's advice on or claim to its
origins.

---

staff, called *Starling of the White House* (New York, Simon and
Schuster, Inc., 1946), in which Starling says that Wilson's temper was
becoming increasingly short at this time. Once, on a golf course, a
boy nearby cupped his hands to his mouth and yelled like an Indian
just as Wilson was addressing his ball. Disgusted, the President said:
"That boy must be training to be a Senator. He's always making a noise
with his mouth and not saying anything."

Who might have gone to Paris with Woodrow Wilson? The newly constituted Republican Senate had chosen Senator Henry Cabot Lodge as its Foreign Relations Committee chairman but Lodge was, of all people, least eligible in Wilson's mind to accompany him anywhere. It is said that he left the Senator cooling his heels for hours in a White House waiting room and that Lodge eventually got up and left without seeing the President—at a time when Wilson needed every ounce of support he could muster for his pet project. Lodge had lately been an acidulous critic of Wilson's internationalism, a close friend of T.R., a thoroughgoing economic conservative, and to Wilson, an intolerant partisan. Yet Senator Lodge might have been friendly to ratification of peace terms he had helped to frame; as chairman of the powerful Foreign Relations Committee he was precisely the last man in Washington a Chief Executive should have snubbed in the circumstances.

But if Lodge had been impossible for Wilson to swallow, there were others who might have helped modify the adamant position the Republican-controlled Senate eventually took on the peace treaty. There was a possibility in the brilliant Elihu Root, once Secretary of State under T.R. and a patriot of less partisanship than most, a former Senator from New York with plenty of friends in the Senate chamber, a famous international lawyer and a specialist on world arbitration. Yet Wilson spurned him, apparently dismissing him in such patronizing terms that the President's faint praise eventually found its way to Root himself and set up yet another needless roadblock to ratification.

There was also William Jennings Bryan, Wilson's first Secretary of State, whose training in international law was, to say the least, questionable but who still possessed a certain political magic on The Hill. Or William Howard Taft, ex-President and Supreme Court Justice, a man of deep integrity, a fine legal mind, and an outspoken advocate of an active international community of nations to insure the peace. But Taft was a Republican and had said, Wilson thought, some nasty things during the 1918 campaign. Wilson simply wouldn't have Taft on his team.

There were a few others, among them astute and friendly Senators, not in any way inimical to the tremendous new idea of a world co-operation and undoubtedly eager to cash in on whatever headlines Wilson would make abroad. But the President couldn't see them and, in point of fact, rarely spoke about such matters with anyone now except Colonel House and Secretary of State Lansing.

Woodrow Wilson quickly settled upon associate delegates from whom he could expect little more than sycophancy, or at least this was the way his Paris delegation appeared to the Republicans. Colonel House and Secretary Lansing would, of course, be there. House was indispensable. Lansing could not be overlooked because he was technically the President's adviser on foreign policy and his advice could, of course, be disregarded since he owed his tenure to the man he was advising. Henry White would go along, a quiet, gentlemanly career diplomat whom Wilson trusted and who was, at least nominally, a Republican, though he had taken little or no part in domestic politics. General Tasker H. Bliss, a military expert of untapped but formidable talent, joined the party. And, secretaries and aides aside, this made up Wilson's delegation!

John Blum points out that the President's disdain of public opinion equaled his aloofness from The Hill and pragmatic politics.[27]

> Only the newspapers could continuously interpret his negotiations in Europe to the American people; he had, as he knew, no facility in dealing with the press; but for his official press representative in Paris he chose George Creel, whose wartime work had seemed to many journalists a form of censorship. Wilson had to agree, furthermore, to holding the important meetings of the conference in secret. This disturbed the journalists, who had mistakenly assumed that open diplomacy meant public negotiation. Unwilling to discuss his unsuccessful opposition to the secrecy imposed, Wilson further alienated the press by making consistently uninformative his official news releases. He simply saw no need to explain or justify himself.

27. Blum, *op. cit.*, p. 161.

The Treaty of Versailles was, then, molded from the American point of view almost single-handed by a naïve professor of political science who had neglected to take Congressional representatives with him. It was created in an atmosphere of personality politics from the ego of one American mind.

The spirit of his Fourteen Points was to be occasionally discernible in the Treaty of Versailles. The Treaty would eventually define as nearly as it could ethnological groupings on the map of Europe. With minor reservations, Wilson's hope for the self-determination and independence of small, indigenous nations carved from kingdoms was fulfilled. As he had forecast, the Covenant of the League of Nations would be an indispensable part of the Treaty and, to him, "the hope of the world."

The Treaty of Versailles was one of five peace treaties ending World War I, but it was the most important because it dealt largely with Germany whereas the other four disposed of Austria, Hungary, Bulgaria, and Turkey. Germany was never consulted openly during the making of the Treaty of Versailles and, when it had been written, the Germans were told simply to sign it—or else.

Although Wilson's Fourteen Points were essentially sacrificed to Old World hates and precedent, to power politics far beyond the strength of the President to withstand, his main objective—a League of Nations—became part and parcel of the Treaty. Reparations payments by Germany, the most ruinous demands of the Treaty, were to be suspended in 1931 largely at the insistence of President Hoover. And many hundreds of volumes have been written to say that the Treaty was either too harsh, too soft, or relatively just in its dealings with the defeated and the long downtrodden. No one can ever come near the truth of it.

The League of Nations, then, became the focal point for hardening Republican opposition to Wilson and all his works. It was on this ground, with growing isolationist support, that the great post-Treaty battle was fought out.

On a quick trip back to the States early in 1919 to attend to domestic affairs, the President was confronted with a devastating document, the handiwork chiefly of Henry Cabot Lodge. Senator Lodge revealed the day before Wilson was to return to Paris a resolution signed by thirty-seven Republican Senators, four more than the thirty-three votes needed to sabotage ratification of any foreign treaty.

The resolution or memorandum or "round robin," as it was variously called, declared that the Covenant as it stood was unacceptable to the Republican Senators and that major reservations would have to be adopted before these thirty-seven Senators could see their way clear to ratifying any treaty containing the Wilsonian brand of League. It was too late now to compromise, though Wilson desperately tried. His was an unpopular cause in isolationist America; he had played his cards very badly indeed.

In the two months of his first stay in Europe, Woodrow Wilson had been acclaimed its savior. His picture had hung everywhere with American bunting draped about it: "Vive Wilson!" had welcomed him in every language in every city of Western Europe. He had had a Messiah's welcome when he first came. Now he was returning to cruel reality.

The torment began when he was in Washington. First there was Senator Lodge's defiant "round robin," which was still to be met. Then there were reports from Paris that his staff had conspired in his absence to separate the Covenant from the Treaty, the League of Nations from peace with Germany. He had insisted they were inseparable and could not be negotiated apart. In his absence, Clemenceau and Lloyd George (or as Colonel House called him, "George") had reverted to type. Orlando of Italy was making imperialistic demands. The French were insisting on an independent republic of the Rhineland, French rights in Syria, and other geographical concessions. The British wanted most of the other Arab states, and the Italians were anticipating possessions promised them in the secret Pact of London.

This Pact of London (often mistakenly called the Treaty of London) was one more diabolical roadblock against Wilson's idealism. A maze of secret arrangements and treaties had been entered into by the Allied forces prior to America's entry into

the war. If these treaties were to be respected, Wilson's Fourteen Points would be all but nullified. One of these secret
treaties was the Pact of London, signed privately in 1915 by
Britain, France, and Italy, assuring Italy that, if she entered the
war on the Allied side, the Trentino, the Brenner Pass, Istria,
Trieste, parts of Dalmatia, some Adriatic islands, and a share
of Anatolia would be hers. These territories were defined and
delimited in the Pact of London with what Herbert Hoover
calls "the precision of a New England farm."[28]

The secret treaties, particularly the Pact of London, now
rose to haunt Wilson, for Italy had, in his absence, insisted
privately that the secret contract of 1915 be implemented and
if France and Britain lived up to its terms, as they were legally
bound to do, self-determination of the Adriatic peoples—the
Yugoslavs—was a dead issue. America had not, of course,
been a signatory to any of the secret treaties which had been
agreed to long before U. S. entry. It is even possible that the
precise contents of the Pact of London were unknown to Wilson, though U. S. intelligence services were undoubtedly aware
of it. Added to this dilemma was fresh insistence, in Wilson's
absence, on the heaviest of reparations from the Germans,
something the Fourteen Points had promised would not
happen.

As the President's ship, the *George Washington,* reached the
French coast, Colonel House came aboard and talked until
midnight. Mrs. Wilson reports the effect on her already apprehensive husband:[29]

> I heard my husband's door open and the Colonel take his
> leave. I opened the door connecting our rooms. Woodrow
> was standing. The change in his appearance shocked me. He
> seemed to have aged ten years, and his jaw was set in that
> way it had when he was making super-human effort to con-
> trol himself.
>
> I asked, "What's the matter? What has happened?" He
> said: "House has given away everything I had won before
> we left Paris. He has compromised on every side, and so I

28. Hoover, *op. cit.,* p. 78.
29. *Ibid.,* p. 196.

have to start all over again and this time it will be harder . . .
he has yielded until there is nothing left."

From the hour of his return to Europe, Wilson's health and
hope began to go downhill. Negotiations went from bad to
worse, from worse to hopeless, then climbed tantalizingly up
the glass hill again, only to slide back. Old European hatreds
rose like cork to the surface, refusing to stay down.

On April 3, after a fortnight of atmospheric malignancy, the
President came down with the flu. It soon infected his prostate
and bladder, although on the word of his physician, Admiral
Grayson, it was in no way connected with his paralytic stroke
five months later. Under the terrible strain of anxiety and unending frustration, fatigue beyond human limits, the man who
had brought a stomach pump to the White House, whose frail
body had never been able to function properly on less than
nine hours' rest per night, broke in health, never fully to re-
cover.

Early in April the ill President called for the *George Washington* to take him home again. When this became public
knowledge, the high hopes he had held for a democratic
Europe melted like sand castles in the surf. Though his health
improved sufficiently to cancel the April sailing, the President
was never able to regain the tactical stature he had had on his
triumphant first arrival.

A further woe now struck his idealistic statesmanship. The
treaty was harsh and scarcely the democratic instrument he
had forecast. But to make things worse, Clemenceau and
Lloyd George were now insisting that the blockade of Germany be renewed until the Germans were forced by starvation
and economic despair to sign the peace treaty as it stood. This
bloodthirsty coercion, understandable in men whose sons and
gold had perished by the millions against the tyranny of a
repeating aggressor, Wilson could not stomach. Yet, in the
end, he was forced to sign his name to a compromise com-
muniqué of the Supreme Council of Allied Powers stating that
resumption of the blockade would not be made "without a
decision from the Council." It must have been the most galling
of his many compromises.

The German delegation was bluntly told that, for all practical purposes, it must sign or suffer the consequences. The Germans replied, after careful perusal, that they could not in all conscience sign something as degrading as the terms handed them; that they had appealed for an armistice on the President's false promises of fair, democratic treatment. Rather than become traitors to the fatherland, the German delegation resigned en masse on June 20.

But a new German delegation appeared on June 28 and this new set of ministers came to the Hall of Mirrors at Versailles and signed away tens of billions of dollars in reparations payments, all of Germany's overseas possessions and mandates, as well as what was left of her strength and honor. The Hun had had it coming; now the Hun was getting it, old-style. The only fragment of the mirror of democracy lay in the formation of the President's dream: a League of Nations. This he must now return to his native land to defend and save from domestic politics.

Wilson left France forever on June 28, 1919, arriving in New York on July 8. When he landed he began at once to plan a nation-wide crusade to ratify a treaty over which the Senate was already in full and acrimonious debate.

While formal submission of the Treaty to the Senate took place July 10, Wilson's major effort began in September when he undertook his cross-country battle for ratification. He would take it to the people, for he had always believed in the common sense of the common people; they would now sustain him if their elected representatives would not. Stubborn to the end, the Scotch-Irish blood had one more battle left; it would be the most stirring, the most courageous, and the most pathetic battle of his fading life, which it was to cost him.

The League of Nations was continuously and violently attacked on the floor of the Senate throughout the spring, summer, and early fall of 1919. Lodge was a ringleader; as his team seemed more and more likely to win the final vote he slowly gained adherents, even among Democrats. They could feel the country's progressive antagonism to Wilson, to internationalism and all its works; it was a reaction against far-from-dead power politics and secret diplomacy of Europe, which had won the decisive rounds at Paris. Isolationism, traditional in America, was reasserting itself: Wilson was playing for his life's highest stakes with a stacked deck.

On September 25, 1919, the President was making his crusade back from the Pacific Coast when suddenly he collapsed at Pueblo, Colorado. The courageous battle was over. Unlike the candor attached to President Eisenhower's later heart attack, ileitis, and stroke, President Wilson's doctor and press secretary did not take the public into their confidence. Mystery, confusion, misunderstanding, and even misrepresentation marked the paralytic stroke with which the slight old man was now seized.

Colonel House wrote in his diary on October 21, 1919, that the President's condition was such that no one was seeing him except his physician and Mrs. Wilson.[30] This date was almost a month after the stroke; yet no mention of the true nature of the illness had yet been made to a hushed but inquisitive press and an even more curious Senate. The President's entire left side was now all but useless.

Three months after the seizure, House was to write privately again that the President "is much sicker than the public is led to believe." A Thanksgiving proclamation went into the sick room via Mrs. Wilson and came back with a signature almost illegible. David Lawrence states that the sick man extracted a promise from those closest to him that his condition would never be made public so long as he was President of the United States.[31] In the context this was an impossible assignment.

Incredibly, the true severity of his illness did not become public knowledge until long afterward and not official until Wilson was no longer in the White House. Woodrow Wilson

30. Col. Starling later wrote: "When he was to go for a ride, some of us [Secret Service] organized a group to stand at the gate as he returned, and we told them to cheer as he passed through. The first time it happened, when we went to lift him from the car after driving around to the back, there were tears in his eyes. 'You see,' he said to Mrs. Wilson, 'they still love me!' "

31. David Lawrence, *The True Story of Woodrow Wilson* (Garden City, Doubleday and Company, Inc., 1924), p. 290.

never recovered from the stroke. He lingered in the torment of frustration, physical and mental, until February 3, 1924.

The Senate voted on the Treaty of Versailles on November 19, 1919; the motion for unconditional ratification failed by seven votes of the necessary two-thirds.[32] Another vote on March 19, 1920, changed little, even with Senatorial reservations abhorrent to the stricken President. The Senate never ratified the Treaty, the only nation of any consequence to refuse.

On January 10, 1920, the League of Nations opened for business in Geneva without the United States, and on April 18, 1946, it disbanded, replaced by a stronger and more practical policing organization, the United Nations. It is doubtful if the UN as it is today could have existed without the idealistic dream and its partial fulfillment in the League. Yet the one major power to repudiate that dream was Woodrow Wilson's own country.

That the President himself was deeply responsible cannot be denied. For he had overlooked a fundamental tenet of the Presidency as true as any other—that a President does not work in an executive vacuum but in a complicated relationship between the people on the one hand and the legislature on the other; that politics, an irrevocable part and parcel of the presidential office, is a fact painfully and perennially true, whether the man in the White House likes it or not.

32. Looking back to the time, the wonder is that ratification came as close as seven votes, a tribute to Wilson's personal standing.

Franklin Roosevelt'ʿ

MARCH 4, 1933, was a Saturday, misty and raw with a seasonal wind and sullen sky. But sky and wind were nowhere as forbidding as the state of the nation. Panic gripped the financial community. No one's money seemed safe. So many millions were out of work that one family in two was directly affected. Trade was as close to a complete standstill as trade can get, the United States as near economic collapse as a growing young country can become and not find itself in physical revolution. This was indeed a cold and forbidding inauguration of a President of the United States.

With the economic and social motors groaning toward a breakdown, there were few Americans indeed who could foresee what it would mean to swear in the good-looking man who had to wear steel braces to stand for his inaugural. What the country could not know was that this man who now took the sacred oath was to accomplish his own kind of bloodless revolution, far more effective and drastic than anything America had seen in her short term of almost uninterrupted capitalistic-industrial expansion. What the terrified capitalist-financiers pleading with the new President could not possibly imagine was how this one individual would irrevocably and drastically change their world, without ignoring a single democratic rule or precept during the unprecedented legislative process. What no one, not even Franklin Delano Roosevelt himself, knew at this historic moment was that his first hundred days in the White House would be the most amazing, prolific, fecund,

216

9

Amazing Hundred Days

and revolutionary period of concentrated social and economic reform in the history of his people. After his tenure as Chief Executive, his country would never be the same again.

March 4, 1933, was the last of the traditional March inaugurals. January 20 would soon replace the later date, as the lame duck Congress would soon be replaced as an antique. The new President was saying to the traditional ceremony: "The only thing we have to fear is fear itself." This was undeniable. Like the old children's card game in which there used to be two cards in the same set, one marked "Confidence Impaired" and the other "Confidence Restored," the tall, handsome orator was now saying that prosperity or depression were largely matters of confidence. Wealth was in one way only the rapidity of circulation; the number of times money changed hands in a calendar month showed how freely it was being spent and whether there was or wasn't confidence in the future. Confidence had been impaired; the new President knew that somehow confidence must now be restored to lubricate the machinery and start the wheels turning again.

If impaired confidence could be changed to restored confidence, the lubrication of hope might set people to buying again, taking normal business risks, stop their hoarding of gold. The business cycle might begin to improve after three and a half ghastly Depression years.

"This nation asks for action, and action now . . ." rang the voice. A cheer went up from those present and a small warmth stirred in the nation shocked to economic immobility, frozen by impaired confidence and fear.

Throughout the United States, millions of Americans were listening to an inauguration over a crazy gadget called the radio, in its adolescence but soon of enormous political use to the very voice they were now hearing. His fireside chats would usher in a whole new means of admirable political communion. The golden baritone, the impeccable delivery, the ingratiating command of spoken language (though his speeches would not read as well as they sounded) were already beginning to provide a lubrication of hope in a stricken, frozen, almost completely paralyzed American economy as near violent revolution as capitalistic countries can get before someone declares martial law. Indeed, martial law had already been declared among normally prudent Midwestern farmers who would rather dump their milk than sell it for a few pennies a gallon.

Half a million of those who listened by radio to the new President or read in the papers of his promise of action now, after months and months of rank inaction, sat down in the next few hours and wrote him personal letters addressed to the White House. Eleanor Roosevelt found the inaugural "very very solemn and a little terrifying" but those 500,000 who wrote the new President letters were for the most part less realistic since they knew less about the man they had elected who was, as most Presidents are in their maiden months, a new leader not yet unfrocked by time and record.

"In this dedication of a nation we humbly ask the blessing of God," said the golden voice over the radio. "May He protect each and every one of us. May He guide me in the days to come."

While the trumpets' flourish was still fresh in memory and the huge inaugural parade was being shown in the nation's newsreels, these letters from American humanity kept pouring in to the White House by trucksful:

Yours is the first opportunity to carve a name in the halls of immortals beside Jesus.

People are looking to you almost as they look to God.

It seemed to give the people, as well as myself, a new hold upon life.

Your human feeling for all of us in your address is just wonderful.

God bless you and yours. We are now on the road again.

At last we have a leader who knows what it is to lead.

It was the finest thing this side of heaven.

Eleanor Roosevelt shuddered that her husband got his biggest hand when he said he might have to assume wartime powers to solve the nation's fantastic economic problems. She knew her husband's strengths and weaknesses, his vast lack of pragmatic economic knowledge (he had failed in several busines enterprises), and her Theodore Roosevelt blood gave her a conservative reverence for the democratic process not even desperate economic panic could entirely erase.

Who was the man who now stood on the inaugural platform? What sort of person, what kind of background, what roots of precedent were there to bend the twig? Franklin Delano Roosevelt was a relative of T.R. (as was his wife), a man of Dutch ancestry, a native of Hyde Park, New York, where his family had been landed gentry ever since Dutchess County had been so properly named. An only child, Franklin had been born when his father was fifty-four years of age, twenty-six years older than his mother; young Franklin was, consequently, so thoroughly spoiled that in Groton he was to many of his young associates a downright prig. Harvard followed, then law school, during which period he had married the scarcely beautiful but bright Eleanor Roosevelt, his cousin.

The Roosevelts had been unhesitatingly drawn to politics. From the first they lived in an atmosphere of the idea, particularly the political idea. In 1910 Franklin was elected to the New York State Senate, where he led one battle after another against Tammany Hall and soon found himself a leader of the independent Democrats in New York State. He fought for Woodrow Wilson's candidacy in 1912, and Wilson appointed him Assistant Secretary of the Navy. He became the Democratic candidate for Vice-President in 1920 with James Cox of Ohio. They lost badly to Harding's tidal wave of Republican "normalcy," a reaction against war, the internationalist Wilson, and his bloody battle for the League of Nations.

The following August at Campobello, New Brunswick, Canada, F.D.R. was suddenly stricken with infantile paralysis which paralyzed him from the hips down. Only by courageous and determined effort did he regain some use of his legs; but he never again walked unaided. At the 1924 and 1928 Democratic National Conventions he placed the name of Alfred E. Smith, the Governor of New York, in nomination. Smith made it in 1928 only to lose to Herbert Hoover, at least in part because Smith was a Catholic and an anti-Prohibitionist. But while Smith was losing nationally, Franklin Roosevelt was winning the Governorship of New York as Smith's successor. He was re-elected in 1930; by 1932 he was himself a foremost candidate for the Democratic presidential nomination, though his record as Governor was relatively undistinguished until the legislative hearing of charges of Tammany corruption which led to the resignation of Jimmy Walker as Mayor of New York.

As Governor, Roosevelt presided over the Walker hearing and it seemed at first that the Governor feared Tammany's power in an election year, for little or no aid and comfort was given those who sought to expose Walker or Tammany's patent misrule. Suddenly, however, the dapper little New York Mayor admitted that he had as much as misappropriated certain funds for which he could not account and Roosevelt asked him if he didn't think that was wrongdoing.

"Well," Mayor Walker admitted, "it may have been unethical."

"But Mr. Mayor," said Franklin D. Roosevelt, "what is unethical *is wrong.*"

Walker resigned that night, September 1, 1932. The Governor had defied Tammany. From that moment on F.D.R. was a man marked for destiny. He had arrogantly snubbed the power of Tammany Hall, which had controlled almost a hun-

dred votes in that summer's Democratic National Convention.
He had stood on the side of the angels and he had won.

Like Cleveland and T.R. before him, his reform record in
the face of Tammany Hall as a Democratic Governor of New
York had shot him to the top as a favorite for larger matters.
(William G. McAdoo, Woodrow Wilson's son-in-law, had
switched from John N. Garner of Texas to F.D.R. at the convention, and Smith had fumed while Roosevelt was nominated.)

It is difficult to keep remembering always that Franklin D.
Roosevelt was a cripple from his early manhood and that he
never walked unaided after 1921. For his amazing energy
began to show itself to the nation in the hour of his nomination when he flew to Chicago to accept the honor, rather than
be notified officially at home, as had been the custom. He was
the first presidential nominee to fly in a plane.

The Wall Street stock crash of October, 1929, had by the fall
of 1932 fused a far deeper business depression than America
had ever undergone before. Since Herbert Hoover had been
President throughout this period, he was blamed for most of
it at an emotional pitch seldom reached by the ordinarily
placid American. To put it bluntly, a large segment of the
country hated Herbert Hoover with all its being and did not
hesitate to tell him so. This was not a partisan matter, moreover; if a Republican in Centerville, Illinois, had lost his life
savings and his livelihood, he could scarcely be blamed for
believing that President Hoover was less than a genius and
for becoming caustic about it.

In addition, Hoover kept referring to Prohibition of legal
liquor, including light wines and beer, as "that noble experiment," but by no means promised to repeal it if re-elected.
Roosevelt, on the other hand, made no bones about his dislike
for Prohibition and forecast its quick repeal after November. If
any political weight had been required to tip the scale in his
behalf this was more than enough. The Iowa Quaker simply
couldn't have won in the circumstances. Every move he made
seemed inept and gauche.

With victory inevitable, Roosevelt did not campaign as vigorously as contemporary memory would have us believe. Looking back at the printed record, he seems to have taken few renegade stands on big issues of the day, preferring instead to generalize on his "New Deal," a persuasive appeal to the unfortunate, the underdog, the "average man" (whoever he was), the disenchanted, and the thirsty.

The rank smell of rot and stagnation deepening over the capitalistic system of free enterprise in America and the Western world progressively reduced President Hoover's chances. He had the misfortune to be working with a hostile Democratic Congress from 1930 on. He was also the victim of his own training and personality. Intelligent and well educated, Hoover possessed an engineer's mind and a wealthy man's economic outlook. Since his wealth had been earned (while Roosevelt's had been handed to him), the ironically perverse logic of human nature decreed that F.D.R. would have more regard for those who earned their living than would the self-made Hoover, who was incapable of apostasy.

Whatever kindliness and friendship had ever existed between President Hoover and F.D.R. quickly fell apart as the campaign progressed.[1] The two had known each other for many years, in a joint crusade during World War I and the reconstruction of Europe that had made Hoover a world-famous humanitarian. Admiration which had led F.D.R. to advocate Herbert Hoover for President in 1920 was by 1932 thoroughly vitiated. Governor Roosevelt had, however, a very private reason for disliking the man now President of the United States and his election opponent, or he thought he had.

In the spring of 1932, President Hoover had invited the annual Governor's conference at Richmond to dine at the White House. The spring of 1932 had been Roosevelt's critical time in the search for Chicago delegates, and one of the chief arguments against his candidacy was that he had had polio and wasn't physically up to the demanding job of being President. Knowing how long it took F.D.R. to move from an auto-

1. Frank B. Freidel, *Franklin D. Roosevelt*, Vol. III (Boston, Little, Brown and Company, 1956), p. 323.

mobile, up steps, or any distance at all under his own locomotion, the Roosevelts arrived quite early at the White House. With Mrs. Roosevelt on one arm, grasping a cane with the other, F.D.R. managed to make the East Room under his own power, but the effort exhausted him. His crippled lower limbs ached and throbbed for relief.

Protocol required that all guests stand until President Hoover and his wife should appear to greet them, but the Hoovers did not appear for a very long time. On several occasions, Roosevelt was offered a chair, but always declined for fear the whispering campaign about his polio disability might be somehow intensified. For almost forty minutes he stood there in absolute torment, the steel braces cutting into his legs and beads of perspiration dotting his face, which never ceased to smile. Frank Freidel rightly points out[2] that a man as essentially decent and humane as Hoover could never have been as deliberately cruel. Yet F.D.R. never ceased to be suspicious, and things were never quite the same between the two former friends.

Personalities aside, the Republicans faced grass roots revolts from every quarter. William Allen White observed that "only the Democrats will save Hoover. . . . How, I don't know, but they are versatile and can find some way in crises." The Republicans hoped and prayed for the usual Democratic split in what had been a loose political coalition since the Civil War. None came. The Republicans hoped and prayed for a spectacular return to prosperity. The Depression only deepened. The Republicans hoped and prayed that candidate Roosevelt would eventually make a fool of himself, stumble into egregious error in the heat of a skirmish, lose the confidence of certain Eastern business and financial elements whose support he had to have to win. But no campaign error was made. The Republicans hoped and prayed that the agrarian revolt of the solid Republican central West would somehow dissolve and "normalcy" return. But the agrarian revolt proliferated.

Actually, there were some indications of improved economic

2. *Ibid.*

status by the fall of 1932. The *New York Times* index of business activity, made up of steel production, electric power, auto, grain, and lumber prices, car loadings and similar fundamentals, rose from 66 per cent, or two-thirds of normal activity, to 74 per cent, or almost three-fourths, by the end of the year. Herbert Hoover has always insisted that, had 1932 not been a presidential election year, the nation's economy would have righted itself. Hoover always felt that the bottom of the Depression came in August, 1932, and that the *Times* business index, which rose from that base, was mathematical proof of it. But whatever vestige of true recovery had begun, Hoover felt, was destroyed by the politicking of Franklin D. Roosevelt and vote-hungry Democrats.

Roosevelt, on the other hand, agreed with Claude Bowers,[3] a historian and an ardent editorial writer, who wrote the Democratic candidate that the Republicans would attempt to inflate wheat prices through manipulating the commodity market. They would then have a persuasive case that prosperity was "just around the corner." F.D.R. replied to Bowers that he agreed about the Republican game and that their strategy was now "perfectly plain."

In any case, bullish sentiment in either Wall Street or newspaper business indexes did not soak down to the mass of the voting public, least of all the huge armies of city unemployed and farm malcontents. Milk was bringing Iowa farmers only 61¢ a hundred pounds and one of Governor Roosevelt's constituents sent him a voucher showing that she had netted but 39¢ on the sale of a month-old calf. It was simply ridiculous, or would have been had it not been so tragic.

Then there was the drama of the so-called Bonus Army in Washington. More than 10,000 unemployed war veterans were, by the summer of 1932, encamped in the nation's capital, many of them in a shantytown along the Anacostia. They wanted a bonus for their war duty and they were undoubtedly a dangerous lobby and certainly an eyesore in the political show window of America. President Hoover investigated, offered them their rail fare home, was rebuffed, then instructed the United States

3. *Ibid.*, p. 326.

Army to evict them. Many, as it turned out, were in truth Communist agitators and fewer than half were actual war veterans.

Unfortunately for Hoover and the Republicans, however, the Army Chief of Staff at that hour was General Douglas MacArthur who, dazzling in medals and self-righteously vigorous in new uniform, brought out tanks and soldiers with gas masks and fixed bayonets, as though the ugly encampment were a host of German snipers.

In its enthusiasm under MacArthur, the Army greatly exceeded Hoover's order to evict. It may well have been a necessary executive move, but as executed it was abysmally bad politics. Nothing could have been better calculated by the Democrats to increase so expertly President Hoover's mounting unpopularity. Resplendent General MacArthur had, in less than an hour, dramatized as no Democrat had been able to dramatize, the desperation, degradation, and danger of the economic ill health of a nation as close to revolution as it had ever been.

But MacArthur's conquest of the Bonus Army alone would not have defeated Herbert Hoover. The Bonus Army simply represented in microcosm the times and stresses, unprecedented in their severity, range, length, and depth. Controls over giant corporations had been relaxed in the reaction against Wilsonian democracy and reform. Rugged individualism had combined with new, high protective duties, and consequent postwar overproduction had shot America's prosperity to dizzy heights. The powerful engine had been running at top speed, but no one had thought to check the brakes.

The October, 1929, collapse of the stock market, where every other businessman and many a housewife had had a tenuous margin account, had broken the bubble. Boom prosperity collapsed with startling rapidity, bringing with it the worst Depression the country had ever known. This was no local bank panic, to be quickly recovered. It was a long-term disease in the body economic, and radical measures were needed to cure it. They were not forthcoming under the Republicans.

In the beginning of 1929, peak year of the Hoover prosperity ("two chickens in every pot, two cars in every garage"), only 3 per cent of the population had been unemployed. By 1930 this figure had risen to 9 per cent, tripling in one year. By 1931 the unemployed of the country were 16 per cent of its working force and by 1932 one breadwinner in four was out of work and many of the employed were teetering or nearly bankrupt. On the Saturday that Franklin D. Roosevelt was sworn in, it was likely that almost 30 per cent of the employables of the United States were without regular jobs. No one will ever really know.

The consequent effect of such a disastrous shortage of income was nowhere more dramatic than in the businesses of real estate and farming. Mortgages were now being repudiated so rapidly that some banks could not keep up with the clerical paper work involved in foreclosing, which was often delayed because there was no one to whom the house could be sold, anyway. Similarly, the American farmer couldn't sell his produce for what it cost him to raise it. He would never starve, as his urban contemporary might and did, but he was as near to true revolt as a conservative American farmer can get and remain law-abiding. In the circumstances, only the fortuitous appearance of Roosevelt and the hopes he engendered prevented a farmer-labor political coup, or worse.

On October 25 at Baltimore, candidate Roosevelt let go with one final blast against Hoover and the "Four Horsemen of the present Republican leadership: the Horsemen of Destruction, Delay, Deceit, Despair." It was an interesting speech from many points of view. It was Roosevelt's most belligerent campaign document and into it the Democratic candidate ad libbed an implied criticism of the Supreme Court which, he said in passing, was controlled by reaction, like the Presidency and the Congress.

Hoover replied bitterly; but F.D.R. controlled his temper, and his election eve broadcast, a moderate and statesmanlike fireside chat from Poughkeepsie, was a classic upon which all politicians might well base their final nonpartisan utterances. That night he was talking like a President of the United

States, and Hoover was like a desperate and overmatched contender. The nation sensed it, too, and there is not the slightest doubt that the quiet confidence, the supple philosophy, the warmth and intimacy of one contrasted so sharply with the waspish finale of the other that F.D.R. gained many a voter the night before the prostrate, angry nation went to the polls.

Was President Roosevelt regarded as a potential great from the moment of his election? Far from it. Walter Lippmann, one of the shrewdest observers, who later became his champion, wrote to the independent Republican Senator William E. Borah, who had repudiated Hoover:[4]

> It'll be a great relief to have the election over, and to me at least, though I have the deepest reservations about Franklin Roosevelt, a relief to be rid of the present administration. It's so utterly discredited that it no longer has any usefulness as an instrument of government. And even assuming that Roosevelt isn't any better than Hoover, a new man for a little while will be better than a man who's worn out and used up.

This, beyond doubt, was what many millions of Americans felt as Franklin Delano Roosevelt stood to take the oath of office on the misty, raw Saturday which was March 4, 1933. Forgotten now was the monumental landslide of November 6, in which the Democrat had ravaged the incumbent Republican by 472 votes to 59 in the electoral college and 22,821,857 to 15,761,845 in total popularity. That this electorate now expected something more creative than what it had been getting in the White House needed no proof. Just what that something would be no man in his right mind could have accurately forecast in the blackest inauguration since Abraham Lincoln's first in 1861.

Fundamental problem for every reasoning citizen on March 4, 1933, was the collapsing banking system of the United States. Before anything else could be coped with, a radical incision had to be made to open the fester that was blocking and

4. Letter from Lippmann to Borah, November 3, 1932.

polluting the flow of currency. The infected economic blood-stream of the nation had slowed to a dangerous level. It might well halt altogether if "confidence impaired" wasn't quickly exchanged for "confidence restored." It was, most men knew, largely a matter of confidence.

Hoover had asked in February that the President-elect come to a White House conference on the spreading bank runs and their resultant panic and chaos. But Hoover had hastened to make it plain that the conference was to be on his own terms, on measures he had already proposed and wanted Democratic sanction for. He seemed to want the new President to repudi-ate the "New Deal" before it had begun, and the foremost New Dealer would have none of it. What Roosevelt wished above all else was to avoid responsibility without power; he was smart enough politically to refuse the conference and yet be held blameless by an adoring constituency which had just given him the greatest political majority in U. S. history.

A string of newly nationalized banks in Ohio and Michigan had just closed their doors and the flow of money in the great Cleveland-Detroit-Chicago industrial area was by now almost completely frozen. What banks were not affected were never-theless in danger of runs. But a run on a bank was nothing new in itself. There had been contagious runs on banks as long as there had been U. S. panics, which was about once every generation. What made this situation unique was the solidity of the frost and its widespread effect. Something had to be done and done immediately to induce a thaw in the frozen assets of a good share of the nation's banking institutions. Until that thaw set in, little would move in the normal currency circulation of commerce, industry, or finance. Fear was the catalytic agent in the frost. Fear had first to be removed before there could be any glimmering hope of better economic health.

President Roosevelt had already decided on two main lines of attack before coming to Washington for the inaugural. These two points boiled down to the removal of the catalytic agent, fear. To accomplish this, F.D.R. proposed to call an immedi-ate special session of the Congress, then declare a national bank holiday—that is, to close all the banks in the country so that no more would fall to the gathering panic of bank runs. The President also planned to invoke a forgotten provision of a wartime act known as "trading with the enemy." This act had never been repealed. Under its provisions, a President had the right to control gold, which was by now being hoarded at a frightening rate because people were instinctively afraid of paper money.

The special session was called for Thursday, March 9, and William H. Woodin, the new Secretary of the Treasury, a marvelous guitar-playing imp of a man with an extraordinary sense of humor and courage far in excess of his physical frailty, promised faithfully to have the emergency banking measure written up in time for Congressional action. Woodin began working on it half an hour after the inauguration on Saturday. He worked at it for three days and nights without much sleep and almost no food, which held little interest for him even in normal circumstances.

On Sunday, after lunch, the new Cabinet met. Within four hours, Roosevelt issued the first two of many emergency measures designed to thaw the icy grasp of fear in which America's hope was encased. Before sundown Sunday, a special session had been summoned and, more important because it bought a week's precious time, the bank holiday had been proclaimed.

To their credit, Hoover's departing bank experts stayed on to help. Ogden Mills, Woodin's predecessor, told the group of financial brains who now assembled in the Treasury to produce a workable program to save the nation's banks and, said Mills, "if they can't, let the President and Mr. Woodin tell us to get the devil out of here and get some men who can."[5] Raymond Moley put it best: "We'd forgotten to be Republicans or Democrats. We were just a bunch of men trying to save the banking system."

Since Moley had been one of the chief brain trusters during the campaign and was now Assistant Secretary under Woodin

5. From personal conversation with Ogden Mills soon after the crisis week.

—who was himself the bogyman of "socialism"—the first moments of the New Deal in office appeared pretty silly all around. From an objective point of view, Franklin D. Roosevelt's early, initial steps in the remarkable "Hundred Days" could not have been closer to the tenets of free enterprise capitalism if Adam Smith himself had taken them. It was by common necessity a national crusade, with the temper of America similar in many respects to that in wartime nonpartisanship. The banking system was at the core of capitalism and its present trauma affected every nerve and muscle of an American economy indisposed to radical measures.

Many progressives felt there was now a golden opportunity to create the first true national banking system the country had ever had. Senators Costigan of Colorado and La Follette of Wisconsin paid a White House call the night before the special session opened and begged the new President to go all the way while he had the chance. Most of Congress was convinced that the New Deal would, then and there, seize such a golden opportunity. Senator Cutting of New Mexico believed that a national bank could have been proclaimed without a word of protest and the frustrating decades of progressive hope might at that very moment have been consummated. But, La Follette said afterward, Roosevelt's mind was made up and could not be changed. He stilled his visitors: "That isn't necessary at all. I've just had every assurance of cooperation from the bankers."

These aren't the words of an apostate flirting with opportune radicalism. They are the words of a man born to capitalistic free enterprise and loath to rend it or toss it overboard without a better substitute. They give an entirely different picture of Franklin D. Roosevelt from the admittedly biased editorial pages of his time. Arthur Schlesinger, Jr., says of this amazing period of the bank holiday:[6] "The very moneychangers, whose flight from their high seats in the temple the President had so grandiloquently proclaimed in his Inaugural address, were now swarming through the corridors of the Treasury."

6. Arthur M. Schlesinger, Jr., *The Coming of the New Deal* (Boston, Houghton Mifflin Company, 1959), p. 5.

What the bank holiday did was far more than halt a run on what was left of the country's deposits. It was as though the week without banks put a period after the word "panic." By the end of three days, few Americans could or would change a twenty-dollar bill and nobody seemed to care. The country was in becoming holiday mood. Fear was disappearing. It was as though a great weight had been lifted. Psychologically nothing else would have worked as well.

The bank holiday closed the door on the ugly past. When the banks reopened the following week, it was as though an expert new driver were behind the wheel, which truth was to be made crystal clear to all by summertime. A newsman from the *New York Herald Tribune* went in to see Woodin the night before Congress was to convene. He asked the Secretary of the Treasury if the new banking bill were finished. The Secretary was sitting on the front edge of his desk, strumming his guitar and singing in a squeaky croak, because he'd had little or no sleep for half a week.

"The bill is finished," said the musical Secretary, swinging his legs in rhythm, "and my name is Bill, and I'm finished too."

The following noon the special Congress assembled, less than one week after inauguration. Only one copy of Mr. Woodin's bill was available. There had been no time to print it, for Roosevelt was making pencil corrections right up to noon.

By unanimous consent, House debate was limited to one hour. At 4:00 P.M. the measure passed unanimously without a roll call. Scarcely a handful of those present had seen the bill and almost no one really comprehended it. In the Senate, windy Huey Long from Louisiana pressed for amendments and was shouted down. At 7:30 P.M., by a vote of 73 to 7, the most remarkable piece of quick banking legislation in U. S. history was passed. It was immediately motorcycled to the White House, where it was promptly signed in the fading light of the same afternoon in which it had been born, a truly remarkable tribute to the democratic process under stress.

It was thought better to let the public adjust to the new

measure over the weekend, so the banks didn't open on Friday, March 10, but on Monday, March 13. There was an orderly, almost festive air to business that day; and from then on the circulation of the body financial improved in geometric proportion, with consequent improvement in business as icy fear melted. The danger of total panic had been averted. The new President, thought by many to be more radical than any since Jackson, had done it with old-fashioned capitalistic methods. But he had also done it with a sure legislative hand. He was a man in control. Here was a steerer, an accomplisher; not a drifter or bright but vague wisher.

New Deal strategists had first proposed that the special session of Congress be summoned to liquidate the banking emergency only, then sent home. But the new-found spirit of accomplishment, the momentum and eagerness already plainly exciting the nation seemed to the new resident of the White House too great an opportunity, too exhilarating a forward motion to waste.

For one thing, F.D.R. had pledged during the election campaign to cut all Federal expenditures by 25 per cent in order to help revive the fading American economy. Led by the Scotch-blooded budget director, Lewis W. Douglas, Roosevelt now sought to balance the budget, badly dislocated by the "spend-thrift Hoover," who had taken emergency steps to prime the economic pump and get the stream of U. S. currency moving again. Roosevelt said, perhaps prophetically: "Too often in history liberal governments have been wrecked on the rocks of loose fiscal policy."

Within a week, against the strongest left-wing liberal opposition in Congress, Roosevelt's budget was balanced, largely through reduction of veterans' pensions, salary cuts of 25 per cent for all Congressmen and other Federal employees, and trimming of every frill and frosting from the Federal cake. Since left-wing liberal Senators in particular owed many a political obligation to the powerful veterans' and civil service lobbies, as well as to union labor, a 25 per cent salary cut was not taken lying down and the wonder is it went through at all.

But F.D.R. won his point, and in the end cut $510,000,000

from Federal expenses and balanced the budget. This was
done largely on the passionate urging of economy-minded Lew
Douglas, who had accomplished this unique balancing act
without any increase in taxes. Roosevelt said to Moley: "In
twelve years he'll be a good Democratic candidate for President." But by the end of twelve years both budget balancing
and Lew Douglas were dead issues and Moley was an anti-
New Deal columnist.

The second Sunday of the Roosevelt Administration found
chief magician Louis McHenry Howe and the President sipping
their coffee and chain-smoking in an atmosphere of badinage
at their evening meal. Suddenly Roosevelt looked at his friend,
the political wizard who as much as any other man had made
F.D.R. President of the United States, and said: "I think, Louis,
this would be a good time for beer." Howe snorted in delight,
left the table, returned with a copy of the Democratic campaign platform, and between them they then and there wrote
on the dining-room table a brief message to Congress favoring
immediate modification of the Volstead Act to legalize light
wines and beer.

The following morning, Monday, March 13, the special session of Congress received the beer message. On Tuesday, ignoring a covey from the Woman's Christian Temperance Union
and the Anti-Saloon League, the House voted for beer with
3.2 per cent alcoholic content. (Some German beers approach
10 per cent alcohol by volume, but the avid American public
didn't remember and didn't care anyway, so long as it had
something legal to slake its long thirst.) The Senate agreed on
Thursday, with only a pretense of a hearing for the Dry lobby.
Within a week's time, the two most powerful lobbies on The
Hill—the veterans and the prohibitionists—had been utterly
routed by this increasingly incredible New Deal.

It was little wonder that a new Treasury bond issue was
oversubscribed before lunch time the next day. Nor was it
amazing that the nation's security and commodity markets in
Wall Street, where the vast trouble had first started, immediately showed a pronounced bullish mood on reopening following the bank holiday hiatus. Confidence and buoyance were

contagious throughout the land. Banks were for the first time in months taking in more money than was being withdrawn. The disastrous runs and danger of new runs had all but ceased. Walter Lippmann could write:[7] "At the beginning of March the country was in such a state of confused desperation that it would have followed almost any leader anywhere he chose to go. In one week, the nation, which had lost confidence in everything and everybody, has regained confidence in the government itself."

The President added the open press conference and the fireside chat to his widening techniques, speaking directly to the people as he had to the Congress. The press conference was an amazing idea in itself. Up to then there had usually been the traditional "White House spokesman" who stood between newspapermen and the President. Now only a desk cluttered with mementos, most of them marine, some of them boyish, stood between them.

F.D.R. told his first White House news conference of more than 100 excited newsmen that he had been warned that what he was about to try would be impossible, but he was going to try it just the same. The first news conference came during the banking crisis, on the eve of the opening of the special session. It was so fresh, so frank, so friendly, such a break with precedent, such a step toward true democratic give and take, that when it was over the hardened news people broke into sharp, spontaneous applause. As an institution, the presidential press conference was here to stay.

Then, on Sunday night, March 12, the President gave the entire nation the first of his fireside chats by radio. It was an explanation in amazingly simple language of the bank crisis, why it had happened, why the banks had been closed, why they were being opened. Will Rogers said that F.D.R. made everybody understand the highly complicated subject, "even the bankers." Republicans who had feared F.D.R. now sent him ecstatic letters and telegrams. Hearst wrote: "I guess at your next election we will make it unanimous!" A *New York Times* reporter wrote: "There is no more resemblance between the

7. "Review of Reviews," May, 1933.

citadel of aloofness Mr. Hoover built and the friendly, welcoming air of the executive offices now than there would be between a formal embassy tea and old-home week at Hyde Park."[8]

The fireside chats were an immediate success because Roosevelt was an absolute master of public speaking technique, particularly radio technique. He projected. He was a pleasure to listen to. He put complex things into plain language. He was thoroughly at home in front of a microphone, the first and only contemporary to be so, for Truman and Eisenhower never mastered either radio or TV delivery, and radio broadcasting absolutey petrified Hoover.

But the most striking contrast was between the Hoover approach and Roosevelt's to the bonus veterans in Anacostia. Hoover had sent the army. Roosevelt sent his wife. The veterans were offered three meals a day; dentists and doctors came and ministered to them; the President saw their delegations; a large convention tent was put up by F.D.R. for their meetings; and Louis Howe drove Eleanor out there one muddy afternoon and, after a long walk through shin-deep mud, Mrs. R. led them in the singing of "There's a Long Long Trail a-Winding," though of recent presidential wives she had the poorest musical ear. Within ten days, most of the Bonus Army had been absorbed into the Civilian Conservation Corps and Roosevelt's skill at handling difficult situations was once again crystal clear.

But the most important point of all was that what Roosevelt had done legislatively he had done through existing Constitutional means. Hamilton Fish, no left-wing liberal, called the Roosevelt Administration "an American dictatorship based on the consent of the governed without any violation of individual liberty or human rights." He could not have defined F.D.R.'s métier more clearly. Here was a President using the Presidency in a new way. Here was a Chief Executive who seemed to be saying to the duly elected representatives of the people: "I ask for dictatorial powers never before granted in peacetime. I ask for them because this isn't any ordinary,

8. *New York Times,* March 19, 1933.

routine adversary—this is The Great Depression, and we must use extraordinary measures to reduce it."

Up to mid-March, the President had done nothing at all along the lines of the New Deal reforms he had hinted at during his campaign. On Thursday, March 16, however, less than two weeks after his inauguration, Roosevelt asked the Congress for a new Federal concept for the American farmer—national planning for U. S. agriculture.

This was but the first of a long series of fundamental changes in the American economic system and the government's role of prying into the private business, even the private lives, of its citizens. As T.R. had felt, it *was* the government's business to step in when a company got too big for its breeches, so F.D.R. opened now the greatest barrage in U. S. history on capitalistic license and snobbery. The great agricultural planning reorganization was simply the first, and it was a shock to many a conservative when it came.

With this and other impending New Deal reform and planning measures came a kind of public servant wholly new to the Capitol. Hard times had made available tremendous pools of talent in law, engineering, and education—men who operated at the theoretical level of thought. Government had seldom wanted them before; now it needed them by the thousands to help blaze the New Deal's wilderness trails and by the thousands they came. Arthur Schlesinger says: "Each prominent New Dealer acted as his own employment agency," and Washington was soon bubbling with intellectual ability and bright young minds the like of which it hadn't seen since the Jacksonian revolution.

Washington had never seemed to be much like a real city, said Anne O'Hare McCormick of the *New York Times*. Now it had been "annexed to the United States." Raymond Tucker wrote in *Collier's*:[9] "They [the New Dealers] have transformed it from a placid, leisurely Southern town, with frozen faces and customs, into a gay, breezy, sophisticated and metropolitan center." Arthur Krock found this bright, merry group of sing-

9. "National Air," *Collier's*, 93:22 (January 27, 1934).

ing, drinking, uninhibited public servants "hearty eaters and colossal workers." Krock also wrote what everyone in Washington soon knew: "The President is the boss, the dynamo, the works."[10]

F.D.R. had been inaugurated on Saturday, March 4. Between that hour and the adjournment of the Seventy-third Congress on June 16, 1933, the people and their elected legislators had been subjected to an unceasing barrage of fresh ideas from the President of the United States, the like of which had never been seen before in Washington. In the fantastic Hundred Days of the special session, both houses of Congress were sent legislation so radical in concept that even now their ready accomplishment defines the unbelievable.

Many at the policymaking levels of the nation, especially on the liberal-progressive side of political thought, had known Franklin Delano Roosevelt all his adult life and thought they had his measure. They were mistaken, and they did not hesitate to say so. For in the incredible Hundred Days this same Roosevelt they thought they knew had made ten major speeches, sent fifteen legislative messages to Congress, and received for signature in record time fifteen pieces of major legislation almost precisely as he had demanded them.

Had he been a dictator, his will could not in a hundred days have been more perfectly accomplished. He was using the Presidency for the first time as the powerful instrument some of the nation's founders had foreseen it a century and a half before.

Raymond Moley, who was there, says it was a trying time, however, for subordinates.[11]

None of us close to FDR lived normal lives. Confusion, haste, the dread of making mistakes, the consciousness of responsibility for the economic well-being of millions of people made mortal inroads on the health of some of us, like Bill Woodin and Joe Robinson (who soon died), and left the rest of us ready to snap at our own images in the

10. *New York Times,* March 12, 1933.
11. Raymond Moley, *After Seven Years* (New York, Harper and Brothers, 1939), p. 191.

mirror. Only Roosevelt preserved the air of a man who'd found a happy way of life.

Moley adds that there was "a vastly greater amount of give-and-take in his attitude toward the 'Hundred Days' Congress than the country realized." And it is nonsense to suppose that as sensitive a human being as Franklin D. Roosevelt did not lose sleep on occasion when he considered what he alone had done to his country and what fantastic powers he had now accepted as virtual dictator of the economic system.

For, in the course of just over three months, the President's "rubber stamp Congress" passed the following major measures:

March 9: Emergency Banking Act
March 16: Legalized beer
March 20: Government Economy Act
March 31: Civilian Conservation Corps
April 19: Abandoned gold standard
May 12: Agricultural Adjustment Act
May 12: Emergency Farm Mortgage Act
May 12: Federal Emergency Relief Act
May 18: Tennessee Valley Authority Act
May 27: Truth-in-Securities Act
June 13: Home Owners Loan Act
June 16: National Industrial Recovery Act
June 16: Glass-Steagall Banking Act
June 16: Farm Credit Act
June 16: Railroad Coordination Act

Roosevelt had repudiated the traditional gold standard and the traditional marriage between investment banking and deposit banking. He had regulated stock buying. He had put the government's name behind virtually all the bank deposits in the country, guaranteeing them under the Glass-Steagall act. He was in a position to wreck permanently every precept of free enterprise, and some would say in the end that he had accomplished it, to serve his own political ambitions. It required, as Moley put it, "no neurotic temperament to see that these unprecedented monetary and credit controls could be utilized so unwisely as to throw the economic system completely out of kilter for the same human reasons that they might be utilized so skillfully as to help stabilize it."[12] Long steps had been taken toward the exercise of credit control, monetary control, and the unification of the state and national banking systems.

Usually in national crises in American history, the power of the executive has faded into an amalgam of national patriotic effort in which the legislative has suddenly come alive and public opinion has stoked the fire quite nicely. This was so as F.D.R. came to power; the events helped make the man, though it had to be the right man in the right place at the right time. And F.D.R. was surely the one.

Just the same, there's no evidence that Roosevelt looked upon his suddenly granted dictatorial powers as permanent, despite screams in the enemy camp. He regarded what he must do as a desperate measure and his dictatorship of the Hundred Days as the best and only means of riding out the storm. He could not have done it in a different aura or context.

Through the emergency banking acts he had, however, permanently altered the concept and practice of the handling of money in this country and of gold as its god. Through legalization of beer, and later full repeal of the Eighteenth Amendment, he began to bring the nation back to its senses in its regard for law, though the bloody gang tradition engendered by Prohibition has never fully left us. Through the economy acts he fulfilled for a time one of the strangest political planks that could be imagined in association with the New Deal, for deficit financing and unbalanced budgets soon became the rule of his long tenure and the stamp of his policy.

But beginning in May all of the quick remedies were overshadowed by the first of the great reform bills which had more to do with fundamentals than with palliatives. The sudden throbbing of the nation's circulation now enabled the President to carry over some of this momentum into permanent

12. *Ibid.* p. 279.

changes that had been coming for generations, among them American social security measures and economic protections and restrictions bordering on Socialism long accepted as part of European life. The first of these had to do with agriculture and real estate.

Through the Agricultural Adjustment Administration, F.D.R. now began to conduct a vast experiment in controlling the production of the farm and the prices farmers got for their produce. The President proposed to tax the consumer for the benefit of the producer. The farmer would for the first time in history be practically guaranteed a minimum income—and the eating nation would pay for it. Gone forever, it would seem, was pure supply and demand. With it, hoped F.D.R. and Henry Wallace, the theorizing farm lieutenant, there would be an end to the unmanageable surplus which annually depressed the market at the very moment the farmer harvested it.

Mortgages, especially farm mortgages, were next examined. The Federal Home Owners Loan Act soon made the government of the United States the largest mortgage banker in the world. It also saved for millions of Americans, farmers in particular, their firesides and their life savings.

Then there was Federal relief, proposed on a gigantic scale for the first time. Up to now relief had been a local matter. Through his nationwide relief program, F.D.R. gave sanction to the philosophy that the "Federal government must assure all its citizens a minimum livelihood."[13] Combined with later social security measures this giant step was perhaps the most radical departure ever taken by an American President. Certainly it was among the most far-reaching and probably the most shocking to the sentient traditionalist, though there were many still unaware of its awesome dimensions.

Next came the controversial yardstick for electric power, the Tennessee Valley Authority, which put government squarely into the private power business—with the taxpayers' money. Not only did the TVA act of May 18, 1933, set up a public vs. private power argument that hasn't come near settlement, even now, but it also involved flood control, creative

13. Franklin D. Roosevelt Papers.

conservation, regional planning, and homesteading for one area at the expense of millions who would never see or benefit from its vast experiment. The private "public utility" would be engaged in the fight of its life; public competition with private power was now a hideous and seemingly permanent fact.

But it took the National Industrial Recovery Act, parent of the NRA blue eagle, to shatter whatever comforting illusions remained about F.D.R. in conservative minds. In the NRA, Roosevelt was recognizing the hazards of unfettered production and competition, experimenting as no American before him had experimented in the interests of the wage earner, the consumer and, in theory at least, the employer. Social exploration at such stratospheric heights might have given pause to a hardened President in the latter part of his second term. Coming in the first hundred days of Roosevelt's first administration it was all the more wonderful and fantastic. Discretionary powers in the hands of the man in the White House were now too staggering to be understood or comprehended by the average voter. Yet somehow they suited Roosevelt, whose courage, said a contemporary, was "absolute."[14]

The Glass-Steagall Banking Act not only secured the people's money but committed the government to cracking down (an NRA cliché) on irresponsible securities and promotions, and regulation of the primary capital markets, such as Wall Street, where the Securities and Exchange Commission soon became a financial policeman.

Through the Farm Credit Act and the Railroad Coordination Act, Roosevelt moved to show the power of centralized government in a shrinking world; unification and co-operation would henceforth replace disinterest and dispersal as national policy, even after he was gone. The Federal government was now in everybody's business.

Although F.D.R. co-operated with members of his party and his own official family and was more keenly aware of the importance of political mechanics than any President but Lin-

14. From conversation with Mrs. Frances Perkins, F.D.R.'s Secretary of Labor.

coln, his native tendency to be independent made itself painfully evident every now and then. Things could look altogether different from one day to the next from where the President sat, whereas they might seem to be relatively changeless to a man like James A. Farley, Postmaster General and patronage boss of the Democratic Party in those early years. Farley later complained bitterly that Roosevelt did not keep his word as President and as leader of his party. But Edward J. Flynn, a New York political leader, wrote something all politicians ought to read on the subject of commitment—and failure to keep one's word when President of the United States:[15]

> The office of President, as everyone knows, is one of great power, but it also has been pointed out that no President can keep all the commitments he makes. This is readily understandable in President Roosevelt's case. He did make commitments that in many cases he did not keep. It is only fair to say that in most instances there was a good explanation for this failure. What might be wise to do one week might not be wise in the next. The President's judgment in such matters has to be taken.

The point involves much more than patronage and private political commitment in the story of F.D.R.'s Hundred Days. He had campaigned on comparatively conservative ground; his early handling of the banking crisis had been along most orthodox, capitalistic lines. Yet as the special session opened vast opportunities for him to make permanent changes in the American system, many of them generations overdue, he did not fail to repudiate the past, forget his campaign promises (the balanced budget is a good example), break with leaders of his own party, and, in some cases, replace them with men who were more keenly aware of the vast revolution that had begun.

Revolution it was! A rereading of the contemporary story of the Hundred Days does nothing to destroy the amazement one feels at how much was accomplished, for good or ill depending on the reader's point of view, between March and

15. Edward J. Flynn, *You're the Boss* (New York, The Viking Press, 1947), p. 164.

June, 1933. Walter Lippmann put it this way: "In the Hundred
Days from March to June we became again an organized
nation confident of our power to provide for our country and
to control our own destiny."[16]

A year and a half later, when many an intelligent American
still did not grasp the scope and vision of the Roosevelt revolution, Winston Churchill wrote in an American magazine:[17]

> The courage, the power and the scale of [Roosevelt's]
> effort must enlist the ardent sympathy of every country, and
> his success could not fail to lift the whole world forward
> into the sunlight of an easier and more genial age. Roosevelt
> is an explorer who has embarked on a voyage as uncertain
> as that of Columbus, and upon a quest which might con-
> ceivably be as important as the discovery of the New World.

This is the professional historian speaking, the man who has
read all there is to read about the past and who will make
history himself in the bloody years just ahead, part of them in
friendly partnership with the same Roosevelt he now assesses.
It is doubtful if, in the history of any country, one hundred
days ever encompassed as many permanent changes in the
fundamental structure and pattern of a nation's way of life
as took place between the inauguration on a misty, cold Saturday in March and the sticky hot June recess day, 1933, when
the great flowering came to an end, though other blossoms
would appear.

Certainly, as Churchill said later of Franklin Roosevelt,
"his life must . . . be regarded as one of the commanding
events in human destiny."[18] His incalculable effect on the
Presidency is proved, if in no other way, by the fact that, as
with Lincoln and Washington, the Roosevelt legend is not
based strictly on fact, but on what the people want to believe
of him.

As he said himself, his generation had "a rendezvous with
destiny." No man ever sat in the White House more aware of

16. As told to the *New York Herald Tribune* Forum, 1933.
17. "While the World Watches," *Collier's*, 94:24–25 (December 29,
1934).
18. As quoted in the *New York Herald Tribune*.

that rendezvous nor more capable technically of using his office to steer an unwavering course toward its fulfillment, though to accomplish the end meant asking for and being granted dangerous dictatorial powers no President had ever asked nor been granted before his time.

Harry Truman

THE *New Yorker* said of Harry Truman that there was something comforting and homely about his face, as though you
were looking down at a bespectacled shoe salesman in your
home town. That this observation has some truth, no one can
doubt, for the nation's press and radio scarcely took any
notice of Truman during the first agonizing hours of his Presidency. A giant had succumbed to a cerebral hemorrhage in
Warm Springs, Georgia, and the giant's equal would not be
seen again. Certainly there were few Americans who could
connect the word "President" with this obscure former Senator
from Missouri named Harry S. (for nothing at all) Truman. He seemed to be an enigma by comparison with the already legendary hero of depression and war, the man with
the golden voice and the impertinent cigarette, for whom more
people had voted than for any other human being in history.

Time described Truman, when he was nominated for Vice-
President, as "a gray little man," "mousy-looking," "a likeable
plodder," "a drab mediocrity." But perhaps the fiery Truman,
whose father had had red hair and a violent temper, described
himself best of all. At Kansas City, during the 1944 campaign,
Senator Truman had said of himself: "A statesman is only a
dead politician. I never want to be a statesman."

This "drab mediocrity," this "mouse" was now President of
the United States. He was in charge of the war that was almost
over in Europe but had only just begun to turn against the
Japanese in the Pacific. There was no telling how long it would

10

Commits His Country to War

take the foot soldier to capture Oriental islands inhabited by tens of millions of people trained since birth to die fanatically and willingly for their Emperor-god. The peace conference Franklin D. Roosevelt had so eagerly anticipated and prepared for in the Wilsonian tradition would now be attended by a once party-bossed Midwesterner who by his own admission knew less about the inner workings of F.D.R.'s White House policy than he knew about Sanskrit. Roosevelt simply hadn't taken Truman into his awesome confidence, even though Truman was his Vice-President.

Franklin D. Roosevelt was not one to present a blueprint of his plans. He still vividly remembered the treatment Woodrow Wilson had received at the hands of his fellow countrymen after announcing in advance his rigid Fourteen Points. F.D.R. had, therefore, left Harry Truman little or nothing to go on over the long course. F.D.R. had liked the visionary, the idealistic, the general statement ("Four Freedoms," "Economic Bill of Rights," etc.) in preference to specific blueprints. This the new President quickly and painfully knew to his own disadvantage.

On this point, President Truman was to write later that his first three hectic months in the White House were a nightmare of exhausting policymaking by day and grinding homework until midnight each night, for weeks on end, in an attempt simply to catch up on secret, supersecret, and super-supersecret information the President of the United States must possess as

Commander in Chief of the armed forces and titular political leader of a hundred and fifty million human beings.

President Roosevelt had died on April 12; on May 8 President Truman announced the end of the war in Europe, proclaiming "V-E Day." The little Missourian with the nasal voice and the petulant hands that chopped as he spoke had scarcely caught his breath or finished his homework by midnight oil when he was faced with a dramatic and important journey to a town near Berlin, Potsdam by name, for the first postwar peace talks with Churchill and Stalin. He knew neither man and neither man knew him. To make things completely awkward, Churchill's party was defeated in a general election back home just as the conference sat down. A new Prime Minister, Clement R. Attlee, now took the place of the most famous living man on the Western side. Attlee did not know Stalin, Stalin did not know Attlee, and Truman knew neither one.

On the agenda were future relations with conquered countries, vital postwar territorial claims and reparations, and the intricate peace treaties themselves. With Stalin, the senior representative, firmly in the driver's seat, little could be accomplished. The best that could be done was to refer all peace treaty and territorial problems to a council of foreign ministers; to agree that there should be a public trial for all German and Japanese "war criminals"; to dissuade the Kremlin from insisting on Clemenceau-like reparations from a prostrate foe. Most important, however, was an ultimatum to Japan to surrender unconditionally or suffer the consequences of all-out war at the hands of every other nation on earth.

Less than a fortnight later, the new President was called upon to make the first of many grave and great decisions in the field of foreign policy. Once again, as so often happens in history, events were making the man—but the fact remained that the man, however unlikely it had seemed, was apparently capable of understanding the requirements of greatness when greatness was required.

On August 6, 1945, therefore, at the new President's specific order, the first atomic bomb was dropped on Hiroshima, killing or maiming forever at least 150,000 Japanese civilians. Their country had defied the civilized world. The Emperor-god's subjects would feel the consequences. These wholly unprotected civilians were now guinea pigs in the most horribly potent experiment in the history of warfare, an atomic explosion equal to the force of 21,000 tons of TNT. It had been a terrifying, an awesome decision for a new President to make less than four months after taking up the mantle of an undoubted, undeniable hero who could do no wrong in history.

Seeing that Japan was doomed by the atomic bomb, Stalin immediately declared war on Japan. His troops entered Manchuria; by Japanese surrender on August 10 they were at the fringes of Korea, which was being abandoned by defeated occupying Japanese. The Emperor had been allowed to keep his throne but he would have to tell his people, as they looked him in the face for the first time, that he was not their god and must not henceforth be so regarded.

Harry Truman pronounced August 15 "V-J Day"; two weeks later General MacArthur landed in Japan and began an occupation which created the greatest imaginable change in a nation's way of life. Japan was altered from hidebound traditionalism to mid-twentieth century democracy in a matter of months. It would never go back to feudal Orientalism, and its women would for the first time be recognized as human beings instead of chattels. This, too, was a remarkable decision for the green, untried President.

A decision to create a workable world congress had been approached at Yalta, the last major act of Roosevelt's life. A conference had gathered for the first time in San Francisco on April 25, 1945, and two months later the final draft of the Charter of the United Nations had been approved. Wilson's dream of a world assembly had come true; the Senate of the United States, which had repudiated its author, now approved his brain child by an overwhelming vote, 89 to 2. On January 10, 1946, the first meeting of the General Assembly of the

United Nations met in London to tackle peace problems on a global basis.

But soon a new antagonist raised its head; its name was not Germany nor Japan, but the Union of Soviet Socialist Republics. Soviet Russia had been a great wartime ally. But days of Western wonder and awe at Soviet courage in stemming the Nazi tide at Stalingrad had long since faded into disgust at Kremlin aggression and duplicity. Churchill was the first to say it aloud. In Missouri in 1946 he talked openly about the impenetrable "iron curtain" that the postwar Soviets had erected between East and West. By March, 1947, Truman had, slowly and reluctantly, begun to adopt a very different attitude toward the giant world power, once America's friend in battle.

The form of this change came gradually; it came officially in what history calls the Truman Doctrine. This boiled down to a policy of containment of Soviet Russia, already making threatening gestures at Western Europe, the Middle East, and the Orient.

The President first called upon Congress to pledge immediate American economic and military aid to Turkey, Greece, and other eastern Mediterranean friends of democracy. Truman said that henceforth every force available to the United States would be exerted to contain the Soviet Union in its obvious plan of world aggression. This statement that the United States would do all in its power to contain Soviet aggression was the key. Any free people resisting Soviet aggression could hereafter count on military and economic aid from the United States.

But Truman did not limit his country to the negative role of Communist containment.[1] In Cambridge, Massachusetts, on June 5, 1947, Secretary of State General George Marshall, formerly Chief of Staff of all U. S. armed forces, invited European countries in particular to survey their economic and military needs and come to Washington with specific, concrete proposals for help.

1. Marshall Smelser and Harry W. Kirwin, *Conceived in Liberty* (Garden City, Doubleday and Company, Inc., 1955), p. 661.

The invitation, anyone remembers, became known as the Marshall Plan; it is unlikely if postwar Western Europe could have survived the Communist threat had there been no Marshall Plan. What scarcely anyone remembers is that General Marshall had the wit to offer reconstruction aid to Soviet Russia as well, though Marshall fully realized the invitation would not be accepted.

The Marshall Plan quickly combined with the Truman Doctrine to place a very different light on America's new world leadership, something she hadn't wanted and for which she was totally unprepared by nature or education. The vacuum created by the dissolution of the British Empire, for years the world's policeman, was at last being filled by the concrete proposals of a "mousy" President. The Marshall Plan alone would in the end cost the United States $30,000,000,000, or between 5 and 10 per cent of America's entire national income. It was cheap insurance. It worked; and it saved the West from Communism.

By the end of the winter of 1947–1948, Soviet intentions were painfully apparent to all. Czechoslovakia seemed ready to cast its lot with the West: so the Communists quickly seized control and, Hitler-like, obliterated every opposition leader. A Wilson-created nation of American friends was sealed off from the West—Churchill's phrase, "iron curtain," daily expressed more terrible meaning.

On the heels of the seizure of Czechoslovakia by the Communists, a Republican newspaperman in the United States Senate stood up and delivered himself of one of the most important editorials any journalist-statesman ever wrote. The Vandenberg Resolution asked that the United States develop regional commitments with nations outside the Western Hemisphere in order to aid in a system of collective defense.

Senator Vandenberg pointed out, in his logical Dutch way, that such regional understandings and defense units were perfectly legal under the United Nations Charter and that the time seemed propitious for such a move on America's part. The Senate quickly voted 65 to 4 in favor of this unparalleled departure from traditional U. S. isolation and its perennial avoidance of entangling military alliances.

The resolution had no legal status whatsoever—it was merely an expression of the will of the Senate of the United States. But Arthur Vandenberg was the Republican spokesman on foreign policy and, since the Republicans had won both House and Senate in 1946, he was now senior Senator on overseas affairs, though the man in the White House was a Democrat. What this bipartisan resolution said in effect was this: the experience of two world wars "suggests that the best deterrent to aggression is the certainty that immediate and effective countermeasures will be taken against those who violate the peace." This could only mean a United Nations police force and regional defense pacts—such as NATO—against Soviet aggression.

The Kremlin, meanwhile, continued to trouble Harry Truman with a war of nerves over Berlin. In the summer of 1948 the Soviets placed a total blockade on all traffic between Berlin and Western Germany, but the Reds did not reckon with Western endurance and ingenuity. Indeed, the trickery on Berlin solidified the Western front as nothing else had. For almost one full year, the Western powers spectacularly supplied the needs of more than two million Berliners entirely by air. It was an amazing demonstration of Allied air strength, technical prowess, solidity, and stubborn insistence on protecting friends of freedom and democracy. But it had an even more important result.

When the West formally protested the Berlin blockade in the Security Council of the United Nations, the Kremlin promptly vetoed each proposal. Few acts could have so dramatized Russian contempt for justice and fair play. Until the later revolt in Hungary, put down by bloody force and duplicity, nothing succeeded as well in demonstrating to the uncommitted world what the Berlin airlift—and its causes— made ominously clear. The Truman Doctrine, the Marshall Plan, and the Vandenberg Resolution gained increasing stature in world diplomacy. And, in their way, these three declarations helped elect President Truman to a term of his own in November, 1948, despite the fact that every political forecaster had predicted an overwhelming victory for Thomas E. Dewey, the Republican candidate.

With the confidence of the people now clearly behind him, the little haberdasher from Missouri plunged with sureness into world affairs. The first of these creative acts was NATO, the North Atlantic Treaty Organization formed by twelve nations of the Western bloc in the spring of 1949. The treaty obligated its signatories to rearm, to settle their individual disputes peaceably if possible, but by joint military or economic action if impossible. An armed attack on one was to be considered an armed attack on all. The name "Soviet Russia" appeared nowhere in the treaty; it did not have to. Truman won Senate approval by a vote of 82 to 13 after considerable debate about avoiding entangling alliances.[2]

The first pronounced result of NATO was the end of the Berlin blockade, which had been one of the chief causes of the creation of NATO. The second immediate result was a turning of Communist interest to the Asian rather than the European sphere, though Europe and the Middle East were never completely free of Kremlin irritations. This fact was to lead America into the only war she ever failed to win—Korea.

By the end of 1949, Generalissimo Chiang Kai-shek had been forced to move the ragged remnants of his Nationalist army off the mainland of China to the island of Formosa. After five years of civil war, Communism was now completely triumphant in China, whose loss shocked the American people as they had seldom been shocked, for the gentle, anti-Japanese Chinese were traditional friends of America. Communist doctrine now ruled half of the land area of the world and one-third of its population. No longer could American liberals pretend to be friendly to Soviet aims: the aggressions and conquests had become too naked; and their nakedness strengthened the creative foreign policy of President Truman.

The peninsula of Korea had been overrun by foreign invaders on so many occasions few historians could remember

2. Washington's farewell address warns throughout against foreign entanglements, but Jefferson used the words, "entangling alliances."

them all. Korea was the Poland of the Orient; her latest rape had been by Japan. Now that the Japanese were out of power, Korea appealed to the United States in particular to help her to her freedom. At Cairo in 1943, Churchill, Roosevelt, and Chiang Kai-shek had announced a determination that Korea should in due course become free and independent. But in the hurry-scurry of war no formal Allied plan was made for Korean independence.

The Kremlin, on the other hand, had known exactly what it would do. As soon as Russia had declared war on Japan, shortly before the end of the Japanese aggression, Russian troops were sent to occupy northern Korea, which was contiguous to Manchuria, now in Communist hands. Three weeks later, U. S. troops were landed in the south and, for military convenience, Korea was divided at the 38th parallel. This was supposed to be but a temporary arrangement and it was taken for granted that all foreign troops would leave when the Japanese peace treaty had been signed. The United Nations would then take over under a trusteeship until Korea was ready for self-government.

But the Soviets (pretending to act for the Korean Reds) refused to leave when the appointed day came. They claimed that there had already been established a "People's Republic" at Pyongyang and it was no longer sensible to leave the government of Korea to a UN trustee. Suddenly, at the end of June, 1950, after excessive and fruitless talk in the UN over what precisely to do about the stubborn Korean "People's Republic," these same Communists again took the initiative. Their North Korean army crossed the 38th parellel and began a military blitz of the entire nation, in which American (and a few other) forces of occupation loosely patrolled the countryside. The relaxed U. S. troops were overwhelmed.

President Truman was now faced with disaster to the keystone of his foreign policy, his Truman doctrine of containment of Soviet aggression. Already he had lost considerable face with the capitulation of Chiang Kai-shek and the whole of China to Communism. Time—even hours—might be vital to the entire future of the democratic West and to United Nations prestige. But there were problems. For the Federal Constitution clearly states that no President can declare war by himself. The framers of that farseeing document reserved to Congress alone the right to declare war.

The Federal Constitution, in Article II, Section 2, states that the President "shall be Commander in Chief of the Army and Navy of the United States, and of the militia of the several States, when called into the actual service of the United States." In other words, besides running the regular Army and Navy, the President runs the state military when these forces are involved in federalized and not local activity. And what is federalized activity? It must be an act involving the whole United States—in concert. In other words, war; war involving the whole country against another.

But the President himself does not possess the power to *declare war*. This power is clearly delineated in the Constitution. Article I begins with these words: "All legislative powers herein granted shall be vested in a Congress of the United States, which shall consist of a Senate and a House of Representatives." In Section 8 of the same Article, Congress—and Congress alone—exclusively retains certain general powers which include:

11. To declare war, grant letters of marque and reprisal, and make rules concerning captures on land and water.

12. To raise and support armies, but no appropriation of money to that use shall be for a longer term than two years.

13. To provide and maintain a Navy.

14. To make rules for the Government and regulation of the land and naval forces.

15. To provide for calling forth the militia to execute the laws of the union, suppress insurrections and repel invasions.

16. To provide for organizing, arming, and disciplining the militia, and for governing such part of them as may be employed in the service of the United States, reserving to the States respectively the appointment of the officers, and the authority of training the militia according to the discipline prescribed by Congress.

It would be difficult to imagine a more specific document in regard to the declaration of war, raising armies, paying for them, and training, arming, disciplining, or regulating them. Those who drew up the Constitution wanted it clearly understood that not the executive (they were inevitably thinking about monarchy) but the people, and the people alone, should have the power to declare war, raise armies, and pay for the fighting. If the Constitutional Convention could help it, war, the monarchial "sport of kings," would not be for any U. S. Chief Executive.

The Constitution goes further. It strictly forbids the President (the elected monarch of the people) or any individual state from declaring war, or raising its own armies, or playing them as on a chess board, or collecting money to pay for them. These powers are reserved for Congress. In Section 10 of Article I, under the title "Further Restrictions on Powers of States," the Constitution reads:

> No State shall, without the consent of Congress, lay any duty of tonnage, keep troops or ships of war in time of peace, enter into any agreement or compact with another State, or with a foreign power, or engage in war, unless actually invaded, or in such imminent danger as will not admit of delay.

In other words, no individual or state can fight a private war, as no President can declare one without the express consent of both Houses of Congress. War is too dangerous a game to be left to individual whim; the whole people, through their elected representatives, can alone declare and prosecute it, though the Commander in Chief will by law be their President.

When the Communist forces of North Korea crossed the 38th parallel and threatened to engulf the whole Korean peninsula on June 25, 1950, President Truman was faced with an untenable and unprecedented situation. The consequences of a blitzkrieg attack could be momentous, not only in the United States but throughout the world. The UN was the legitimate brain child of an American President; it had been physically born on American soil at San Francisco; its permanent headquarters were in New York. And without quick, sure action on this Korean crisis the UN was doomed, and Truman knew it. Only bold reply would now save the United Nations from sharing a common grave with the League of Nations.

When Truman had sent American troops to Europe to give NATO a transfusion, when he had vitiated the crisis of the Berlin blockade with immediate air action which, nevertheless, lacked Congressional consent, he had been acting as Commander in Chief as the Constitution provided. There had then been heated argument in Congress whether Truman was within his rights to send American soldiers and equipment to Europe in peacetime in support of Berlin and NATO; some isolationist newspapers called for a "Great Debate," and his political opponents tried to tie his hands by cutting off the money to pay for the troops and planes and ammunition. But, says David Cushman Coyle, "the struggle was more political than legal." Mr. Coyle continues:[3]

According to the Constitution, the Congress has the power to declare war, and presumably the intention was to let Congress decide whether to go to war or not. But in fact any powerful element in the country may be in a position to get the United States into a war. Even the San Francisco Board of Education, responding to a widespread feeling in the State of California in 1906, ordered that Japanese children should be segregated from white children in the schools. This action set off a dangerous outburst of feeling in Japan. President Theodore Roosevelt sent a member of his cabinet to San Francisco, not that he had any power to force the Board to withdraw its order, but to satisfy the Japanese that he had tried to undo the insult.

The President can bring on a war by taking actions that are within his power and that create a war situation. Woodrow Wilson, for instance, protested against British and German violations of neutral rights in terms that showed the gradual shift of American opinion from neutrality to an anti-German position. When he asked Congress for a declara-

3. David Cushman Coyle, *The United States Political System* (New York, New American Library, 1954), p. 48.

tion of war, it was too late to refuse. On the other hand, in 1812 the majority of Congress hotly desired war with England. Some historians have thought that President Madison was unwillingly dragged into the War of 1812.

If the Soviet Union had not been instantly and vigorously countered by Truman in Berlin and Korea, both probing raids might have been fatal to the United Nations and indeed to the free world. These were severe and premeditated testings; had the West been tested and found wanting, as at Munich, the whole world might have been on the slide leading to World War III. Harry Truman instinctively knew all this and he acted; and he alone of all the leaders in the free world was in a position to do so.

The Republic of Korea was invaded by as many as 60,000 Communist troops, most of them North Koreans and Manchurians spearheaded by a hundred Soviet-built tanks and protected by Soviet aircraft, some of which were not even camouflaged. The first act on the part of the United Nations came in the Security Council, set up to meet the emergency of such aggressions. The Security Council demanded withdrawal to the 38th parallel and immediate cessation of hostilities while more peaceful solutions could be applied.

But the Reds did not even reply. They simply kept marching toward Seoul, capital of South Korea. They took it two days after President Truman, acting as Commander in Chief of U. S. forces, had on June 27 ordered General Douglas MacArthur to come to the aid of the young South Korean Republic. The U. S. 7th Fleet was simultaneously ordered by the President to protect Formosa and likewise to keep the Chinese Nationalists there from attacking the mainland and spreading the Korean "police action" into general war. The phrase "police action" was Truman's, a conscious rationalization of his Constitutional limitations.

Let the President himself tell what it felt like to be shaken awake from the false dream of peace.[4]

4. Harry S. Truman, *Memoirs*, Vol. II (Garden City, Doubleday and Company, Inc., 1956), pp. 331–34.

On Saturday, June 24, 1950 (it was June 25 in Korea), I was in Independence, Missouri, to spend the weekend with my family and to attend to some personal family business.

It was a little after ten in the evening, and we were sitting in the library of our home on North Delaware Street when the telephone rang. It was the Secretary of State calling from his home in Maryland.

"Mr. President," said Dean Acheson, "I have very serious news. The North Koreans have invaded South Korea."

My first reaction was that I must get back to the capital, and I told Acheson so. He explained, however, that details were not yet available and that he thought I need not rush back until he called me again with further information. In the meantime, he suggested to me that we should ask the United Nations Security Council to hold a meeting at once and declare that an act of aggression had been committed against the Republic of Korea. I told him that I agreed and asked him to request immediately a special meeting of the Security Council, and he said he would call me to report again the following morning, or sooner if there was more information on the events in Korea.

Acheson's next call came through around eleven-thirty Sunday morning, just as we were getting ready to sit down to an early Sunday dinner. Acheson reported that the U.N. Security Council had been called into emergency session. Additional reports had been received from Korea, and there was no doubt that an all-out invasion was under way there. The Security Council, Acheson said, would probably call for a cease-fire, but in view of the complete disregard the North Koreans and their big allies had shown for the U.N. in the past, we had to expect that the U.N. order would be ignored. Some decision would have to be made at once as to the degree of aid or encouragement which our government was willing to extend to the Republic of Korea.

I asked Acheson to get together with the Service Secretaries and the Chiefs of Staff and start working on recommendations for me when I got back. Defense Secretary Louis Johnson and Chairman of the Chiefs of Staff General Omar Bradley were on their way back from an inspection tour of the Far East. I informed the Secretary of State that I was returning to Washington at once.

The crew of the Presidential plane Independence did a wonderful job. They had the plane ready to fly in less than an hour from the time they were alerted, and my return trip got under way so fast that two of my aides were left behind. They could not be notified in time to reach the airport.

The plane left the Kansas City Municipal Airport at two o'clock, and it took just a little over three hours to make the trip to Washington. I had time to think aboard the plane. In my generation, this was not the first occasion when the strong had attacked the weak. I recalled some earlier instances: Manchuria, Ethiopia, Austria. I remembered how each time that the democracies failed to act it had encouraged the aggressors to keep going ahead. Communism was acting in Korea just as Hitler, Mussolini, and the Japanese had acted ten, fifteen, and twenty years earlier. I felt certain that if South Korea was allowed to fall, Communist leaders would be emboldened to override nations closer to our own shores.

If the Communists were permitted to force their way into the Republic of Korea without opposition from the free world, no small nation would have the courage to resist threats and aggression by stronger Communist neighbors. If this was allowed to go unchallenged it would mean a third world war, just as similar incidents had brought on the second world war. It was also clear to me that the foundations and the principles of the United Nations were at stake unless this unprovoked attack on Korea could be stopped.

What President Truman carefully emphasizes here in his *Memoirs* is the point of view taken instinctively by Secretary of State Acheson that this was a matter specifically for the United Nations Security Council; that the Soviet aggression against the Republic of Korea was an aggression against the whole United Nations organization, the entire free world, not simply the United States whose troops happened to be in great majority as Korean occupation forces.

It is clear that the State Department and the Truman Cabinet felt from the first that the President would be on firmer legal and political ground if he moved the target of the

Korean aggression from the United States to the United Nations. As a common defender of Korea through the UN, the United States could justify many adventures, among them swift military and naval reaction by U. S. forces without the specific consent of Congress.

On any other ground the President would be going contrary to Article I, Section 8 of the Federal Constitution, giving Congress and Congress alone the right to declare war. With isolationism on the rise again, particularly in the Midwest, the President simply could not be placed in the position of appearing to commit his country to war without the consent of Congress. The United Nations Security Council provided a handy, legitimate escape hatch.[5]

Emergency meetings of civilians and military were held every few hours. On Sunday night in New York, the Security Council, by a vote of 9 to 0, the USSR not voting, approved a resolution declaring that "a breach of the peace" had been committed by the North Korean action, and ordering the Reds to cease this action and withdraw at once. Technically, the UN resolution took the President off the hook, although U. S. troops already had been in Korean combat by that hour.

One of these weekend emergency meetings boiled down to an undeniable, outstanding truth in Truman's mind,[6]

> . . . the complete, almost unspoken acceptance on the part of everyone that whatever had to be done to meet this aggression had to be done. There was no suggestion from anyone (both Republican and Democratic leaders were present) that either the United Nations or the United States could back away from it. This was the test of all the talk of the last five years of collective security.

No better justification for the Korean "police action" has ever been offered by anyone, or need be. As Lincoln had logically justified suspension of the writ of habeas corpus to save a greater freedom, Truman clearly saw in quick military reaction to naked Communist aggression "the test of all the talk."

5. From a study of the *New York Herald Tribune's* Washington dispatches from June 26 to August 10, 1950.
6. Truman, *op. cit.*, pp. 334–35.

It was now or never: from here on, the United Nations would be simply another toothless League, a Continental Congress; or it would be a true force for peace and security, a Constitution with powers of enforcement.

By carefully placing the onus where it belonged, by insisting that the Soviet crime was a crime against all and not one only, by immediately placing U. S. troops "at the disposal of the United Nations," the President could legitimately sidestep the Constitutional restrictions mentioned in Section 8 of Article I, albeit no such far-reaching military action as Truman's had ever before been taken by an American President on his word alone.

But there was from the first another side to it. Perhaps this can best be dramatized by the perceptive *Congressional Digest* for January, 1951. Senator Taft of Ohio was, of course, the opposition spearhead. He was a thoroughgoing isolationist and he wanted to be President in 1952. He could taste the dissatisfaction of a large segment of the nation with Truman's precipitate action in Korea (soon a losing cause) and he meant to make the most of it politically.

During the "Great Debate," Taft called Truman to account for the extent of the legal authority of the President as compared with the legal authority of Congress to commit troops abroad. Said Taft on January 5, 1951, on the floor of the Senate:[7]

> As a matter of fact, he [Truman] had no authority whatever to commit American troops to Korea without consulting Congress and without Congressional approval. He could not commit our armed forces to the support of the United Nations under the terms of the U.N. participation act which was passed by Congress, for that act only recognized the commitment of troops in the event of the negotiation of a special military agreement with the Security Council "which shall be subject to the approval of the Congress by an appropriate act of joint resolution." The Russians have prevented the conclusion of any such agreements. Congress has, therefore, never acted. The President simply usurped author-

7. *Congressional Digest,* January, 1951, p. 54.

ity, in violation of the laws and the Constitution, when he sent troops to Korea to carry out the resolution of the U.N. in an undeclared war.

The Senator from Ohio admitted it might be argued that Congress, by appropriating money for additional Korean action, had ratified Truman's executive act, ex post facto, but, said Taft, "the war was on and we had no choice but to back up wholeheartedly the boys who were fighting in Korea."

The isolationist press had been screaming as much for months. The *New York Daily News* and *Chicago Tribune* led the attack, along foreordained lines, and a contemporary journalist correctly reported as follows:[8]

A second view held by one Congressional bloc is that as a matter of simple common sense and in the name of unity the President would do well to obtain Congressional approval before engaging in any further major decisions of foreign policy (sending troops abroad). These decisions have had critical results on a scale far surpassing expectations.

The correspondent reported severe Senate criticism of Truman's unique action.[9]

Upon what authority, then, *has* the President been operating in the case of Korea? There appears to be but one answer. His authority as Commander-in-Chief of the armed forces of the United States. The White House has never specifically designated the exact authority it has in mind. But it is significant that no Administration spokesman has undertaken to refute the legal situation outlined in the foregoing. Queries put to the White House by "The Digest" have resulted in "no comment" and the only power now mentioned when the question is put is the power of the President under the Constitution—that is, the Commander-in-Chief power.

But even Truman's enemies, and they were hungry, bitter men, out of power since 1932 and smelling victory, conceded that he had some precedent. The presidential power was, they

8. *Ibid.*, p. 35.
9. *Ibid.*, p. 46.

admitted, a broad one, and there appeared to be no doubt of a President's authority to send American armed forces abroad in times of peace on certain "police actions."

Jefferson had done so against the Barbary pirates. Polk had sent Taylor into Mexico. Pierce had ordered the Navy to bombard Nicaragua. McKinley had sent 5,000 troops to China during the Boxer Rebellion. Teddy Roosevelt had intervened in Haiti, Nicaragua, and Honduras. Wilson had ordered Pershing to Mexico and had fired upon Veracruz. F.D.R. had authorized attack on any unidentified submarine that wouldn't answer U. S. challenges off our coastal waters. There had been dozens more such acts in U. S. history.

But each of these examples, contemporaries pointed out, might be distinguished from the present situation in at least two ways: (a) the enormous scale of operations (10,000 U. S. soldiers in Korea were dead in the first half year), and (b) the fact that this was a citizen army, whereas before, the President had always used professional soldiers who had volunteered for military service and whatever police actions came their way.

"The power to send troops abroad is Constitutionally only an implied one," the *Digest* correspondent went on, reporting opposition moves "limited by precedent and judicial sanction. There is no honest precedent for the situation today. So unless the approval of Congress is sought and obtained, it is difficult to escape the conclusion that the Executive, at best, is operating with an assumed legal authority. The question now seems to be whether one man should be asked or allowed to make the decisions which the times are demanding of America."[10]

The "Great Debate" was joined, therefore, on an issue of far greater permanence than the outcome of the Korean "police action." Constitutional argument went on for weeks on the floors of both House and Senate during January, 1951, over the extent of the legal authority, in the atomic age, of the President alone and of Congress to commit U. S. troops abroad. The flowering opposition took the form of the Coudert-Wherry Resolution, named after a Congressman from New York and a

10. *Ibid.*

Senator from Nebraska, both of them staunch Republicans of strong nationalist leanings.

The fertile brain of Senator Taft actually fathered the Coudert-Wherry Resolution. Kenneth S. Wherry was Senate minority leader (the Republicans had managed to lose their Senate majority) and even more isolationist than the gentleman from Cincinnati. He was happy to comply with Taft's dictation which sought to put the Senate on record "against sending U. S. troops abroad without Congressional approval." The Republican supranationalist bloc saw to it that Frederic R. Coudert, Jr., introduced a similar resolution in the House. Eventually they were joined and immediately sent to committees.

While the committees were debating the Coudert-Wherry Resolution, Senator William E. Jenner (Republican, Indiana) launched into the most violent and virulent attack yet made on Truman's lonely executive act in sending troops abroad. On January 8 Jenner bitterly accused Truman of having "blundered, tricked or betrayed us into a war."[11] Congress must issue Truman an ultimatum, said Jenner, demanding either a declaration of war against Red China or total withdrawal of our forces from Korea. The usual platitudes against UN ineffectiveness (an inconsistent line in Jenner's case) closed the polemic. It had succeeded in opening the wound of isolationism vs. internationalism that the heroisms of World War II had all but healed.

Whatever the inconsistencies of the Taft-Wherry-Jenner forces in the Senate, the total impact of their criticism of U. S. foreign policy was to deprive the administration of maneuverability and any great degree of diplomatic sanction or freedom.[12] Increasing inflexibility had been apparent in right-wing Republicans since Dewey's nomination over Taft in 1948. The fateful (for Taft) last chance of 1952 loomed large. He was "Mr. Republican" to the country's press. He represented the "outs"; he also represented a most natural revulsion to more

---

11. "Facts-on-File," 1951, p. 4 and *passim.*
12. John W. Spanier, *The Truman-MacArthur Controversy* (Cambridge, Harvard University Press, 1959), p. 162.

casualty lists. America had had enough since 1941. In this context, any act of President Truman was suspect.

The initial North Korean Communist drive south had been blunted by a brilliant landing of U. S. Marines at Inchon in the fall of 1950. The North Korean capital of Pyongyang had been taken October 20 and the U. S. 7th Division had reached the Manchurian border on November 20.

But just before the "Great Debate" reached its peak and the Coudert-Wherry Resolution was presented to the Congress as a means of restraining the war-making powers of the Presidency, 200,000 Chinese Communist "volunteers" counterattacked the UN forces. These "volunteers" crossed the Yalu River and pushed back 100,000 UN troops from a score of nations, chiefly U. S. soldiers and armor. The Chinese Reds kept right on going, crossed the 38th parallel, and went seventy miles inside South Korea before a desperate UN defensive stand halted 600,000 of them at Eastertide, 1951.

From the outset, General MacArthur had been handicapped by being unable to use certain modern weapons of war, among them atomic explosives, and having to avoid bombing Red ammunition depots and marshaling yards beyond the border. MacArthur was a professional soldier who did not relish defeat at the hands of swarming Orientals when his own force was hamstrung by the gentlemanly code of the West.

MacArthur, who detested Truman anyway, let no opportunity go by to reach the American people directly through the press and via friendly voices like Taft's, Wherry's, and the *Chicago Tribune's*. For a time there seemed to be two commanders in chief in Korea, President Truman and General MacArthur. It was an anomalous situation which could not go on forever; Truman ended it abruptly on April 11, 1951, by replacing the great Pacific hero with General Matthew B. Ridgway. Peace negotiations began two months later.

MacArthur came home in utter triumph. Millions cheered him. He told a packed joint session of the Congress tearfully that "old soldiers never die, they just fade away," and was then the star of a seven-week Senate inquiry largely engineered by Taft, Wherry, and other anti-New Deal-Fair Deal Senators.

In the end, MacArthur was found not to have been insubordinate, but simply to have disregarded the presidential order to clear policy statements through the Defense Department.

Sporadic fighting continued for more than two years while peace negotiations stalled under expert guidance of the Kremlin. By the election of 1952, Korea was so sore a carbuncle that Dwight D. Eisenhower actually made political capital from a campaign statement that if he won the Presidency his first act would be to fly to Korea and "clear up the mess."

On July 27, 1953, six months and a week after General Eisenhower had been sworn in to succeed Harry Truman, an armistice was signed and all fighting ended in the only major war the United States had ever entered and failed to win. Returned U. S. prisoners eventually told such fearful stories of Chinese Communist inhumanity and torture that all thoughts of MacArthur, of presidential campaign promises, of Senate resolutions, or of executive power to declare war were temporarily overwhelmed in a sea of American revulsion. Since Truman had been the righteous leader against such inhuman barbarism, his cause did not suffer in the long run and the chirping against him fell away gradually as Taft's star declined and finally expired.

Truman always felt justified in sending U. S. troops on this superpolice action. He said on many occasions that his view of the Presidency was the modern view in an atomic world of split-second timing. He later wrote: "The President must have the unfettered right to be in a position to act promptly when an emergency arises. He must, therefore, have the broadest powers, limited only by the Constitution and his term of office."[13]

Efforts to hamper and restrict the office of the Presidency, Truman felt, usually fell into two categories—attempts to cause him to lose prestige and attempts to contract the inherent powers of the President. In the first case, those opposed to quick presidential action in a specific case are often politically opposed to the action itself. They would be against its approval

13. "My View of the Presidency," *Look*, 22:25–31 (November 11, 1958).

even by Congress. This takes political forms, as he pointed out. By holding a President's executive actions up to criticism and scorn, even ridicule, the opposition can cause him—and his party—to lose prestige, and perhaps the next election. As to hampering and restricting the office of the Presidency, many American legislators have honestly felt that the President of the United States should be more of a figurehead than a political leader and statesman; that encroachment by Presidents who take initiative and power into their own hands must at all times be thrust back into what is, for them, literal Constitutional limitation.

But, as Truman pointed out, the Constitution is a flexible instrument. If it weren't, it would have little or no value in an age that has replaced the horse with motors and jets, the messenger with electronic communication, and gunpowder with nuclear holocaust. The former President wrote:[14]

> It is nothing short of a miracle, when you think of it, that the framers of the Constitution had the genius to create an office, the Presidency of the United States, which can function as responsively and as easily in this rocket and atomic age as it did in the age of the stagecoach, the sailing ship, and the powdered wig.
> Most of the powers that a President exercises today are authorized by the Constitution. Other powers have been built up by custom created by time and by events in emergencies met by our stronger Presidents. I have deep admiration for our strong Presidents who clearly understood their powers and acted to meet difficult situations as they arose. Grover Cleveland said in one case, "We are faced with a condition and not a theory." He met the condition.

This is precisely what Harry Truman, the man who looked like a shoe salesman and a mouse to contemporary journalists, did when he courageously committed U. S. troops to a foreign field without the consent of Congress. He was faced with a condition, not a theory, and he met the condition vigorously.

In doing so, President Truman irrevocably widened the concept of the power of the Presidency. From his term on, no

14. *Ibid.*

President could hesitate to quell a modern blitzkrieg on grounds that Congress would first have to debate and vote the issue. By the time such debate had been placed on the calendar, in the critical atomic equation half of America might lie in radioactive ruins and our democracy with it.

POPULAR AND ELECTORAL VOTES FOR PRESIDENTS

Year	Candidate	Party	Popular Votes	Electoral Votes
1789	George Washington	Federalist	Unknown	69
	No opposition	—	—	—
1792	George Washington	Federalist	Unknown	132
	No opposition	—	—	—
1796	John Adams	Federalist	Unknown	71
	Thomas Jefferson	Democrat-Republican	Unknown	68
1800	Thomas Jefferson*	Democrat-Republican	Unknown	73
	Aaron Burr	Democrat-Republican	Unknown	73
1804	Thomas Jefferson	Democrat-Republican	Unknown	162
	Charles Pinckney	Federalist	Unknown	14
1808	James Madison	Democrat-Republican	Unknown	122
	Charles Pinckney	Federalist	Unknown	47
1812	James Madison	Democrat-Republican	Unknown	128
	De Witt Clinton	Federalist	Unknown	89
1816	James Monroe	Democrat-Republican	Unknown	183
	Rufus King	Federalist	Unknown	34
1820	James Monroe	Democrat-Republican	Unknown	231
	John Quincy Adams	Democrat-Republican	Unknown	1
1824	John Quincy Adams**	National Republican	108,740	84
	Andrew Jackson	Democrat	153,544	99
	Henry Clay	Democrat-Republican	47,136	37
	William H. Crawford	Democrat-Republican	46,618	41

* Elected by House of Representatives due to tie vote.
** Elected by House of Representatives (no candidate having polled a majority).

Year	Candidate	Party	Popular Votes	Electoral Votes
1828	Andrew Jackson	Democrat	647,286	178
	John Quincy Adams	National Republican	508,064	83
1832	Andrew Jackson	Democrat	687,502	219
	Henry Clay	Democrat-Republican	530,189	49
1836	Martin Van Buren	Democrat	762,678	170
	William H. Harrison	Whig	549,000	73
1840	William H. Harrison	Whig	1,275,016	234
	Martin Van Buren	Democrat	1,129,102	60
1844	James K. Polk	Democrat	1,337,243	170
	Henry Clay	Whig	1,299,062	105
1848	Zachary Taylor	Whig	1,360,099	163
	Lewis Cass	Democrat	1,220,544	127
1852	Franklin Pierce	Democrat	1,601,274	254
	Winfield Scott	Whig	1,386,580	42
1856	James C. Buchanan	Democrat	1,838,169	174
	John C. Fremont	Republican	1,341,264	114
1860	Abraham Lincoln	Republican	1,866,452	180
	Stephen A. Douglas	Democrat	1,375,157	12
	John C. Breckinridge	Democrat	847,953	72
	John Bell	Const. Union	590,631	39
1864	Abraham Lincoln	Republican	2,213,665	212
	George McClellan	Democrat	1,805,237	21
1868	Ulysses S. Grant	Republican	3,012,833	214
	Horatio Seymour	Democrat	2,703,249	80
1872	Ulysses S. Grant	Republican	3,597,132	286
	Horace Greeley	Democrat-Liberal	2,834,125	—
1876	Rutherford B. Hayes	Republican	4,036,298	185
	Samuel J. Tilden	Democrat	4,300,590	184
1880	James A. Garfield	Republican	4,454,416	214
	Winfield S. Hancock	Democrat	4,444,952	155
1884	Grover Cleveland	Democrat	4,874,986	219
	James G. Blaine	Republican	4,851,981	182

Year	Candidate	Party	Popular Votes	Electoral Votes
1888	Benjamin Harrison	Republican	5,439,853	233
	Grover Cleveland	Democrat	5,540,309	168
1892	Grover Cleveland	Democrat	5,556,918	277
	Benjamin Harrison	Republican	5,176,108	145
	James B. Weaver	Populist	1,041,028	22
1896	William McKinley	Republican	7,104,779	271
	William J. Bryan	Democrat	6,502,925	176
1900	William McKinley	Republican	7,207,923	292
	William J. Bryan	Democrat	6,358,138	155
1904	Theodore Roosevelt	Republican	7,623,486	336
	Alton B. Parker	Democrat	5,077,911	140
1908	William H. Taft	Republican	7,678,908	321
	William J. Bryan	Democrat	6,409,104	162
1912	Woodrow Wilson	Democrat	6,293,454	435
	Theodore Roosevelt	Progressive	4,119,538	88
	William H. Taft	Republican	3,484,980	8
1916	Woodrow Wilson	Democrat	9,129,606	277
	Charles E. Hughes	Republican	8,538,221	254
1920	Warren G. Harding	Republican	16,152,200	404
	James M. Cox	Democrat	9,147,353	127
1924	Calvin Coolidge	Republican	15,725,016	382
	John W. Davis	Democrat	8,386,503	136
	Robert M. La Follette	Progressive	4,822,856	13
1928	Herbert Hoover	Republican	21,391,381	444
	Alfred E. Smith	Democrat	15,016,443	87
1932	Franklin D. Roosevelt	Democrat	22,821,857	472
	Herbert Hoover	Republican	15,761,845	59
1936	Franklin D. Roosevelt	Democrat	27,751,597	523
	Alfred M. Landon	Republican	16,679,583	8
1940	Franklin D. Roosevelt	Democrat	27,244,160	449
	Wendell Willkie	Republican	22,305,198	82
1944	Franklin D. Roosevelt	Democrat	25,602,504	432
	Thomas E. Dewey	Republican	22,006,285	99

Year	Candidate	Party	Popular Votes	Electoral Votes
1948	Harry S. Truman	Democrat	24,105,695	303
	Thomas E. Dewey	Republican	21,969,170	189
	J. Strom Thurmond	States' Rights	1,169,021	39
	Henry A. Wallace	Progressive	1,156,103	—
1952	Dwight D. Eisenhower	Republican	33,778,968	442
	Adlai E. Stevenson	Democrat	27,314,992	89
1956	Dwight D. Eisenhower	Republican	35,581,003	457
	Adlai E. Stevenson	Democrat	26,031,322	73
1960	John F. Kennedy***	Democrat	34,221,485	303
	Richard M. Nixon	Republican	34,108,684	219

*** Senator Harry F. Byrd of Virginia received fifteen electoral votes.

President	Native of	Inaugurated	Vice-President
George Washington	Virginia	Apr. 30, 1789	John Adams
John Adams	Massachusetts	Mar. 4, 1797	Thomas Jefferson
Thomas Jefferson	Virginia	Mar. 4, 1801	Aaron Burr
Thomas Jefferson	Virginia	Mar. 4, 1805	George Clinton
James Madison	Virginia	Mar. 4, 1809	George Clinton
James Monroe	Virginia	Mar. 4, 1813	Elbridge Gerry
James Madison	Virginia	Mar. 4, 1817	Daniel D. Tompkins
James Monroe	Virginia	Mar. 5, 1821	Daniel D. Tompkins
John Quincy Adams	Massachusetts	Mar. 4, 1825	John C. Calhoun
Andrew Jackson	South Carolina	Mar. 4, 1829	John C. Calhoun
Andrew Jackson	South Carolina	Mar. 4, 1833	Martin Van Buren
Martin Van Buren	New York	Mar. 4, 1837	Richard M. Johnson
William H. Harrison	Virginia	Mar. 4, 1841	John Tyler
John Tyler	Virginia	Apr. 6, 1841	—
James K. Polk	North Carolina	Mar. 4, 1845	George M. Dallas
Zachary Taylor	Virginia	Mar. 5, 1849	Millard Fillmore
Millard Fillmore	New York	July 10, 1850	—
Franklin Pierce	New Hampshire	Mar. 4, 1853	William R. King

President	Native of	Inaugurated	Vice-President
James Buchanan	Pennsylvania	Mar. 4, 1857	John C. Breckinridge
Abraham Lincoln	Kentucky	Mar. 4, 1861	Hannibal Hamlin
Abraham Lincoln	Kentucky	Mar. 4, 1865	Andrew Johnson
Andrew Johnson	North Carolina	Apr. 15, 1865	—
Ulysses S. Grant	Ohio	Mar. 4, 1869	Schuyler Colfax
Ulysses S. Grant	Ohio	Mar. 4, 1873	Henry Wilson
Rutherford B. Hayes	Ohio	Mar. 3, 1877	William A. Wheeler
James A. Garfield	Ohio	Mar. 4, 1881	Chester A. Arthur
Chester A. Arthur	Vermont	Sept. 20, 1881	—
Grover Cleveland	New Jersey	Mar. 4, 1885	Thomas A. Hendricks
Benjamin Harrison	Ohio	Mar. 4, 1889	Levi P. Morton
Grover Cleveland	New Jersey	Mar. 4, 1893	Adlai E. Stevenson
William McKinley	Ohio	Mar. 4, 1897	Garret A. Hobart
William McKinley	Ohio	Mar. 4, 1901	Theodore Roosevelt
Theodore Roosevelt	New York	Sept. 14, 1901	—
Theodore Roosevelt	New York	Mar. 4, 1905	Charles W. Fairbanks
William H. Taft	Ohio	Mar. 4, 1909	James S. Sherman
Woodrow Wilson	Virginia	Mar. 4, 1913	Thomas R. Marshall
Woodrow Wilson	Virginia	Mar. 5, 1917	Thomas R. Marshall
Warren G. Harding	Ohio	Mar. 4, 1921	Calvin Coolidge
Calvin Coolidge	Vermont	Aug. 3, 1923	—
Calvin Coolidge	Vermont	Mar. 4, 1925	Charles G. Dawes
Herbert Hoover	Iowa	Mar. 4, 1929	Charles Curtis
Franklin D. Roosevelt	New York	Mar. 4, 1933	John N. Garner
Franklin D. Roosevelt	New York	Jan. 20, 1937	John N. Garner
Franklin D. Roosevelt	New York	Jan. 20, 1941	Henry A. Wallace
Franklin D. Roosevelt	New York	Jan. 20, 1945	Harry S. Truman

President	Native of	Inaugurated	Vice-President
Harry S. Truman	Missouri	Apr. 12, 1945	—
Harry S. Truman	Missouri	Jan. 20, 1949	Alben W. Barkley
Dwight D. Eisenhower	Texas	Jan. 20, 1953	Richard M. Nixon
Dwight D. Eisenhower	Texas	Jan. 21, 1957	Richard M. Nixon
John F. Kennedy	Massachusetts	Jan. 20, 1961	Lyndon B. Johnson

ABOUT THE AUTHOR

Richard L. Tobin began working for the *New York Herald Tribune* the day after he graduated from the University of Michigan and during the next twenty-four years covered, among other things, every aspect of local, state, and national politics. His special assignments during that period included the famous Lindbergh case, the meteoric rise of Fiorello La Guardia, wartime foreign correspondence from Europe, and news of the White House, which the author visited regularly during the administrations of Presidents Roosevelt, Truman, and Eisenhower. Mr. Tobin was also Director of Radio and Television News for the *Herald Tribune* and Public Affairs Director in charge of its annual forum.

For thirteen years, beginning in 1940, Mr. Tobin was on the faculty of the Pulitzer School of Journalism, Columbia University. During the same period he was also a news broadcaster and commentator, both in the United States and in Europe.

In 1958, Mr. Tobin was appointed Executive Editor of the Famous Writers School, a post which he left in 1960 to become Communications Editor of the *Saturday Review*.

In both 1956 and 1960, Mr. Tobin participated actively in national politics as an advisor and publicity manager for Dwight D. Eisenhower and Richard M. Nixon in their campaigns for the American Presidency.

Mr. Tobin's former books include *Invasion Journal* (1944), *Golden Opinions* (1948), and *The Center of the World* (1951). He has contributed to numerous national magazines and lectured extensively around the country on current events.

THIS BOOK WAS SET IN

BASKERVILLE AND CALEDONIA TYPE,

PRINTED, AND BOUND BY

THE HADDON CRAFTSMEN.

IT WAS DESIGNED BY ANDOR BRAUN